Corporate Power, Class Conflict, and the Crisis of the New Globalization

Corporate Power, Class Conflict, and the Crisis of the New Globalization

Ronald W. Cox

LEXINGTON BOOKS
Lanham • Boulder • New York • London

Published by Lexington Books
An imprint of The Rowman & Littlefield Publishing Group, Inc.
4501 Forbes Boulevard, Suite 200, Lanham, Maryland 20706
www.rowman.com

6 Tinworth Street, London SE11 5AL, United Kingdom

British Library Cataloguing in Publication Information Available

Library of Congress Cataloging-in-Publication Data

Names: Cox, Ronald W., 1962– author.
Title: Corporate power, class conflict, and the crisis of the new globalization / Ronald W. Cox.
Description: Lanham : Lexington Books, [2019] | Includes bibliographical references and index.
Identifiers: LCCN 2018050097 (print) | LCCN 2018053906 (ebook) | ISBN 9780739187685 (Electronic) | ISBN 9780739187678 (cloth : alk. paper)
Subjects: LCSH: Corporate power. | Corporations—Political aspects. | International economic relations. | International trade—Political aspects. | Globalization—Economic aspects.
Classification: LCC HD2731 (ebook) | LCC HD2731 .C69 2019 (print) | DDC 303.48/2—dc23
LC record available at https://lccn.loc.gov/2018050097

™ The paper used in this publication meets the minimum requirements of American National Standard for Information Sciences—Permanence of Paper for Printed Library Materials, ANSI/NISO Z39.48-1992.

Contents

Acknowledgments

I want to thank Professor David N. Gibbs in the Department of History at the University of Arizona for providing detailed and very useful commentary on the final version of this project. His willingness to share his time and expertise in the areas of U.S. foreign policy and political economy has helped improve this book. I also want to thank Professor James H. Nolt, whose conversations about the global political economy, and especially global finance and trade, have proven to be extremely helpful in guiding me through key aspects of this project. I am also grateful for the assistance of my colleagues at Florida International University, including Professors Tom Breslin and Julie Zeng in the Department of Politics and International Relations. Tom's sharp observations and extensive knowledge of the political economy of China and East Asia helped me with these sections of the book. As always, he has been exceedingly generous with his time in providing me with help in copyediting earlier versions of this manuscript. Julie's passion for international political economy and considerable experience, skill, and knowledge in dissecting the political economy of China also proved to be extremely helpful in sharpening my arguments. And finally, I owe so much to the steady companionship of my partner, Laura Leigh Rampey, who has always been there to offer suggestions, listen to my ramblings about the direction of my research, and provide a steady love and friendship that transcends everything I've ever written.

Chapter One

The Political Economy of the New Globalization

Corporate power and class conflict have been central determinants of the content, scope, and pace of the internationalization of production that has defined the global economy for the past forty years. This book examines the political economy of corporate power and class conflict by analyzing the relationship between transnational corporations and their "home" states in shaping the political economy of contemporary globalization. The focus will be on transnational firms in the U.S., the E.U., and Japan, where corporations have used their political and economic leverage to restructure the global economy to increase profits, reduce wages, and expand production on a global scale. I will also examine the relationship between transnational corporate power, the rise of China, and the expansion of transnational production in developing countries, especially East Asia, primarily through an analysis of the political economy of global value chains. In these case studies, I examine closely the extent to which corporations have restructured the global economy by engaging in class warfare against working-class and poor people (Cox 1987, 2012; Robinson 2004, 2014; Harvey 2007; Soederberg 2009; Harris 2016; Hart-Landsberg 2013; Smith 2016; Kotz 2015).

My account of contemporary globalization differs from liberal accounts that celebrate globalization as a positive driver of increased wealth that offers mutual gains for rich and poor countries alike. Liberal theories that emphasize positive-sum gains from trade and foreign investment make assumptions that are derived from theories of comparative advantage, which argue that countries are better off specializing in the production of goods and services that they can produce most efficiently and at the lowest costs. The liberal assumptions about trade and investment either minimize or ignore the role of corporate power and class conflict in shaping the content of trade and investment agreements among states. As I will show throughout this book, corporations, relying on their market and political power, have been able to structure trade and investment agreements in ways that privilege and prioritize their own profit-making interests at the expense of workers and societies across both rich and poor countries in the global economy. In the "new globalization," corporate profits have risen as a percentage of gross domestic product while wages have decreased as a percentage of GDP across rich and poor countries alike.

To explain the relationship between corporate power and the "new globalization," I examine the ways that corporations have structured the central features of contemporary transnational production as a project of dominant class interests. This is most apparent when analyzing the increased concentration of corporate power within the market. Corporations have utilized cross-border mergers and acquisitions to create oligopolies that have enabled a few dominant firms to reap disproportionate profits within each of the major sectors of the global economy. Corporate consolidation within the global market has allowed a few firms to limit competition, while aggressively competing with large-scale rivals for ownership of the most profitable assets that are central to the "new globalization." The ascendancy of information technology firms as power brokers within the "new globalization" has shaped the power relationships within the contemporary global economy, where control of the most lucrative source of profits, intellectual property rights, is contested within the market and within the politics of trade and investment agreements. Too often accounts of corporate power have erred by either focusing exclusively on the political influence of corporations to the neglect of increased market power, or, conversely, by focusing on the market power of corporations with little attention to how market power has been shaped by politics. This account seeks to avoid these simplifications by developing a more inclusive historical framework for understanding the growing political and economic power of transnational corporations.

The first aspect of this framework involves an analysis of the dynamics of market power within a global capitalist system. In analyzing these dynamics, we start by asking basic questions about capitalist firms: what are the most profitable and competitive firms globally, what are they producing, and where are they located within the global system? In doing so, we develop what some have called a production profile of capitalism that takes us through various phases of capitalist history and globalization (Gourevitch 2006; Chase 2005). For example, the production profile of capitalist firms after World War II was dominated by the following sectors: steel, automobiles, chemicals, petroleum, and machine tools. The leading multinational firms in these sectors were disproportionately concentrated in the U.S., which they used as their most important platform for producing goods and employing a workforce that contributed high-value-added profits for the dominant firms. The most powerful firms in these sectors benefited from their position within the early stages of the product life cycle, where leading firms incorporated the latest technologies and employed economies of scale that made it more difficult for latecomer competitors to enter into these relatively consolidated markets (Kurth 1979). Today, in contrast, the most dominant global firms are concentrated in the financial and information technology sectors of the economy, if measured by market value (Harris 2008).

The second dynamic of global capitalism is the extent of market power held by dominant firms, often measured in economics textbooks in either four-firm or eight-firm ratios (Cowling and Tomlinson 2005). These measurements capture how much of a sector is owned by just four or eight firms, respectively. In addition to these measurements, there is an important body of scholarly literature that identifies corporate organization of production as a strategy to increase consolidation of corporate power relative to competitors (Prechel 2000; Serfati 2008). Corporations increase their market power by purchasing firms within the same sector, thereby limiting competition and consolidating their ability to control and manage costs. Corporations also increase their market power by strategies of vertical integration, consolidating ownership and control of production activities that serve as cost inputs. Instead of having to rely on the market for acquisition of supplies, corporations may choose to bypass the market by expanding their organizational control over what would otherwise be market relationships. In that sense, corporations trample the market to achieve greater cost certainty and to make it more difficult for competitors to enter their sector of production. These strategies of corporate consolidation are reflected in various waves of mergers and acquisitions that have occurred historically throughout the history of capitalism. Over the past twenty years, there has been a dramatic expansion of cross-border mergers and acquisitions, indicating the extent to which corporate consolidation is expanding well beyond the borders of nation-states (Nolan and Zhang 2010). This is one aspect of the new globalization, as corporations attempt to secure market power through a more consolidated ownership structure that positions firms to take advantage of what are increasingly global production operations involving global value chains (Milberg and Winkler 2013).

In using the phrase "the new globalization," I am not arguing that transnational corporations are becoming more "globalized," a simplistic framing that obscures the extent to which the dominant corporations were always global entities. Instead, following the lead of a robust body of scholarship, I am arguing that transnational firms, beginning in the mid-1970s, began to shift their organization of production toward a transnational platform, with goods being produced across a wider range of countries, alongside a greater reliance on the outsourcing of component parts to distant supply networks and/or foreign subsidiaries. This reorganization of production was highly uneven, more pronounced in some sectors than others, and more characteristic of some firms than others. Information technology firms had a longer history of relying on an international production of component parts than did other manufacturing firms, but other sectors have gradually followed the same patterns, albeit at different intervals and to different degrees (Milberg and Winkler 2013). The process was also uneven because transnational corporations pursued strategies of restructuring that were affected by the domestic politics of their societies, as well as the institutional opportunities and constraints embedded within the context of state-societal relationships. Despite differences in national context, however, transnational firms across the capitalist world have restructured their production across state borders, differentiated only by the timing and degree of such restructuring.

This shift toward transnational production reflected heightened global competition within the leading sectors of the capitalist economy during the 1960s and 1970s. Firms in the U.S. that had previously sought to defend their market position through greater consolidation of ownership activities and through expanded mergers and acquisitions found that such strategies did nothing to improve a steadily declining rate of profit. Fortune 500 firms, an index that includes most of the leading firms in the global economy, were experiencing a decline in their profit rates that had begun in 1965 and continued through 1982. In response, many of the leading transnational firms represented by organizations such as the U.S. Business Roundtable, established in 1972, sought to devise and implement market strategies to reduce their cost margins and thus reverse the decline in the rates of profit (Cox 2012). In Western Europe, transnational corporations formed the European Roundtable of Industrialists in 1982 to accomplish similar goals (van Apeldoorn 2002). The most powerful transnational corporations in Japan had utilized the business organization Keidanren for much the same purpose (Lechevalier 2014).

The intensification of global capitalist competition impacted the strategies of leading transnational firms as early as the mid- to late 1970s. By this time, firms sought to alleviate cost competition through lower-cost foreign inputs. Yet there were considerable political obstacles to relying more on foreign markets for inputs to production. First was the rising wave of left-nationalist movements in the developing world that restricted the access of transnational capital to foreign markets (Prashad 2008). The second were the risks of engaging in foreign direct investments in those markets. Indeed, during the 1970s, U.S. and European transnational firms increasingly relied on risk analysis experts to chart the high costs of foreign direct investment in the developing world, where the rise of nationalism and left-leaning populism led to threats or actual instances of appropriation of transnational capital investments (Maxfield and Nolt 1990).

Still, during much of the 1950s, 1960s, and 1970s, transnational corporations could coexist quite nicely with a wide range of nationalist governments. In fact, nationalist governments that protected their domestic markets through trade restrictions could, and often did, benefit transnational firms who established production facilities designed to produce goods for the domestic market. Transnational firms often benefited from, and supported, protectionist barriers that they could "jump over" to produce for foreign markets. The extent to which transnational capital (and the U.S. state) encouraged and supported import-substitution strategies of developing states has been much underappreciated in the literature of international political economy (Maxfield and Nolt 1990). Prior to the mid- to late 1970s, transnational corporations emphasized foreign direct investment in relatively large markets in the developing world with the goal of establishing production facilities that could sell to domestic buyers. The barriers to trade were less of a problem for foreign corporations able to jump over trade barriers, although they did impact exporters to those markets and firms that did not have the capital and the economies of scale to afford what were often high barriers to entry in those foreign markets.

What we see during the mid- to late 1970s is a more pronounced shift of transnational capitalist firms toward an FDI strategy that involves the production of component parts in an international division of labor that has become much more dispersed across the borders of states. One of the trends that made this shift possible was the debt crisis in the developing world in the 1970s and 1980s. The debt crisis created an opportunity for the IMF, the World Bank and the U.S. state to restructure foreign markets so that they were more favorable to foreign direct investment and/or to the outsourcing of production to independent supply networks at lower costs to U.S. corporations (Ross and Trachte 1990). This restructuring of foreign markets became a precondition for servicing loans that developing countries desperately needed. The political and economic alliances that supported restructuring included core states in the capitalist world economy (U.S., E.U., Japan), transnational corporations with a vested interest in expanding production and financial operations at lower costs, and elites within developing countries that had close ties to transnational capital. These alliances contributed to further opportunities for transnational corporations to rely on foreign direct investment strategies to segment production across state borders.

Corporate reorganization of production was also facilitated by business political mobilization and lobbying that took place in the U.S., the E.U., and

Japan that resulted in favorable changes in corporate taxation, reduced regulatory costs, lower labor costs, and support for corporate restructuring, especially in the U.S., that allowed corporations to sell off corporate divisions in a move from a multidivisional organizational structure toward a multilayered subsidiary structure at minimal cost (Prechel 2000). In this organizational shift, corporations attempted to shrink their organizational bureaucracy toward ownership of high-value-added activities including research and development, patents, branding and advertising. The divisions that once produced actual products or services were either sold off or maintained as independent subsidiaries. Instead of relying on their own divisions to produce goods and services, corporations contracted with independent producers, often in the developing world, to produce goods and services that used to be produced "in-house" by the parent firm (Cox 2012).

Investment banks were central players in the restructuring of U.S.-based corporations during the 1980s. They issued high-yield junk bonds, which were used for leveraged buyouts and hostile takeovers by wealthy financial investors. Especially vulnerable were corporations faced with long-term declining profit rates, which faced high interest rates during the early 1980s, making borrowing difficult. The most seriously afflicted firms saw their book value fall behind their actual market value, making them targets of financial investors. When firms were purchased by investment money during the 1980s, financial investors gained more clout within the corporate boardroom. Financial investors had leverage to restructure corporations by selling divisions and pocketing the proceeds. The restructuring led to a focus on high quarterly profit margins, which meant directives to corporate managers to invest in high-value activities whose rate of return could bring higher stock prices to investors. The role of institutional financial investors in the restructuring of U.S. corporations was facilitated by changes in U.S. tax law that provided a low-cost environment for corporate restructuring and the selling of entire corporate divisions. This was one aspect of the "financialization" of production that helped shape the contemporary production profile of capital-to-capital relations (Milberg 2007).

Another aspect of "financialization" is the degree to which nonfinancial corporations are investing a larger share of their profits in financial speculation. From the 1980s to the present, there has been a significant and steady increase in the percentage of corporate profits invested in financial markets. In restructuring their operations from the 1980s to the present, corporations have shed responsibility for ownership of production activities. Instead, corporate investment has been directed toward high-value activities within the marketplace, including patent ownership, marketing and branding of a product, advertising, and investments in financial asset speculation (Davis

2009). As financial assets have become a more important part of corporate portfolios, corporations have used these assets more aggressively to attempt to shore up the value of their own stock price, and to hedge their bets within a global financial marketplace by dispersing their investments across a range of financial assets. This has allowed corporations to become less dependent on banks for loans to finance operations or investments (Lapavitsas 2013).

A third aspect of the "financialization" of contemporary capitalism is the increasingly central role played by institutional financial investors in linking the operations of a corporation to supply networks in the developing world. As corporations shed divisions during the restructuring that began in the 1980s and continued in the 1990s, more firms looked to independent producers in the developing world to produce goods and/or services that used to be controlled by the parent corporation. Corporations in the high-tech sector, for example, have given up direct control over the production of component parts, and even the finished product, in favor of contracting with producers in key regions or states in the global economy, notably China, to produce products that meet corporate standards. As part of this process, corporations hire institutional investors to help provide the financing and the logistics for establishing the relationship between the corporation and the supply network. Put another way, corporations pay fees to institutional investment networks that facilitate the expansion of global supply chains (Milberg and Winkler 2013).

The internationalization of production, then, has relied on both the politics of the state and the politics of the market. The production profile of the "new globalization" differs from the production profile of the previous era of international relations. From the 1970s to the present, there has been a shift in the dominant global corporations from automobiles, machine tools, chemicals, and steel to a production profile dominated by information technology and global finance, each of which have been key players in the emergence of a burgeoning network of global value chains. This is not to say that the other sectors of the global economy have gone away; quite the contrary. Indeed, most of the manufacturing sectors, to varying degrees, have shifted toward a greater reliance on global value chains, alongside an incorporation of high-technology products within the means of production. This has given the high-technology sectors of the global economy much more structural power within the marketplace and within the politics of nation-states. An examination of the profits of global capitalist sectors supports this analytical framework: information technology firms have the highest market value within global capitalism in recent decades, followed closely by global financial sectors, and finally by the dominant retail corporations and traditional manufacturing firms. High-tech firms have seen a corresponding rise in their inclusion in transnational political coalitions, including trade and investment advisory boards established by governments during the process of negotiating trade and investment agreements with other countries (Cox 2008).

Powerful states, led by the U.S., the European Union, and Japan, have helped to establish the political conditions for the growth of these global supply chains through utilizing leverage in foreign trade and investment agreements. The proliferation of trade and investment agreements from the 1980s to the present has promoted the conditions necessary for the growth of foreign direct investment and the globalization of production by reducing investment barriers across the borders of states. In addition, transnational firms have worked with their host governments, especially in the core states of the global capitalist system, to lobby for an extensive deregulation of investment and a set of protections for intellectual property rights within trade and investment agreements (Cox 2008; Gathii 2011). The role of powerful core states and transnational firms in establishing the rules and regulations governing global institutions such as the World Trade Organization is also extremely revealing. But the politics of transnational production can only be fully grasped by examining the specific political and economic political coalitions that have formed in the most recent phase of global capitalism, which is the purpose of this book.

THE TRANSNATIONAL INTEREST BLOC

The ability of corporations to tap into global financial networks and to establish relationships with favored supply chains is not simply a market-driven process but one that is highly political and characterized by power relationships involving transnational corporate actors, states, institutional investors, and producers in the developing world. To fully grasp the significance of these relationships, I use the term "transnational interest bloc" to identify the political coalitions that have come together to exert their influence in establishing favorable terms for the consolidation of global supply chains. This term requires further elaboration here, as it will form an important conceptual framework for the book.

A transnational interest bloc has several key features that facilitate our understanding of the most important power relationships within the global political economy. The first is the centrality of transnational corporations in political organizations that are based in the dominant states and regions of the world. Transnational corporations have taken the lead in establishing the most important political organizations during the key transition period of the 1970s, when the shift toward global production strategies was just beginning to be conceptualized as a political project (Ferguson and Rogers 1987;

Cox and Skidmore-Hess 1999). The U.S. Business Roundtable, established in 1972, has been central to the political strategy of U.S.-based transnational firms in lobbying the U.S. state for neoliberal policy changes and in articulating the interests of the most globally competitive sectors of transnational capital within U.S.-negotiated regional investment agreements (Dreiling 2000). Similarly, the European Roundtable of Industrialists has played the same role within the E.U., acting as the dominant lobby for transnational corporate interests in both promoting neoliberal restructuring within E.U. member countries and working with E.U. bureaucracies in helping to structure E.U.-led regional investment agreements. Keidanren in Japan has played an equivalent role in organizing the most globally competitive transnational firms in Japan who have taken the lead in promoting neoliberal policy changes in Japan and in promoting favorable conditions for an expansion of Japanese transnational capital in regional investment agreements (Yoshimatsu 1998). Globally, the Trilateral Commission, established in 1973, has been important in bringing together transnational corporations from diverse states and regions of the global economy (Gill 1990).

Each organization has been the subject of a wide range of critical scholarship, but two central points need to be established about these transnational corporate networks. First, these transnational corporate lobbying networks were used to develop political strategies for helping firms to overcome declining profitability that had affected Fortune 500 firms from 1965 through 1982. Second, they sought to establish cooperative mechanisms and institutional structures between firms and leading states in the global economy that would allow for expanded market access across state borders. This was considered especially important in the increasingly competitive and unstable global market environment that characterized the 1970s, when the Bretton Woods system was in crisis, oil price hikes helped contribute to the global recession of 1974, and there was a persistent rise in nontariff barriers to trade by advanced industrial states. In this environment, the leading transnational firms sought to expand their political ties across diverse sectors of the economy and with political elites in the U.S., Western Europe, and Japan (Van Der Pijl and Yurchenko 2014).

An important aspect of the development of transnational interest blocs is the process by which transnational corporations based in the U.S., the E.U., and Japan built political coalitions with state actors during the pivotal transition to neoliberalism in the 1980s. Chapter two will examine the political economy of this transition through case studies of each of these transnational interest bloc coalitions. What starts as a set of alliances between transnational firms and governments based in the U.S., the E.U., and Japan enables the growth of further transnationalization of production that will include substantial parts of the global South. Within the concept of transnational interest bloc, state-capital linkages form around core regions within the global economy, then gradually expand to developing countries where transnational interest blocs produce new alliances, compete for market position, and often allow firms to shed their national identities in favor of shifting transnational accumulation strategies. This has led to the dramatic expansion of foreign direct investment, outsourcing, and subcontracting of global production from the 1980s to the present.

This process has resulted in the second prominent feature of the transnational interest bloc: a proliferation of transnational political organizations in the developing world with ties to their domestic governments and with ties to transnational firms based in the U.S., the E.U., Japan, and China. The extent to which such organizations have become influential political blocs within developing countries is largely a product of the history of capitalist class relations as they have developed within states and societies. In other words, transnational interest blocs are not equally powerful across states, but their power is mediated and contested by conflict with other societal groups, including other business actors, working-class organizations, political party coalitions, and regional/geographic splits that affect political culture, class unity, and the cohesion of the transnational interest bloc (Cox 2008).

The third feature of a transnational interest bloc is the power relationship embedded in the segmentation of production across the borders of states. Transnational firms that own and control patents, branding, marketing, and distribution of a product collect most of the value added from that product in final profits and revenues. These firms are increasingly linked to contractors and subcontractors in the developing world, but the relationships are best characterized as hegemonic and subordinate. Transnational firms at the top of the value chain benefit from their favorable market position and enjoy a hegemonic position in global production networks. Their control over branding and patents enables them to secure a favorable marketing position within powerful retail networks. They are also, being relatively few, able to bargain favorable deals with foreign supply networks, which are forced to compete with hundreds of competitors at the low-cost end of the value chain. As supply networks in the developing world race to move up the value chain, they attempt to establish more cost-effective production of higher-value component parts, which then enables a better bargaining position within global supply chains (Nolan, Zhang, and Liu 2007).

Fourth, transnational interest blocs attempt to use their market power and political organization to increase their access to foreign markets. Market strategies include mergers and acquisitions across state borders and transfer pricing between parent firms and subsidiaries that reduce the costs of operations for the most powerful firms. Political strategies include increased protection of foreign direct investors through laws extending "investor rights" and "patent protections," which have been the central feature of new investment agreements promoted by core states, alongside prohibitions on certain types of government regulations said to "discriminate" against foreign investors.

Fifth, there is conflict between transnational interest blocs based on degree of global competitiveness and sectoral characteristics of production that is often accentuated in divergent trade and investment policy preferences. As I will examine in chapter three, competing transnational interest blocs emerged in the U.S. during the NAFTA and CAFTA-DR negotiations, in the E.U. during the Eastern European negotiations for accession to E.U. membership, and in Japan during the negotiations with Mexico and other Economic Partnership Agreements. The key divisions were often between those firms that were highly integrated and competitive globally, who preferred more robust reductions of trade and investment barriers, and those sectors often linked to agriculture, textiles, and less competitive manufacturing sectors, who supported maintaining minimum levels of protection. These divisions were also replicated in developing countries, especially as developing countries developed more robust linkages with global value chains. Firms in developing countries linked to global value chains and the (often global) financing of those chains favored reducing trade and investment barriers and extending more protection to foreign investors embedded in global value chains. Firms that were less competitive, and more dependent on subsidies and protectionist barriers from their home state, were more inclined to oppose maximum liberalization.

The concept of the transnational interest bloc differs from the concept of "transnational capitalist class," used by a range of scholars whose work I greatly respect, and whose scholarship has provided a solid foundation for my own work on this book (Sklair 2000; Robinson 2004; Harris 2008). However, the term "transnational capitalist class" suggests greater cohesion and levels of organization among the global elite than is presently the case. Transnational interest bloc, in contrast, is a more fluid term that contextualizes the power of transnational capitalist coalitions within a broader set of embedded relationships. These relationships include historical-structural patterns of class conflict, institutional factors that mediate and affect the policy outcomes of corporate-state relationships, the relative power of opposing capitalist interest blocs, and broader patterns of societal cooperation and conflict. The similarities between transnational interest bloc and transnational capitalist class include the extent to which both concepts see capitalist class power as central to understanding the political economy of global capitalism. The concept of transnational interest bloc, however, operates at a mid-range level of analysis that is more sensitive to how fractions and sectors of transnational capital develop and operate in relationship to their location within the domestic and global politics of nation-state conflict and cooperation. For example, in this book I will refer to the "home" location of transnational capitalist coalitions, which I believe is still significant for understanding how transnational firms maneuver in the competitive battle for position within global capitalism. That is not to say that some transnational interest blocs have not outgrown their home location; in many ways they have. But it is to acknowledge the ongoing importance of these political relationships between transnational capitalist firms and the dominant states of the global capitalist economy.

In this book, I document the uneven and differentiated pattern of transnational capitalist coalitions by examining transnational interest blocs in the U.S., the E.U., and Japan. Each of these transnational interest blocs lobbied its "home" state to advance its interests against other transnational interest blocs within global capitalism. While it is true that the line between a U.S., an E.U., and a Japanese-based corporation has become increasingly blurred, the corporate distinctions have not been completely erased or eviscerated. Transnational corporations form transnational interest blocs within nation-state contexts as a step toward greater transnational consolidation of power. In the process these blocs navigate the political realities of their domestic origins, their historical rivalries with other capitalist blocs favored by competing states, and their opportunities to expand beyond the circumstances of their nationally differentiated and constrained political histories. This is especially apparent when examining the way that transnational capitalist coalitions rely on the history of their relationships with their home governments to negotiate favorable investment agreements in locations where their government has established previous colonial or imperial relationships. These historical-structural patterns of colonial and imperial domination still matter in helping to establish the hegemonic politics of a transnational interest bloc.

This framework also has the advantage of being more sensitive to sectoral variation among competing transnational corporations. Students of corporate political and economic organization have established convincing arguments that sectoral variation matters in terms of corporate strategy. Capitalists who own and manage assets that are more tangible, fluid, and permeable, such as financialized assets, are able to move those assets with fewer constraints relative to firms that own more tangible, long-term, and sunken assets that represent fixed investments. The fact that dominant transnational firms are increasingly "financializing" their assets through capital investment strategies that often eschew direct investment gives them more power and flexibility in an age of relatively open financial markets than their competitors that are undertaking more risky investments in finished plants and equipment. The degrees of separation of these firms are increasingly blurred in this new age of globalization, but nonetheless there are important firm-level differences that are reflected in how transnational capital manages their establishment of global value chains.

To illustrate these points, consider the variation among several sectors of the new globalization in how production is managed within global value chains. The high-tech computer and electronics sectors occupy a central position within the market and political structures of global capitalist accumulation. These firms were the earliest to adopt a complex global value chain strategy that involved extensive and far-reaching segmentation of production across state borders. In the U.S., the E.U., and Japan, all the leading transnational computer, electronics, and networking firms began to thoroughly internationalize their production from the late 1980s to the late 1990s. In the U.S., "Apple, Lucent, Nortel, IBM, 3Com, Hewlett Packard and Maxtor sold much of their domestic and offshore production facilities to large contract manufacturers and rapidly moved toward outsourcing their circuit board and product assembly" by the late 1980s and early 1990s (Pratap 2014, 54). In the E.U., transnational firms, including Ericsson, Philips, Siemens, Nokia, and Alcatel, followed this lead by the late 1990s, as did the Japanese firms NEC, Fujitsu, and Sony. In these cases, the parent or "headquarter" firms delinked from in-house production to focus on high-value ownership of intellectual property rights, branding, marketing, and advertising. In the process, the most elaborate and complex value chains were created in these sectors, which became the central drivers of the new globalization. Parent firms established value chain linkages with large-scale contract manufacturers in their home countries and later across Asia, specifically in high-end and high-value locations such as Taiwan, Hong Kong, and Singapore, where legal agreements were established with original design manufacturers (ODMs) and original equipment manufacturers (OEMs). The ODMs undertook product design, development, and manufacturing under the direction of the parent firm, while the OEMs carried out production and assembly operations by supervising an extended array of supply networks, increasingly concentrated in the developing world, again with disproportionate emphasis on the location of supply networks within East and Southeast Asia.

The automobile sector also took advantage of global value chains to ease a rate-of-profit crisis associated with the high cost of in-house production and assembly. This sector, unlike their computer and electronics counterparts, did not rely on contract manufacturers, but instead carried out final assembly operations in their own plants and with their own equipment. This final assembly stage, however, has increasingly been structured so that the assembly plants perform simplified final assembly processes within (or adjacent to) the largest markets where the finished vehicles are sold. This means concentrating the final assembly "around bolting or fixing various fully developed modules or systems" (Pratap 2014, 67). The acquisition of such modules or systems is increasingly dependent on a supply network dominated by relatively few large-scale suppliers, with a strong emphasis on East Asia as the center of intermediate parts production. The global capitalist crisis of 2008 resulted in a greater consolidation of this supply network, with finished assembly processes that are still heavily concentrated inside and around the major global markets of the U.S., the E.U., and Japan.

The increasing reliance of global brand apparel manufacturers on complex global value chains is another indication of the significance of sectoral differentiation. Textiles and apparel were initially outsourced by leading firms from North America and Europe to Japan as early as the late 1950s and early 1960s. By the late 1970s and early 1980s, rising wage costs shifted the locational strategy of leading global brands from Japan to outsourcing investments in East Asia, which was soon followed during the late 1980s by shifts to lower-cost locations in Southeast Asia. However, it was not until the Northern countries fully abandoned their restrictive and preferential import restrictions by phasing out the Multi-Fibre Arrangement in 2005 with the adoption of the Agreement on Textiles and Clothing within the World Trade Organization that the current system of more complex global value chains established itself as a dominant and pervasive tendency. This long-term economic and political restructuring has allowed for an even more segmented and globalized market restructuring whereby the top global brand name firms have concentrated their ownership on branding, marketing, and distribution while establishing an elaborate value chain network that includes ODMs, OEMs, and a wide range of low-cost and dispersed supply networks (Pratap 2014, 80).

As my case studies of the U.S., the E.U., and Japan will make clear, capitalist coalitions operating in distinctive sectoral, historical, societal, and institutional contexts have driven the adoption of neoliberal policies during the new globalization. But the actual neoliberal policies have differed because of the intersection between transnational corporate policy preferences, their sectoral characteristics, and the societal context in which these transnational corporations operate. Some scholars have advanced the useful term "variegated neoliberalism" to describe the way that neoliberal policies have been developed and adopted in different capitalist states (Brenner, Peck, and Theodore 2010; Macartney 2010). This means that capitalist neoliberal policies are contingent on the distinct histories of nation-states, including past levels of class struggle and institutional differentiation. Similar to "variegated neoliberalism," the concept of transnational interest bloc operates at a mid-range level of analysis that allows us to ground the formation of transnational capitalist coalitions within specific histories, and to be sensitive to the extent to which those histories still shape the orientation and objectives of rival capitalist interest blocs. On the other hand, the transnational capitalist class terminology operates at a high-range level of analysis, which is less equipped to examine the specific contextual factors that enhance, limit, or impede the power of transnational capital.

I will argue throughout this book that capitalist coalitions have used transnational interest blocs to enhance their power within states and within national and global markets. The sheer growth and magnitude of this power may well allow for the eventual consolidation of global power by a more unified transnational capitalist class. But thus far the primary vehicle for transnational capitalist expansion of political and economic power has been alliances with political and economic actors within and across nation-states. This process can best be explained by the transnational interest bloc concept, which suggests differentiation, competition, and fluidity of political and economic relationships that is heavily mediated by historical-structural circumstances. Both the transnational interest bloc and the transnational capitalist class terminology can be useful, depending on the context and purpose of the usage. I would acknowledge that the growth of transnational interest blocs throughout the world has contributed to forums that invite greater collaboration among transnational capitalist coalitions akin to what one would expect when using the term "transnational capitalist class." Still, the use of "transnational interest bloc" has clear advantages in differentiating and specifying the more specific, mid-range political and economic networks that sectors of transnational capital occupy within global capitalism.

TRANSNATIONAL CORPORATIONS AND DEMOCRACY

Transnational corporations are not new to global capitalism. However, the scale and scope of their power, both within political systems and within the global capitalist marketplace, have been key factors in the erosion of legitimacy of capitalist political institutions during the "new globalization." The point here is not to romanticize the history of capitalist states, built and reshaped over centuries through colonialism, the slave trade, imperial wars, cyclical depressions, and battles between capitalists and workers. Rather, the point is to contrast what some observers have called the period of "regulated capitalism," from 1945 through 1973, with the period of the "new globalization" from the mid-1970s to the present (Kotz 2015). To be sure, regulated capitalism was rife with hierarchies of exploitation and oppression that have been endemic to capitalism as a system. However, this period of capitalism was unique in that global capitalist growth was sustained over roughly three decades alongside growing wages and incomes for workers in much of the global North and the global South. The concentration of wealth by capitalist ruling classes was less pronounced than in earlier phases of capitalism. Workers' wages as a percentage of GDP were higher in this period (in most capitalist states) than in any previous period of capitalist history. The growth of trade union movements in Western capitalist states, as well as the growth of socialist and communist movements globally, contributed to the reduced polarization of income (Bosch 2015).

In contrast, the period of the "new globalization" has brought capitalism much closer to its earlier pre-1945 history. This includes a greater concentration of wealth on a global scale and within nation-states. While the rise of India and China has lifted hundreds of millions out of poverty, the rate of global capitalist exploitation has intensified across the global capitalist system. This can be measured by the fact that wages have declined as a percentage of capitalist revenues across most of the capitalist world during the period of the new globalization (Dao, Das, Koczan, and Lian 2017). To be sure, this process of wage immiseration has been more pronounced in some capitalist states than others and has occurred unevenly across the time frame of the new globalization. Nonetheless, transnational capitalists have generally succeeded in lowering wages (as a percentage of revenues) and reducing the costs of taxation and regulation in the new globalization, in a wide range of locations within the global capitalist system (Oxfam Briefing Paper 2016). This has been achieved through the segmentation of global production and the relocation of substantial sectors of the global working class, especially in manufacturing, from the global North to the global South. This has meant a more precarious existence for workers in both the global North and South, as the reserve army of the unemployed has been enlarged and utilized to increase exploitation of workers (wages reduced as a percentage of revenues/profits) across the capitalist system.

The political and economic power wielded by transnational corporations in this new globalization has been used in an attempt to reverse the declining rate of profit from 1965 to 1982. The declining rate of profit is typically measured by examining profit rates as an overall percentage of capitalist investment costs. There are numerous contending theories as to why capitalism as a system is prone to periodic declines in the rate of profit. I am not going to wade into the specifics of those contentious debates here, other than to say that the recent work of Marxist economists provides a useful starting point for explanation and understanding. Defending a classical Marxist interpretation, Michael Roberts, in his book *The Long Depression*, argues that the decline in the rate of profit occurs as the incorporation of fixed capital in production (technology, equipment, machinery) outpaces the ability to exploit the living labor of workers, from whence profits are thought to be derived (Roberts 2016). Fixed capital is in this view "dead labor" in that the costs of fixed capital have to be recouped by utilizing the "living labor" of workers. For this process of exploitation to occur, wages paid to workers lag well below the surplus value that they produce for the capitalist owner.

For Marxist economists, and for Marx himself, capitalism is inherently prone to crises emanating from the tendency of the rate of profit to fall. This is due to the inherent contradiction between the tendency of capitalists to constantly expand the ratio of fixed capital ("dead labor") used in production relative to the use of "living labor." Marxists call this process an increase in the "organic composition" of capital, where the ratio of "dead labor" rises in relationship to "living labor." This reduces the ability of capitalists to extract surplus value from workers to recover the costs of investment. The essential aspect of this theory is that worker exploitation is the source of surplus value for capitalist owners. As capitalists integrate advanced technology, machinery, and automation into the production process in an effort to compete with other capitalists, labor exploitation has to rise sufficiently to pay for the costs of incorporating this fixed capital (Roberts 2016).

Capitalists, as Marx discussed extensively, especially in Volumes 2 and 3 of *Capital*, can utilize various techniques to temporarily reverse the tendency of the rate of profit to fall. These include the penetration of foreign markets for capitalist investment, which provides new sources of surplus value to exploit. Another temporary fix is to increase the rate of exploitation of workers by increasing productivity while wages stagnate or lag behind. A third method is to lower the costs associated with doing business by reducing the costs of regulation, taxation, and various revenue payments made to "third parties." This includes the capitalist revenues that are distributed to governments, merchants, "middlemen," and the managerial and service classes that are necessary to distribute the finished product. Capitalists may also acquire access to new sources of revenue through profit-making opportunities made possible through privatization of previously publicly owned property. The ability of capitalists to buy out their competitors through mergers and acquisitions can also allow them to acquire expanded access to revenues and markets. Or a great depression will result in the devaluation of capitalist assets, creating low-cost opportunities for capitalist investment that can temporarily reverse the tendency for the rate of profit to decline.

However, each of these tendencies, in Marxist theory, is only a temporary fix before the rate of profit begins to decline again. This is because the various tactics used by individual capitalists to reverse the tendency of the rate of profit to decline will be mimicked by their competitors, creating market saturation and increasing the competitive pressure on individual capitalists to increase the ratio of "dead labor" to "living labor." That is, capitalists will move toward investing in new technology and new marketing and investment opportunities only to have their behavior mimicked by other capitalist competitors, which contributes to rising organic composition of capital and oversaturated capitalist markets. Capitalists then respond by looking to further reduce the costs of investment, even if it means turning against the very capitalist institutions that have historically provided the social infrastructure, property laws, and welfare spending that have provided some overall stability (and legitimacy) to the capitalist system.

This era of the new globalization, underpinned by what many observers have called the ascendancy of "neoliberal capitalism," has epitomized the rapacious tendencies that have been inherent to capitalism throughout its history. Capitalist firms, seeking to reverse the tendency of the rate of profit to fall, have sought to leverage their political and economic power to lower their costs of production and to increase the exploitation of workers on a global scale. In undertaking these efforts, they have relied on strategies of "neoliberal capitalism," as both ideology and policy, at the level of the nation-state and within the global capitalist marketplace (Harvey 2007). Transnational corporations advocating a set of neoliberal capitalist "solutions" have risen to political and economic hegemony in very diverse nation-states and regions throughout the world economy. But these transnational firms do not all look and behave in exactly the same way. They have emerged from specific domestic, regional, and global histories that have structured and impacted their articulation of neoliberal policies. In other words, transnational corporations occupy distinctive transnational interest blocs that derive from their geographical and socioeconomic histories. These histories include patterns of institutional governance (relationship between corporations and the state), class struggle, and sectoral characteristics that help to shape corporate interests and policy preferences.

In order to analyze transnational interest blocs effectively, there has to be attention to both structure and agency. Transnational corporations have expanded their global production networks across a wide range of sectors, regardless of their geographical location. Structurally, these transnational firms are responding to the central dynamics of global capitalism: a tendency of the rate of profit to fall. They are attempting to counter that tendency by relocating production to cheaper locations, selling off corporate divisions that are too costly while retaining ownership of the most profitable activities, and leveraging their global power over states and other market actors. Corporations utilize their political relationships with nation-states to maximize their profit-making opportunities. At the same time, their opportunities are both directed and constrained by the socioeconomic context from which they operate.

The move toward neoliberal capitalist policies has been pervasive across the U.S., Western Europe, and Japan. Transnational capitalist coalitions in each of these locations, in different ways and at different time periods, have pushed for the adoption of neoliberal policies by their host governments during this new globalization. The effect has been the deregulation of financial markets, privatization of public services, greater concentration of wealth, reduced protection for workers and the poor, and easing of business regulations. The dominant political parties, whether liberal, conservative, social democratic, or socialist, have tended to support these neoliberal policy measures (Marliere 2010). That has meant a steady decline in legitimacy for capitalist states in much of the Western world. Whether measured by voting participation rates, public opinion polls, or levels of confidence in political parties or entire political systems, the Western capitalist states are increasingly considered illegitimate by the voting public—especially working-class populations (Mair 2013). State elites are perceived to represent the interests of the wealthy and the "political class" rather than the interests of groups within civil society. Political scientist Peter Mair has captured these trends in his analysis of Western political systems. Tracing the legitimacy of these political systems from the early 1990s to the present, Mair finds that working-class people are participating less in voting, have higher levels of distrust of governing institutions, and see all political parties as representing the interests of entrenched elites and the wealthy (Mair 2013).

Declining state legitimacy is a direct outgrowth of the power of transnational interest blocs to advance neoliberal policies that are opposed by substantial sections of the population. This has led observers such as Wolfgang Streeck to argue that we are witnessing a "crisis of capitalist democracy" that is leading to a complete evisceration of democratic institutions—an increasingly unregulated capitalism that abandons even the pretense of democratic accountability (Streeck 2017). The rise of transnational corporate power has delegitimized states by stripping away social protections for the working population and the poor. This has served to enhance the power of capital, but it has created an ongoing crisis of governance and legitimacy. At the same time, despite adherence to neoliberal policies, states have not been able to generate the conditions for a long-term increase in the rate of profit for transnational capitalist firms. By 1998, according to Roberts, the rate of profit was in decline again, and corporate investment in productive activities was supplanted by speculative investments on financial markets—the very ingredients that led to the global depression of 2008, the worst capitalist crisis since the depression of the 1930s (Roberts 2016). Well after this depression, capitalist firms are still hoarding cash, unwilling to invest their capital into productive activities necessary to create jobs. The assessment seems to be that the rate of return on such investments is too low to be worth the expenditure. Meanwhile transnational corporations search for new opportunities to further reduce their costs of doing business by pushing for yet more neoliberal measures, including more opportunities for financialized profit accumulation in lieu of productive investments.

Cyclical crises of capitalist accumulation provide the backdrop to understanding the timing of corporate political mobilization. What James Kurth called the political economy of the product life cycle is important for grasping the tendencies of capitalist economies to go through periods of growth and stagnation (Kurth 1979). Discoveries of revolutionary technologies can reverse (temporarily) the tendency of the capitalist rate of profit to decline, typically with the assistance of capitalist governments. Capitalist pioneers of innovation benefit from the earliest incorporation of new product technologies in the production process. Railroads, the steamship, electrical generation, chemicals, and refrigeration allowed capitalists at the turn of the nineteenth century to aggressively expand trade and investment outside the home market, helping to alleviate the long-term decline in the rate of profit that marked the stagnation of the capitalist world economy from 1873 to 1896. But such a recovery from long-term stagnation had to be coupled with imperialist strategies deployed by dominant capitalist states to pry open foreign markets. Similarly, the recovery from the second global capitalist depression of the 1930s was only made possible by World War II, the largest, deadliest, and costliest global war in capitalist history. U.S. government spending on the war effort helped intensify and expand the (already developed) application of assembly line production techniques to the mass production of manufactured goods, including autos, steel, iron, chemicals, and machine tools.

"Regulated capitalism" pivoted around these newly expansive industries until the technologies spread across the global capitalist system, generating more capitalist competition for market access and squeezing capitalist profits in the process. Similarly, the growth of information and communications technology spearheaded the transformation of the capitalist production process that is central to the new globalization and the growth of neoliberal capitalism. The segmentation of production would not have been possible without the development of these new technologies. At the same time, capitalist states have been crucial in enabling the transfer of these technologies to the private sector, often through government-financed research and development that was used for military production in the U.S. and then transferred to the private sector to facilitate the growth of corporate profits. Capitalist states, as we will see in this book, have also been central to the process of private-sector accumulation by promoting favorable conditions for foreign direct investment though "investment agreements" negotiated with foreign states. The terms of these agreements, often referred to wrongly as "trade agreements," emphasize the protection of intellectual property rights and investment guarantees that facilitate corporate restructuring and corporate profits. Transnational interest blocs have used their growing power within the global capitalist system to advance their interests in these new investment agreements.

The power of transnational interest blocs has contributed to the growth of global value chains, which has been structured within a hierarchal relationship of corporate power and based on an increasingly global exploitation of labor within those value chains. Transnational capitalist coalitions have worked to establish the preconditions for these supply chains by consolidating their political and market power within global capitalism. However, such consolidation has always been tied to deepening exploitation of workers, the degradation of the environment, and a steady weakening of a regulatory infrastructure whose purpose is increasingly tied to the narrow, short-term interests of global capitalist profit. As such, the current neoliberal capitalism built around global value chains, and central to what I term the new globalization, is beginning to fracture due to its inherent contradictions. Several scholars have discussed this process within a wide range of critical frameworks. I will contribute to that discussion in chapter five of this book, where I bring the crisis of neoliberal capitalism and the new globalization up to date by examining the recent stagnation of global value chain production and the rise of nationalist coalitions that are mounting a challenge to the power of transnational interest blocs.

This book analyzes the power and significance of transnational interest blocs in the following chapters. Chapter two examines how transnational interest blocs in the U.S., the E.U., and Japan have used their political and market power to facilitate the creation of global value chains through the aggressive promotion of neoliberal policies during the 1980s and 1990s. Chapter three analyzes the growth of transnational interest blocs in the developing world through the growth of global value chains, forged through a process of corporate restructuring, further financialization of production, and the proliferation of investment agreements championed by transnational capitalist interest blocs. Chapter four examines the political economy of value extraction within global value chains by examining the distribution of profits and wages, as well as the increasing reliance on developing countries, especially in Asia, to produce manufactured goods and component parts that are central to the new transnational system of accumulation. In chapter five, I examine the current neoliberal crisis, the concentration of corporate power in the information technology sectors, the rise of far-right parties, and the delegitimization of the capitalist state. In this context, I analyze the opportunities for workers to use their leverage in global value chains to wrest a larger share of revenue from transnational capitalists. In chapter six, I argue that my analytical framework, transnational interest blocs, explains the dominant trends in global capitalism better than competing approaches in international relations or international political economy. I also suggest ways that this theoretical framework could be used to promote linkages between theory and practice in helping social movement activists challenge corporate power more effectively.

Chapter Two

Transnational Interest Blocs in the U.S., the E.U., and Japan

This chapter will examine the role of corporations in promoting an economic and political restructuring of business-state relations within the U.S., the E.U., and Japan from the 1980s to the present. Corporations established the terms of this restructuring by wielding their power within markets and within political systems. This meant the ascendancy of a national and global architecture of corporate power that has promoted deregulation, lower taxes on corporations and the rich, weakened trade unions, and the creation of global value chains that has dispersed production across nation-states. Within this period of neoliberalism, corporations have engaged in class warfare against working people, which has accelerated inequalities within nation-states. The rising power of transnational corporations is central to understanding these trends. Here I will outline the hierarchy of transnational corporate power that exists within global value chains, followed by a closer examination of how transnational corporations have used their economic and political power to enhance their profits at the expense of workers and the poor within nation-states and on a global scale.

Transnational corporations are the dominant political and economic actors in global politics today. Their dominance is manifested by their coordination of global value networks that are responsible for about 80 percent of global trade (Kim et al. 2018, 5). The conceptual framework of global value chains was initially limited to an analysis of the producer and retail networks involved in the production and distribution of a good or service. Over time, scholars have sought to deepen our analysis of the political economy of global value chains by expanding our understanding of the range of economic and political actors involved (Nielson et al. 2014). The more expansive use of the term, global value networks, is designed to include both the production and distribution networks involved in global value chains and the vast and growing array of intermediaries that are necessary to coordinate, facilitate, and complete the requirements of global value chains. These intermediaries include management consultants, legal services, recruitment agencies, traders, financiers, and standard-setters, as well as the political governing structures that help to establish global value networks. In this book I will use the term "global value chains" interchangeably with "global value networks" in order to capture the broader political and economic relationships surrounding the construction and operation of global value chains.

Traditional trade statistics have dramatically understated the prevalence of global value chains by looking primarily at foreign direct investment operations to capture intra-firm transactions. Today, intra-firm transactions represent about 35 percent of global trade. However, transnational firms over the past two decades have relied much more on contracts, leases, franchising, and arms-length transactions than on ownership of foreign subsidiaries. This has created a vast web of transnational production networks in which transnational corporations own the most valuable aspects of global value chains, including patents, branding, and marketing, while managing the segmentation of production across a range of actors. Transnational firms, located at the top of a value chain pyramid, procure their finished product in production networks that typically span several developing countries, disproportionately concentrated in Asia. The dramatic rise in intermediate good exports as a percentage of overall exports reflects the growing predominance of transnational value chains. As of 2009, "world exports of intermediate goods exceeded the combined export values of final and capital goods for the first time, representing 51% of non-fuel merchandise exports" (Gereffi 2014, 434).

Concentration of ownership at the top of global value chains means that only a few transnational corporations dominate the most profitable ownership activities within industrial sectors. This enables lead firms, disproportionately located in developed OECD countries, to capture most of the value from global value chains (Banga 2013, 3). The rest of the value allocated is dispersed among a much more competitive supplier network, much of which is now based in the developing world. The hyper-competition among suppliers forces down the cost of inputs, intermediate goods, and labor used in the production of finished products. The ability of transnational corporations at the top of global value chains to secure a disproportionate share of value cannot be explained by their innovation and value added in production. Transnational firms leverage their dominant position within the global marketplace to secure profits that are disproportionate to their contribution to global value chains. Transnational corporations that manage production networks have concentrated their market wealth and power in global capitalism during the neoliberal era. Nolan and Zhang (2010) examined the small number of firms that dominate the global market share in a variety of industrial sectors:

	Number of firms	*Global market share*
Large commercial aircraft	2	100
Automobiles	10	77
Fixed-line telecoms infrastructure	5	83
Mobile telecoms infrastructure	3	77
PCs	4	55
Mobile handsets	3	65
Pharmaceuticals	10	69
Construction equipment	4	44
Agricultural equipment	3	69
Cigarettes	4	75*

Figure 2.1. Transnational Corporations and the New Globalization
Source: Nolan and Zhang 2010, 99.

	Number of firms	*Global market share*
Large commercial aircraft		
Engines	3*	100
Braking systems	2	75
Tires	3	100
Automobiles		
Auto glass	3	75
Constant velocity joints	3	75
Tires	3	55
Information Technology		
Micro-processors for PCs	2	100
PC operating systems	1	90
Glass for LCD screens	2	78

Figure 2.2. Transnational Corporations and the New Globalization
Source: Nolan and Zhang 2010, 99.

Figures 2.1 and 2.2 indicate the extent to which transnational corporations that control the highest-value activities within global value chains, which Nolan and Zhang label "system integrator" firms, dominate entire sectors of production. Figure 2.1 indicates the market share of "system integrator" firms in their corresponding production sector. Figure 2.2 breaks down the market share of firms that produce component parts within global value chains. These firms, often labeled original equipment manufacturers or subcontractors, coordinate an increasingly vast supply network to produce finished goods that will be incorporated into a finished product that is owned, marketed, and distributed by system integrator firms. The value of Nolan and Zhang's chart is the extent to which it captures the extreme levels of concentration within global value chain production.

There has been a steady increase in cross-border mergers and acquisitions (M&A) that have contributed to the consolidation of ownership in global value chains. Cross-border M&A have been led by firms within developed economies who have sought to increase their market consolidation within industries and within global value chains. Firms targeted for acquisition have been those that had already outsourced their production to developing countries (Smith 2016, 73). The consolidation of ownership has resulted in greater control of high-value activities among a very small number of lead firms. This has created a greater differentiation between the market power of lead firms, increasingly consolidated within the U.S., the E.U., and Japan, and a more dispersed, subordinate, and hyper-competitive supply network in the developing world that provides cheap labor. Firms at the top of global value chains are the dominant players in a transnational interest bloc that has shaped the contours of the new globalization.

I use the term "transnational interest bloc" to frame an understanding of how transnational capitalist coalitions have used their economic and political power to shape global value chains. In my view, "transnational interest bloc" best captures the power relationships that have been central to creating, operating, and sustaining global value chains. Recognition of this power structure is central to understanding the political economy of value allocation within global value chains and production networks. Transnational interest blocs are led by transnational firms based in the market economies of the U.S., the E.U., and Japan and linked to policy networks through business associations that have promoted the conditions necessary for the establishment, maintenance, and growth of global value chains. These blocs have been the most important actors in drafting domestic legislation that has contributed directly to global value chains. Most importantly, this has included the active involvement of transnational interest blocs in drafting trade and investment agreements that have facilitated the growth of global value chains.

Transnational interest blocs have both common and conflicting goals depending on their position within the global economy. Transnational corporations ally with each other across the boundaries of states to promote investment agreements that facilitate their ability to expand their linkages to global value chains and production networks. As such, we can identify transnational interest bloc coalitions that share a common interest in lowering barriers to trade and investment restrictions that inhibit flows of capital. However, transnational interest blocs also involve competition between rival transnational firms, who seek to use their ties to governments to provide them with subsidies, tax incentives, and research and development money that will give them an advantage in global market competition with rival interest blocs. The fluidity of this cooperation and competition means that transnational interest blocs are not defined by their relationship with one government, but instead maneuver for position within multiple governments based on the goal of maximizing global market share and profits. Transnational blocs will also be divided according to levels of global competitiveness, levels of global integration, and sectoral characteristics that will at times generate interest bloc conflict over the terms of trade and investment agreements.

Transnational interest blocs also include business associations, government bureaucracies, ministries, and legislative alliances in the developing world that have long-standing ties with transnational firms based in the U.S., the E.U., and Japan. The transnational ties between business associations in the North and the South have deepened since the 1980s, coinciding with the politics of the debt crisis in the developing world. The debt crisis gave transnational actors in the North and South a political opportunity to extend their investment ties through the promotion of neoliberal trade and investment policies. These policies favored the interests of transnational actors and extended ties between transnational political coalitions in the North and South, while promoting the establishment, maintenance, and growth of global value chains.

Transnational interest blocs are shaped by the specific historical and institutional context in which they are established. Transnational firms that are linked to global value chains have different histories based on their distinct institutional and political contexts. An institutional and political culture that varies from one nation-state to another has helped shape the different trajectories of interest bloc coalitions. Similarly, the ability of transnational interest blocs to establish political and economic linkages to developing countries has often been dependent on the extent to which the socioeconomic class structure and the institutional political structure have been favorable to the growth of global value chains.

The volatile and shifting nature of transnational interest bloc formation will be analyzed by examining the patterns of bloc formation within the context of the U.S., the E.U., and Japan. In order to be more precise about the particular relationship between the transnational interest bloc and government policies that have furthered the growth of global production networks, I will emphasize the role of transnational interest blocs in working with governments in the U.S., the E.U., and Japan to promote policies favorable to the growth of foreign direct investment, subcontracting, and outsourcing of production that were central to the establishment of these blocs. During their formative stages, transnational firms used their location inside the borders of the major core economies to develop an extensive network of relationships with their respective governments. Initially this linked the formation of transnational interest blocs to state policies that promoted neoliberalism, including the establishment of regional and global investment agreements that have been aggressively promoted by the most powerful governments in the developed world.

TRANSNATIONAL INTEREST BLOCS AND THE UNITED STATES

The shifting production strategy of U.S.-based transnational corporations was a response to a systemic crisis in global capitalism that deepened during the 1970s.[1] From 1965 through 1982, Fortune 500 corporations faced a declining rate of profit. Heightened global competition between U.S., German, and Japanese firms eroded market share for previously dominant U.S.-based firms. In response, U.S. firms engaged in economic and political strategies to bolster their competitiveness. These included a wave of mergers and acquisitions during the 1960s when some firms dramatically expanded their ownership activities by forming conglomerates and diversifying into a wide range of business activities. By the end of the 1960s, it was evident that this strategy had failed, and firms began looking for other solutions to their competitiveness problems. Some firms in the textile and electronic sectors had already started segmenting their production by outsourcing their supply networks as early as the 1960s. Automobile firms started outsourcing the production of component parts as early as the 1970s in response to increased global competition.

However, the foundations of the qualitative and quantitative shift by transnational corporations to global value chains began in the 1980s and accelerated in the 1990s and the 2000s. This shift in the structure of globalization, which I refer to as "the new globalization," was part of a lengthy political and economic process that was aided by the ascendancy of neoliberal ideology during the 1980s. Corporate activism during the 1970s contributed substa tially to the rise of neoliberal ideology, which argued that too much government regulation, taxation, and interference by the state in the private market had reduced corporate profits, slowed growth, and limited job creation. Corporations in the U.S. dramatically increased their political lobbying networks during the 1970s with the goal of reducing their costs of production through reducing taxes and regulations. The formation of the Business Roundtable in 1972 is especially important in understanding the politics of the "right turn" in U.S. economic policy. The Roundtable started as an industry association determined to weaken the power of unions within the construction sector. But when it was renamed Business Roundtable, its agenda became more ambitious, including efforts to lobby the U.S. government to establish corporate-friendly trade and investment agreements. The Business Roundtable membership included the largest and most powerful transnational firms, based in the U.S., whose members were looking to the U.S. government for favorable tax policies and for the promotion of foreign investment in an effort to forestall the ongoing decline in the rate of profit.

Corporate lobbying networks in the U.S. achieved their most significant victories in shaping congressional legislation during the 1980s. These victories included the neoliberal package of reduced taxation on the wealthy and on corporations, reduced business regulations, reduced enforcement of worker health and safety regulations, and tax breaks specifically geared toward corporate reorganization. Corporations, led by the Business Roundtable, lobbied for congressional legislation that would make it less costly for corporations to restructure their businesses. The passage of the Tax Reform Act of 1986 included provisions that would allow corporations and businesses to restructure their operations by selling off unprofitable divisions. The act "provided tax free mechanisms to transfer capital among parts of the corporate family." Concretely, this provision allowed corporations to more easily shift their corporate structure from multidivisional forms (MDF) to multilayered subsidiary forms (MLSF). Corporations could replace divisions that were previously owned by the firm and managed by the central office with subsidiaries that would be legally independent of the corporation while still being financially controlled by the corporate parent. This allowed corporations much greater flexibility in financing their operations given that divisions, which were previously wholly owned by the firm, were shifted to the status of subsidiary corporations that could raise money on their own through stock sales.

The shift in corporate structure from the MDF to the MLSF allowed corporations, at tax-free rates, to restructure their operations by shedding legal responsibility for corporate divisions that were previously managed by the central office. This facilitated the global restructuring of the corporation, with the central office of the parent company establishing a far-flung network of subsidiary firms that would produce a range of products at arm's length from the legal obligations of the parent corporation. Within this structure, corporations could easily shift ties from subsidiaries to independent suppliers and contractors to further restructure the corporate form.

Such a restructuring strategy would not have been possible without the fourth wave of mergers in U.S. history during the 1980s. This merger wave, unlike the conglomerate trend of the 1960s, was characterized by firms purchasing firms in the same industry and downsizing other activities that were deemed peripheral to future profit streams. The Tax Reform Act of 1986 included a provision that allowed corporations to use their acquisitions of other firms to qualify for tax-free status, as long as the acquisition "was in the same or a related product line as the existing business" (Prechel 2000, 257). This law followed an extended period of reduced enforcement of antitrust policy during the Reagan administration. Reagan's treasury secretary, attorney general, and commerce secretary supported an antitrust policy that would relax provisions of the Clayton Act which specified that mergers and acquisitions should be prohibited when "the effect of such acquisition may be to substantially lessen competition or tend to create monopoly" (Prechel 2000, 257). Within this context, the Reagan administration's first antitrust chief in the Justice Department, William Baxter, "rewrote the antitrust guidelines to raise the level of market concentration that triggered a Justice Department challenge to conglomerate mergers, vertical combinations between suppliers and customers, and horizontal mergers between competitors" (Prechel 2000, 257).

The mergers and acquisitions wave of the 1980s began a process of restructuring by U.S.-based transnational firms that intensified during the 1990s and 2000s. With each passing decade, corporations have used favorable changes in U.S. antitrust and tax laws to facilitate the establishment of global production networks, which have been essential in efforts to attempt to stabilize profit rates after two decades of steady decline. Since 1986, U.S.-based corporations have relied on imports from global value chains for a steadily higher percentage of inputs in production. In the manufacturing sector alone, "offshoring intensity of material inputs reached 14.5% in 2006, up from 11.6% in 1998, 6.2% in 1984 and 4.1% in 1974" (Milberg and Winkler 2010, 6). However, not all firms are created equal in their linkage to global value chains. Corporations involved in the production of electrical equipment, telecommunications, computer and electronic products, motor vehicles, transportation equipment, and apparel were disproportionately involved in offshoring of material inputs. Firms in these sectors, by 2006, were relying on the offshoring of material inputs for as much as 20 to 25 percent of non-energy inputs used in their final product (Milberg and Winkler 2009, 16). Aggregate numbers reveal a similar picture of a U.S. economy that is much more firmly tied to offshoring and global value chains than has been the case historically. By 2004, "52% of U.S. imports were intra-firm" and "intermediaries accounted for 38% of U.S. imports" (Milberg and Winkler 2010, 280). A simulation model of U.S. trade found that "vertical specialization—the sequential vertical trading chain stretching across many countries, with each country specializing in particular stages of a good's production sequence—accounted for over 50% of the growth of US trade in the period 1962–1997" (Yi 2003, 91).

Just as the U.S. state has provided transnational firms with favorable changes in domestic tax and antitrust legislation, the U.S. state has also been very important in negotiating reductions in trade and investment barriers with developing countries to facilitate the emergence of global production networks. U.S. corporate investment in global value chains has been facilitated by greater access to foreign stock and bond markets, which has given U.S. transnational firms the ability to link directly with foreign producers through the creation of subsidiaries or through minority shares in production networks dispersed across a range of locations and countries. A greater percentage of U.S. corporate profits from the early 1990s to 2006 have been directed to financial investments in stock and bond markets, including a rising percentage of these investments in the emerging markets of the developing world (Krippner 2005, 184–186). At the same time, corporations are paying out more revenues as dividend payments to shareholders, while reducing wages paid to U.S. workers and while investing less in productive plants and equipment in the U.S. (Serfati 2008, 40–42).

In the U.S., transnational corporations that were most aligned with these newly emerging production structures lobbied the U.S. state to change tax laws in ways that facilitated corporate restructuring. This was also true in U.S. foreign economic policy, where political organizations led by the Business Roundtable became vehicles for promoting the liberalization of capital markets, policies which benefited globally competitive U.S.-based financial interests as well as nonfinancial corporations that sought to increase reliance on foreign markets for the production of intermediate goods and component inputs that would be designed, branded, and distributed by the parent firm. The liberalization of foreign stock and bond markets helped to connect producers of intermediate goods in the developing world to value chains that extended back to the U.S. and other developed country markets. Transnational firms would link with foreign producers, either in the form of joint ventures, subsidiaries, or independent contractors, to produce products incorporating the technological specifications and packaging required by the parent firm. Foreign producers at the higher end of the production chain could raise money for their costs of doing business by tapping newly emerging domestic stock markets, which could be financed in part by global institutional investors as well as domestic financiers who wanted to realize profits from the newly emerging transnational production networks. Other foreign producers, at the lower end of the production chain and not capital-intensive enough to enter domestic stock exchanges, would produce component parts at cheap costs at the bottom of the supply chain, with an overwhelming dependence on cheap labor to realize the slimmest of profit margins.

A political model of corporate influence in U.S. foreign policy can be linked to the position of corporations along the global value chain, which I have labeled a transnational interest bloc. U.S.-based transnational firms at the top of the value chain have the strongest representation within the Business Roundtable, arguably the most influential corporate political organization in U.S. foreign policymaking—especially U.S. foreign economic policy and trade policy. In the negotiations that provided the legal framework for NAFTA, the membership of the Roundtable overlapped with the trade advisory committee established by the U.S. Special Trade Representative to negotiate the details of the agreement. Corporate sectors that were disproportionately represented in the negotiation were those sectors most involved in a global restructuring of production, including industrial and consumer electronics, telecommunications, pharmaceuticals, computers, agribusiness, auto manufacturers, and the most globally competitive textile and apparel manufacturers (Chase 2005). U.S. retail corporations and the leading commercial and investment banks also supported the agreement. The opening of the Mexican financial markets allowed U.S.-based institutional investors holding mutual, pensions, and insurance funds to tap into the Mexican market as a condition for the restructuring of Mexican debt. At the same time, the privatization of Mexican state-owned industry provided opportunities for the expansion of supply networks linking U.S. transnational corporations to subcontractors in the Mexican market. This was especially true in auto parts and electronics produced in the maquiladora sector. This sector expanded rapidly after the passage of NAFTA, alongside other manufacturing sectors that are closely linked to intermediary trade in U.S.-led global value chains (Yang 1998).

The U.S. state played a significant role in establishing the political conditions necessary for a greater consolidation of supply networks in Mexico. A 1982 change in U.S. banking regulations, the Export Trading Company Act, allowed commercial banks to invest directly in import-export firms as part of their foreign operations. In addition, there were further changes in U.S. banking regulations due to a relaxation of Federal Reserve requirements that allowed commercial banks to gradually expand the percentage of their capital investments in stock and bond markets (Bhargava and Fraser 1998). Finally, the Brady Plan of 1989 allowed Mexico to finance some of its debt by a "debt for equity" swap in which commercial banks could purchase equity stakes in shares of Mexico's newly privatized firms as a substitute for outright repayment of debt obligations. The privatization of Mexican firms during the 1980s helped create a transnational political coalition that linked U.S.-based financial corporations—in commercial and investment banking as well as institutional investors—to a newly emerging Mexican supply network that was increasingly owned by a relatively small number of Mexico's wealthiest financial investors. Represented politically by the Mexican Council of Businessmen, the largest thirty-seven Mexican firms dominated the privatization of state assets, accounting for 80 percent of the value of all privatizations between 1982 and 1991 (Moody 1995, 101). The Business Roundtable and the U.S. Chambers of Commerce worked closely with Mexican investors to support privatization initiatives during the 1980s that became institutionalized with the passage of NAFTA.

In the case of Mexico, a transnational political bloc could emerge more easily than was possible in other contexts due to the historical ties between U.S. capital and Mexican capital, especially in the Maquiladora sector, which had been established as a legal arrangement in the 1960s, and in agribusiness, where large-scale Mexican firms and financial interests were already deeply connected to U.S. agribusiness firms in the purchase of machinery, fertilizer, and trade relationships. This process was connected to the ongoing transformation of global agriculture toward more elaborate supply chains that linked to food processing, marketing, and distribution networks dominated by large-scale U.S. agribusiness corporations and structured in important ways by the rising power of corporate supermarket retail chains (Spieldoch 2010).

In the NAFTA negotiations, there were two groups of transnational capital that formed distinctive interest bloc preferences, which were ultimately codified in NAFTA. The first bloc was composed of the high-tech, financial, and pharmaceutical sectors, which wanted a NAFTA free of any preferential trade and investment barriers. These sectors advocated far-reaching globalization of the NAFTA market due to their global competitiveness and the extent to which they had already globalized significant aspects of their production. A second sector, which was led by automobile producers, especially the big three U.S.-based producers—General Motors, Ford, and Chrysler—advocated preferential tariff protection for auto firms that produced at least 62.5 percent of their content in North America. These firms saw NAFTA as a path to lower their cost of restructuring in the short term as they moved toward more integrated global production strategies. Consumer electronics firms and parts of the U.S. textile and clothing industry also fell into this second category, advocating for preferential terms for their industries as part of the NAFTA agreement. Likewise, the most powerful U.S. domestic agricultural interests, while supporting unfettered access to the Mexican agricultural market, supported a continuation of quota restrictions to protect the higher value-added processing activities associated with U.S. domestic production.

These transnational interest blocs emerged initially as linkages between transnational corporations, their lobbying associations, and the state(s) in which these corporations were based. Over time, other transnational interest blocs have emerged within the historical and institutional contexts determined by patterns of interaction between dominant transnational corporate interests and the state. The next two sections will detail the emergence of transnational interest blocs in the European Union and Japan.

TRANSNATIONAL INTEREST BLOCS AND THE EUROPEAN UNION

Transnational corporations in Western Europe faced many of the same pressures from globalization experienced by their counterparts in the U.S. The twin problems of rising unemployment and slow growth in the 1970s and 1980s provided the context for the rise of transnational corporate lobbying organizations. The most significant was the European Roundtable of Industrialists (ERT), which took its name from the Business Roundtable in the U.S. Formed in 1982, the ERT consisted of several of the most globally competitive European firms, as well as the so-called European "national champions," whose success had been closely linked to their particular relationship with their home country government. During the early years, the ERT devoted itself to establishing a close working relationship with the European Commission of the European Economic Community (EEC). Their objectives at first were to try to expand the European Market as leverage for European-based large-scale capitalists against increasing competition from Japan in particular, but also from the competitive pressures of globalization more broadly. The ERT, between 1983 and 1987, supported a neo-mercantilist policy that included expanded market access to the EEC alongside protectionist measures for European capital against non-European firms, especially the U.S. and Japan (van Apeldoorn 2002, 83–114).

The firms within the ERT that most favored the neo-mercantilist strategy were based in France and were less globalized than their counterparts in Britain. In fact, the political divisions within the ERT can largely be explained by the institutional and socioeconomic histories of particular firms. Firms that were less globalized and more dependent on their home states for subsidies and financing were most likely to support protectionist strategies of European market expansion. More globalized firms that were more dependent on trade and foreign investment, as well as the most competitive global firms, were more likely to support a neoliberal European market expansion. Corporations supporting neoliberal policies wanted freer trade and investment opportunities within Europe and within the larger global economy. As these firms became more powerful within the ERT by 1987, the policy orientation of the organization shifted from neo-mercantilist to neoliberal. This can be explained in part by the overall rise in the transnational orientation of ERT member firms, which increased their reliance on foreign trade and investment in response to increased globalization. The internal politics of the ERT also contributed to such a shift in policy orientation, as British and German firms took a larger role in setting the agenda for the ERT by 1987, in comparison to the previous influence of French-based firms (van Apeldoorn 2002, 94–100).

The formation of a powerful transnational interest bloc within the ERT was apparent by the mid- to late 1980s. At that time, the ERT had established a long-term working relationship with the European Commission that became instrumental in shaping the framework for the creation of the European Union. The formation of the ERT reflected the views of the most dominant and profitable firms within Western Europe. The timing of the organization's formation reveals the extent to which large-scale European capital was responding to the ongoing declining rates of profit. The member firms of the ERT sought to expand the opportunities of European capital by promoting the establishment of the European single market. The goal was to lower and to eventually remove the barriers to trade and investment so that European producers could create more efficient economies of scale across the European Economic Community (EEC). The EEC had allowed member states to establish differential standards pertaining to trade and investment, which meant that European firms had to tailor their investment strategies around the requirements of national economic policies. The ERT began to articulate an agenda and a full-blown set of policy proposals that would have an impact on the eventual adoption of the European single market. This process was codified through the adoption by the European Commission of the Single European Act of 1986, which established the outlines and the timetable of European integration.

The ERT was influential in developing the policy agenda for European integration, which it had hoped would be achieved by the European Commission as early as 1990. Instead, the process was delayed until the adoption of the European Union through the Maastricht Treaty of 1992. Between the drafting of the Single European Act of 1986 and the establishment of the E.U. in 1992, the ERT aggressively lobbied member governments of the EEC, through their home governments as well as the Council of Ministers, in support of single-market policies that would establish a large-scale transportation infrastructure to facilitate an expansion of trade, cross-border investment, and enhanced integration. The ERT also worked to establish an overarching agenda in consultation with the European Commission, which drew directly from the ERT's policy reports to craft the final version of European integration that would be embodied in the Maastricht Treaty of 1992. The first pillar of the treaty involved unfettered movement of goods, services, capital, and labor among the member states of the newly formed E.U. The second pillar was the emphasis on "competitiveness" and "benchmarking" whose goals were to establish uniform standards governing industrial competition policies. In practice, this meant breaking down barriers to investment and privileging large-scale capital. The third pillar involved plans for the European Monetary Union (EMU), which was pushed by transnational capitalists in the Association for the Monetary Union of Europe (not all firms within the ERT agreed with the monetary union initially). The fourth pillar involved the further expansion of the European Union to Eastern Europe, where large-scale capital could further exploit economies of scale by creating low-cost production networks in countries targeted for their cheap and easily accessible labor (Bohle 2006).

An analysis of the firms comprising the ERT indicates a division between those firms favoring a liberalization of the European market without external protection and those favoring liberalization with external protection. The information technology sectors, including computers, semiconductors, telecommunications, and microelectronics, advocated liberalization as a strategy for global competitiveness. The CEOs in these sectors, represented by the founder of the ERT, the CEO of Philips, championed the European single market as a platform for mergers, strategic alliances, and technology-sharing viewed as crucial in the battle for global markets. Firms in these sectors, as well as large-scale banking and financial firms, wanted a liberalized European market as a gateway for encouraging further globalization. Firms with large economies of scale—automobiles, chemicals, machine tools, and electronics—also supported European integration. However, these sectors, unlike their counterparts in information technology, differed on the degree of support for external protection of the European market. Firms that were less competitive and benefited from domestic protectionism saw European market expansion as necessary but wanted to retain subsidies and levels of protection against non-European importers (Drahokoupil 2009).

The divisions between European firms over the degree to which European integration should be accompanied by external protectionism were evident within the ERT membership. German steelmakers were advocates of an external market expansion that ended state subsidies, quotas, and trade barriers against competitors. On the other hand, "national champions Usinor and Sacilor in France, Finsider in Italy, and British steel in Britain, supported protection against low-cost German and Dutch competitors in the transition to a single market" (Chase 2005, 160). European firms that were more globally competitive were in favor of neoliberal strategies of integration that allowed for lowering their costs against global competitors. Cost-cutting strategies included cross-border mergers, use of part-time or relatively low-paid labor in cheaper markets, and greater access to foreign markets by reducing barriers to entry. It was here that the information technology (IT) sector led the way in promoting global restructuring. The IT sector was more nimble than its counterparts in traditional large-scale industry, and the use of IT products became increasingly important for industries looking to lower their costs of producing goods. At the same time, financial investors sought to take advantage of policies harmonizing capital movements (Chase 2005, 160). Those sectors that were more mobile took the lead in promoting neoliberal restructuring that had ripple effects on the balance of power between capital and labor.

The firms that comprised the ERT sought an expansion of the European market conducive to capitalist restructuring. Expanded trade, competition policy, and integration of Eastern European markets facilitated the reorganization of European capital. The ERT lobbied aggressively for a single European market, which was eventually adopted in the Treaty of Maastricht in 1992. The unified market contributed to a growth of intra-firm trade within corporate production networks in the E.U. In fact, the growth of intra-firm trade eclipsed the growth of trade in finished products, mirroring the larger trends within the global economy. The ERT also lobbied for a shift in the orientation of "competition policy" by the European Commission. The Directorate General for Competition was initially established in 1957 with the creation of the European Community. The purpose of this bureaucracy was to develop a set of procedures, guidelines, and regulations pertaining to the concentration of business power within the market. In practice, this bureaucracy was weak and rarely used its regulatory powers until the turn toward neoliberalism enabled by the approval of the Single European Act in 1986. Since that time, competition policy has been reinterpreted to allow the Directorate General (DG) much more authority and discretion to act as a regulatory and enforcement agency. The DG has used its newfound power to intervene against cartels, and to limit and restrict state subsidies and protectionist policies that were deemed to inhibit private-sector competition. In practice, the "competition" policy has been more effective in limiting national subsidies to industries than in blocking mergers. State aid to industries has steadily declined from 2 percent of EC GDP in the 1980s to 1 percent during the 1990s to 0.5 percent in the years 2004–2008. On the other hand, the vast majority of mergers and acquisitions have been approved. From 1990 through 2012, the EC approved almost all requests by E.U.-based corporations for mergers and acquisitions. "Only 22 out of 5,068 or .43 percent of mergers notified in the period of 1990 through 2012 were blocked" (Wigger and Buch-Hansen 2014, 122–123).

Transnational corporations have been able to use this new trade and regulatory environment to dramatically increase their levels of corporate consolidation within the E.U. During the late 1990s and early 2000s, the telecommunications and technology sectors led the way in a merger and acquisitions wave that reached its peak in 2001. The financial sector was a close second in merger activity during this time. The third-highest merger activity was concentrated in the industrial sectors, especially manufacturing, as high-technology products were being integrated at an accelerated pace into steel, machinery, chemical, and consumer goods production. As much as one-third of the E.U. merger activity involved mergers between E.U. and non-E.U. firms, indicating the speed with which E.U. transnationals were integrating with their counterparts in the U.S. (European Central Bank 2006, 36–37). As transnational firms were increasingly dependent on cross-border integration, support for neoliberal globalization increased and support for protectionism declined. At the same time, high-technology producers and financial investors became the key drivers of an accelerated globalization. Industrial firms and nonfinancial corporations relied increasingly on the integration of high-technology products and financial investors to restructure their global operations. Consistent with these trends, E.U. corporations looked to expand their production networks and value chains to low-cost locations, especially in Eastern Europe. This process was facilitated by the terms of E.U. accession that were required for Eastern European countries to become members of the E.U.

Transnational corporations comprising the ERT were in favor of the expansion of the European Union to include Eastern European countries. The terms of such expansion were crafted by the European Commission with the assistance of the ERT from the period of 1993 through 2004, when eight Central and Eastern European countries joined the E.U. (the Czech Republic, Estonia, Hungary, Latvia, Lithuania, Poland, Slovakia, and Slovenia). The process of Eastern European integration required that Eastern European countries implement liberalization and privatization reforms in a manner that favored Western capitalist interests (Bohle 2009). The politics of the eastward expansion of the E.U. were on much more restrictive and conditional terms than had been the case for Western European expansion. Aspiring Eastern European states were expected to liberalize and to privatize their economies as a precondition for the accession process. In turn, during the transition period, Western European countries were able to enact protectionist measures in the imports of steel, textiles, clothing, chemicals, and agricultural products, areas in which the Central European states held a comparative advantage (Caradaica 2013, 28).

The outlines of the accession process were first established in the Copenhagen criteria of 1993, which stipulated that accession countries had the obligation prior to accession "to adapt their economic and political institutions to the conditions of a free market, guaranteeing of human rights, institutional stability and so forth" (Haller 2011, 145). The ERT worked with the European Commission in establishing the framework or the preconditions for Eastern European integration. These included favorable policies in the areas of privatization, foreign direct investment, low taxation, reform of labor markets, and liberalization of property laws so that "competition policy" encouraged protection of access to Eastern European markets for foreign investors and traders. The terms of the integration of Eastern European regimes into the EU can partly be explained by attention to the external power of the ERT and the European Commission in establishing the terms of accession. But we also have to consider the internal political economy of the Eastern European countries in order to fully explain the timing and content of economic reforms.

The accession process did not follow the same path in all of the Eastern European countries. The European Commission did use the strength and size of the E.U.-15 to bargain hard for a full array of liberalization and privatization measures as a precondition for E.U. accession and membership. However, the internal political environments within the various candidate states played a role in determining the pace, content, and eventual direction of these neoliberal reforms. Some scholars have used the term "embedded neoliberalism" to describe the tendency of the larger market economies in Eastern Europe to structure access to their markets for foreign investors around state subsidies, tax breaks, and partnerships with domestic investors, state bureaucrats, and mid-level managers. These subsidies were promoted by a transnational interest bloc led by manufacturing firms in Western Europe who were able to join with domestic partners in the four Visegrad countries (Hungary, the Czech Republic, Slovakia, and Poland) to promote a foreign direct investment regime that provided "tax exemptions, direct subsidies for specific investments, import protection, building of infrastructure, investment in skills, and reforms of the labor code towards more flexible regulations" (Bohle 2009, 174). These relationships were made possible by the historical and institutional context that established the preconditions for the growth of transnational interest blocs that tied Western transnational corporations with their business, professional, and managerial partners in these Eastern European countries.

Over time, the Visegrad countries shifted their political and economic strategies in efforts to meet the requirements of the E.U. accession process. At first all of the countries emphasized import protection and tax holidays, but then they had to shift their subsidy packages to be in line with E.U. "requirements on common external tariff and state aid" (Bohle 2009, 174). As a result, the subsidies shifted away from tariff protection to emphasize a different variety of incentive packages, which included "preferential treatment in acquiring land, cash benefits, investments in the infrastructure and training of the labor force, and . . . a thorough deregulation of the labor codes" (Bohle 2009, 174). These embedded subsidies created a downward set of competitive pressures among the Visegrad countries themselves, which competed aggressively with each other to extend more favorable cost reductions to transnational corporations. This has meant vigorous competition among the Visegrad countries to lower taxes, with reductions in the corporate tax rates occurring regularly in Hungary, Slovakia, the Czech Republic, and Poland from 1999 through the first decade of the turn of the century. These tax reduction measures were accompanied by competition in investment incentives and a deregulation of the labor market—making it easier for employers to terminate labor contracts. In addition, there has been a steady retrenchment of the welfare state—including reductions of social benefits such as pensions, a reduction in overall social spending, and tightening of health-care and education spending and benefits.

Transnational interest blocs have pursued a political and economic agenda that has simultaneously pressured states to increase corporate subsidies and corporate welfare alongside a steady reduction in social welfare spending. Transnational lobbying networks led by the American Chambers of Commerce have supported this agenda, as have sectors of transnational capital that have sought to lower their costs of production by shifting toward associational agreements with production partners in Eastern Europe. The establishment of transnational value chains has become deeply embedded within a set of corporate-state interest blocs that have provided ample incentives for a restructuring of transnational production. The ripple effects on the social fabric of these Eastern European countries are being felt with the rise of far-right political parties that have encouraged workers to blame lower incomes and growing inequalities on the cosmopolitan features of the EU accession process, including immigrant workers and the EU bureaucracy, rather than the dominant corporate interest bloc coalitions that have profited from lower wages and reductions in social spending.

Transnational corporations have been able to use their production platforms in Eastern Europe to exert greater pressure on workers in Western Europe, including a weakening of the social wage and a renegotiation of the terms of employment in Germany and elsewhere. This has meant an increasing differentiation of workers within German industry, "with only core workers keeping their high levels of employment protection" (Bohle 2009, 179). German employers in automobiles, telecommunications, chemicals, pharmaceuticals, machinery, and electronics have already seen downward pressure on wages and overall job protections. Over the past decade, working-class wages in Germany have been stagnating, indicating that the dominant transnational corporate employers are at the very least using their enhanced leverage associated with relocation of production to create a more favorable bargaining position with German workers. At the same time, there has been a shift within the German state to tighten the rules and to increase the requirements associated with state assistance in providing temporary subsidies for workers attempting to transition between jobs. According to economist Michael Roberts, "about one quarter of German workers now receive a 'low income wage,' using a common definition of one that is less than two-thirds of the median, which is a higher proportion than all 17 European countries, except Lithuania" (Roberts 2017).

While the Visegrad countries of Eastern Europe have exerted the most direct competitive pressure downward on social wages, job protection, tax rates, and welfare expenditure, neoliberals have lavished the most praise on the policies of the Baltic states, whose governments have opened their markets with fewer restrictions, fewer subsidies, more cuts in government spending, more privatization, and even lower taxes than the other Eastern European countries. The speed with which the Baltic states have radically restructured their economies has been praised by E.U. technocrats, the IMF, and transnational corporate investors—especially in finance, which views the deregulation of financial markets in the Baltic states as a good model for the rest of Eastern Europe. The extent to which Latvia, Estonia, and Lithuania have deregulated their labor market and have met the terms of a pure "competition state" has meant that labor unions have been "all but completely marginalized . . . [while] trade union density as well as collective bargaining coverage is among the lowest in Europe" (Bohle 2009, 172–173). Of all the Eastern European countries to ascend to E.U. membership, the Baltic states and the Visegrad have been welcoming to foreign investors, but the Visegrad economies have used their subsidies to attract higher-end capital embedded in value chain relationships, while the Baltic states have relied on low-cost capital accumulation by pursuing policies that reward production in low-cost component parts or services. In Estonia, this has meant a production profile of information technology services, telecommunication services, and low-cost production of component parts for machinery and transport vehicles. For Latvia, there has been an emphasis on financial services, component parts production, wood products, refined petroleum, wheat products, and packaged medicants ranking at or near the top of their list of exports. Lithuania has also emphasized component parts production for motor vehicles and machinery as well as exports of services in information technology.

Transnational interest blocs have worked successfully to restructure the European economic landscape through the acceleration of global value chains. Transnational corporations in financial services, telecommunication services, information technology services, and machinery and transport corporations have used the Baltic states to extract low-cost production of services and components. The price has been the growing gaps between an upper class and managerial class in the Baltics that benefit from these relationships and a working class that has steadily lost ground in wages, social benefits, job security, and job protection. The shredding of the social safety net has been tacitly endorsed by the E.U.'s emphasis on "competition policy," which encourages new member states to adjust their economies to liberalize trade and foreign investment. In the bigger market economies of Eastern Europe, the Visegrad, governments have relied on a range of subsidies to attract more productive investments, yet the terms of such investment have meant a simultaneous reduction in wages, job security, job protection, and increasing precarity for the Eastern European working class. At the same time, an entrenched managerial/professional class has benefited from these policies by working to position themselves as junior partners within transnational interest bloc value chains. Only one Eastern European country, Slovenia, has succeeded in minimizing these trends, only gradually opening its economy and keeping strategic sectors in the hands of domestic nationals. The overall effect, however, of the Eastern European restructuring has been to elevate the political and economic power of transnational interest blocs in most of the leading sectors of European capital accumulation, while weakening the position of the working class.

TRANSNATIONAL INTEREST BLOCS AND JAPAN

During the mid-1980s, the corporate power structure that characterized post-WWII Japanese capitalism began undergoing a steady transformation with the adoption of neoliberal policies. In order to fully grasp the dynamics that have contributed to the ascendancy of neoliberal ideology in Japan, I will first review the outlines of the system of Japanese corporatism that developed during the 1950s and deepened during the "Japanese miracle" of the 1960s, which helped to catapult Japan to the strongest sustained growth rates in the capitalist world—contributing to its emergence as a leading competitive industrial economy through much of the 1970s and 1980s, before a severe and prolonged economic recession during the late 1980s led to a long-term structural crisis. The mid- to late 1980s marked the beginning of a transition from a Japanese corporatist/Fordist economic system to a neoliberal corporate structure whose changes are similar, but not identical, to those identified in the U.S. and E.U. case studies.

The post-WWII development of Japanese capitalism led to the consolidation of market power by groups of dominant Japanese corporations bound together by horizontal linkages (cross-shareholding between partner firms) and preferential financing by large-scale Japanese banks. The horizontal corporate groups, known as *kigyo shudan*, linked Japanese corporations within a network of overlapping shareholders that served to shield member firms from the "short-term threat of takeover" while facilitating "long-term investment decisions" (Cowling and Tomlinson 2011, 572). Japanese banks enabled these corporate groups by providing "access to cheap funds and assistance in financial and foreign markets" while occasionally undertaking "industrial rescues" (Cowling and Tomlinson 2011, 572). The dominant corporations within these kigyo shudan relied on a group of subcontractors to produce component parts for the major firms. Known as *keiretsu*, this supply network was a crucial component of a Japanese "just-in-time" production system that enabled low-cost delivery of component parts from small-scale firms to large-scale corporate manufacturers.

The domination of Japanese assembly corporations within this structure of corporatism is well established in the scholarly literature. Japanese firms in the hierarchy of these corporate groups have been able to leverage their market size and power to extract low-cost production from subcontractors, who operate on tight cost margins and are dependent on the parent contractors for sales. The parent firms in this vertical supply chain also exert influence over their suppliers through equity ownership stakes in the subcontractors, which has resulted in significant managerial control of supply chain business practices, including "the subjugation of keiretsu partners by assemblers dictating contract conditions and imposing technologies and processes upon them" (Cowling and Tomlinson 2011, 573). Three-quarters of subcontractors depend on one assembly corporation for "over 50% of their orders," a statistic that reflects the market power of the "parent" corporation in the keiretsu hierarchy (Cowling and Tomlinson 2011, 573). The market power of the lead firm in the history of Japanese corporatism can be seen as a precursor to the globalized production system that is increasingly tethered from its domestic context in favor of global outsourcing of component parts. In other words, the Japanese "just-in-time" Fordist system of production anticipated many of the features of the "new globalization."

One aspect of the Japanese system has long been the subjugation of labor within the hierarchical market relationships dominated by lead firms. Japanese workers have been represented by "production-first" unions whose roles in the production process have facilitated corporate strategies in implementing a "performance-based pay and promotion system and a relative absence of job rules" (Price 1994, 68). Corporate managers have worked closely with union officials to ensure that workers are disciplined within a tightly run structure of production targets, job "flexibility," and "lean production." In practice, this has meant that Japanese workers are enlisted as participants in quality control and productivity improvement efforts but in the context of a hierarchical decision-making structure that vests considerable discretion with the company manager. In this system, workers in the top-tier firms were given relatively high wages and "lifetime employment" guarantees but were expected to be utilized across a range of jobs and to be rewarded based on managerial assessments of performance output. This system of worker subordination to a managerial-dominated workplace within a corporatist supply structure had roots in an employer offensive in Japan during the early 1950s, led by auto firms such as Suzuki. At that time, Japanese business owners mobilized, with assistance from U.S. occupation authorities, to roll back gains that had been won by Japanese workers from 1946 to 1949, who used work stoppages and strikes to win progressive reforms, including workers' representation on management councils, a greater role for workers in company decision-making, and a greater say in hiring and firing. The employer offensive of 1950 reversed these gains and subordinated the more independent, militant Japanese unions to a company union structure that solidified management control. The result was an imposition of a more restrictive, hierarchical system of capital domination over labor that has only been intensified by the gradual adoption of neoliberal changes within capital-labor relations in Japan.

As has been extensively documented, the Japanese state played a crucial role in financing this corporatist system that privileged a hierarchy of Japanese assembly corporations and Japanese banks within an embedded supply chain structure of production. The Japanese Ministry of Trade and Industry provided subsidies, research and development funding, and capital investment to favored industries. These mercantilist strategies contributed to the high growth rates of the Japanese economy during the so-called Japanese economic miracle of the 1960s and further entrenched the power of the Japanese corporate groups within the economy. At the same time, the Ministry of Finance provided an allocation of credit that became essential for the growth of Japanese corporate investment. The Japanese government deployed "a wide array of tools to promote savings" and "savings subsidized investment by depositing money into savings accounts that earned lower-than-market rates of interest, thus raising the demand for credit and giving the government the leverage to allocate credit to priority sectors" (Bello 2017, 3). This state-supported and state-subsidized credit system provided banks with investment funds that "they could lend to firms at below-market rates and still maintain reasonable spreads (margins between deposit rates and lending rates)" (Bello 2017, 3).

This Japanese corporatist system could be sustained so long as the Japanese capitalists could expand their access to export markets necessary to finance growth. However, by the mid- to late 1970s, the intensified competition among Western industrial corporations served to drive down global growth rates, resulting in a mismatch between increased production of corporations in the core of the global economy and declining market shares. From 1950 to 1973, the world economy grew at a rate of 4.9 percent per year, while from 1974 to 1989 the growth rate was only 3 percent annually (Bello 2017, 3). The declining growth rates of the 1970s and 1980s were exacerbated by the rise of the newly industrializing countries of East Asia, particularly South Korea and Taiwan. As economic historian Robert Brenner has noted, "the shares of world exports of goods held at this point by all non-OPEC, non-Japanese Asia had risen to 13.1 percent, higher than that of the U.S. (11.7 percent), Germany (12.7 percent) or Japan (8.5 percent)" (Brenner quoted in Bello 2017, 3). These trends exacerbated a long-term decline in capitalist profit rates across all of the core regions of the global economy, including Japan.

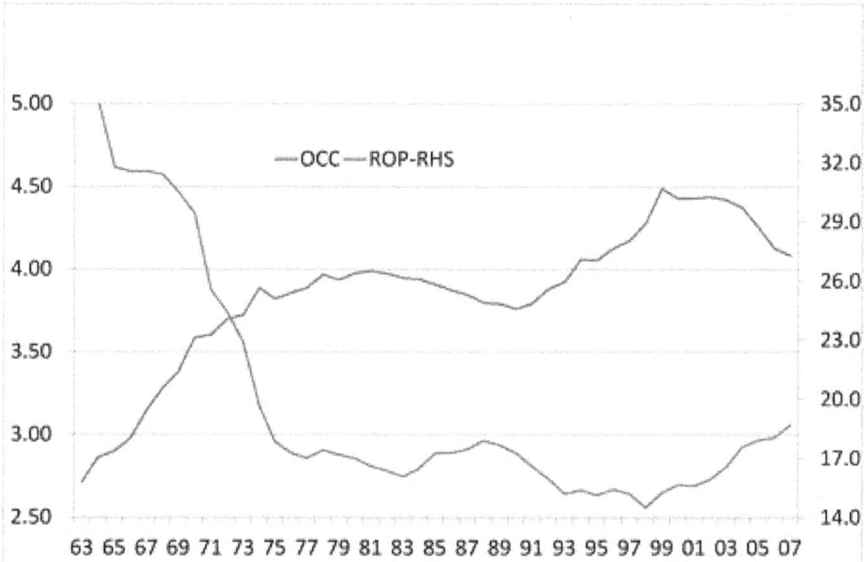

Figure 2.3. Japan: Rate of Profit (%) and Organic Composition
Source: Roberts 2012.

The effects of this profit crisis led corporations in Japan, alongside their counterparts in the United States and Germany, to organize politically and economically to attempt to reverse the profit rate decline. In all three cases, the most globally competitive firms advocated lower-cost foreign direct investment strategies to reduce the costs of doing business in the home markets.

Japanese corporations, represented by the lead Japanese corporate lobbying organization Keidanren, worked closely with Japanese officials in the Ministry of Trade and Industry (which became the Ministry of Economy, Trade and Industry by 2001) and the Ministry of Finance in a concerted effort to promote favorable conditions for the expansion of foreign direct investment. The Japanese state had long provided extensive subsidies to Japanese corporations for FDI activities, but prior to the 1980s the FDI subsidies were directed primarily toward FDI in resource extraction activities. During the first two decades of Japanese subsidization of FDI, from the early 1950s through the early 1970s, the state directed most of its FDI support toward raw materials processing sectors (e.g., paper and pulp, steel mills) that were closely linked to the needs of processing plants in Japan. By the mid-1960s, the state financing of FDI included support for the textile sector as it entered a phase of structural decline that resulted in a greater outsourcing of production to lower costs. At this time, subsidization of FDI was also directed to heavy industries dependent on cheap energy, especially after the 1973 "oil shock" dramatically raised energy costs. By the mid-1980s, there had been a further shift in FDI subsidization toward leading Japanese corporate export sectors whose competitiveness had been threatened by intensified global market competition and an appreciation of the yen. The electronics and automobile sectors' share of loans from the Japanese Export-Import Bank "jumped from 2 percent and 12 percent, respectively, in 1985 to 22 percent each in 1999" (Solis 2003, 105). By the mid-1980s, Japanese corporate exporters in high-tech and manufacturing worked closely with the Japanese state in a transnational interest bloc to promote a transition to lower-cost FDI in foreign markets that would begin to shift the lower wage production of the keiretsu supply chain from Japan to lower-cost locations in East and Southeast Asia.

The relationship between capital and labor in Japan has been mediated by the corporatist policies of the Japanese state, which has consistently provided support for Japanese corporations through subsidization of domestic and foreign investment activities. The role of the Japanese state in supporting the internationalization of Japanese capital from the mid-1980s to the present is consistent with earlier Japanese strategies of "managed globalization" in that Japanese subsidization levels for corporate activities has always been very high by comparative standards. The Japan Export-Import Bank provided "close to $69.5 billion in public loans for overseas investment between 1953 and 1999," which amounted to "almost 10 percent of all Japanese postwar FDI during this time period" (Solis 2003, 103). However, it was not until the mid-1980s that the Japanese state began to work closely with Japanese corporations in the high-tech and manufacturing sectors to provide subsidization that would facilitate the process of relocating Japanese domestic production within these sectors to foreign locations, aggressively targeting FDI expansion to East and Southeast Asia. This strategy of "managed globalization" has retained significant features of the previous system of Japanese capitalism: a corporatist set of linkages between the Japanese political parties, bureaucracies, and leading Japanese corporations. However, this new globalization differs from the old in the neoliberal restructuring of the Japanese keiretsu value chain networks. By the mid-1980s, leading Japanese corporations, led by firms such as Toyota and Matsushita, dramatically expanded FDI into Southeast Asia, alongside the relocation of parts of their supply network:

> At least $15 billion of Japanese direct investment flowed into Southeast Asia between 1985 and 1990, with Indonesia receiving $3.1 billion, Thailand $3.7 billion and Malaysia $2.2 billion. . . . It was, however, not just the scale of Japanese investment over this five-year period that had an impact—it was also the strategy that accompanied it. The Japanese government and the keiretsu planned and cooperated closely in the transfer of corporate industrial facilities to Southeast Asia. One key dimension of this process was the relocation of not just big corporations like Toyota or Masushita, but also the small and medium enterprises that supplied them with services and components. Another key dimension of the process was the functional integration of complementary manufacturing operations that were spread across the region in different countries. (Bello 2017, 9)

There were several economic and political factors that contributed to this relocation of Japanese production to low-cost Southeast Asian locations. The first was the overproduction in the Japanese export sector, indicated by a steady fall of exports relative to gross domestic product especially after 1985, when the Japanese yen had appreciated in value. Japanese firms looked to compensate for underperformance in the export sector by relocating production in Southeast Asia, facilitated by loans from the Japanese government. Second, the Japanese state relaxed capital restrictions, which helped Japanese corporations rely less on Japanese banks for financing, thus breaking one of the links in the kigyo shudan or the horizontal corporate groups that had characterized the previous decades of Japanese capitalism. Japanese corporations in high-tech and manufacturing started to shift toward the Tokyo, New York, and London bond markets for financing instead of relying as heavily on Japanese banks. In turn, Japanese banks began to shift financial activities toward real estate investment and speculative finance, which contributed to the bubble in Japanese real estate markets that eventually crashed by 1990, leading to a decade-long period of stagnation.

Third, the shift toward greater FDI investment by Japanese firms into Southeast Asia was part of a long-term lobbying effort on the part of the most mobile sectors of transnational capital, including high-tech and manufacturing firms as well as transnational banks, to deregulate capital markets in developing countries. This process of global financial deregulation was promoted by Japanese transnational firms and the Japanese financial sector, alongside transnational capitalists in Western Europe and the U.S., with the goal of increasing lower-cost foreign direct investment and portfolio investment in the Southeast and East Asian region through the mid-1990s. Japanese foreign direct investment can be divided into two categories: capital-intensive investment, which was more expensive and constituted a much larger percentage of overall FDI, and labor-intensive investment, which emphasized low-wage labor in subcontracting arrangements. Capital intensive FDI was directed toward the U.S. and Western European countries, while labor-intensive subcontracting was directed toward developing countries in Asia.

The internationalization of Japanese production has been facilitated by state strategies of subsidization, access to cheap credit, and restructuring of the relationship between Japanese corporate groups and their supplier network. At the same time, during the 1980s the state continued to provide incentives to large-scale Japanese private banks to expand their lending to speculative activities, including investments in the real estate sector. City banks, long-term credit banks, and trust banks built up enormously risky loans that could not be repaid after the real estate crash of 1990. By 1992, the London *Financial Times* "estimated that the total of bad loans in Japanese banks [stood] at around 42–46 trillion yen (roughly 10 percent of the total 450 trillion yen in loans)" (Itoh 2000, 92). By January of 1998, "a survey by the Ministry of Finance revealed that the total of bad loans still amounted to 12 percent of total loans by various banks, or 76 trillion yen" (Itoh 2000, 92).

The Japanese government underwrote and perpetuated the bad loans held by Japanese banks throughout the 1990s by providing access to cheap credit at taxpayer expense, followed by a massive program of public subsidization, underwritten by substantial increases in Japanese state debt, financed through the Japanese bond market. The "Bank of Japan reduced the official interest rate from 6 percent in 1990 to 1.75 percent in 1993 to 0.5 percent in September 1995," in an effort to "mitigate the difficulties of banks and other financial institutions with huge bad loans" (Itoh 2000, 92). In addition, there was a substantial public subsidization of Japanese banks throughout the 1990s that had reached the highwater mark of 70 trillion yen in subsidies by 2000 (Itoh 2000, 103). These policies were backed by a dramatic escalation of public sector debt, which is reflected in the growth of budget deficits financed by government bonds. Japan's public sector debt worsened during the 1980s and resulted in neoliberal measures including the privatization of state-owned enterprises alongside cuts in social security and education spending. The crisis of the 1990s deepened these trends, as the value of government bonds outstanding increased from 166.3 trillion yen in 1990 (about 37.9 percent of GDP) to 327 trillion in 1999, which was "almost seven times the annual tax revenues of the state" (Itoh 2000, 98). As Itoh has observed, the political terms of this dramatic increase in bond debt "works as a powerful means of income redistribution from the great number of taxpaying workers to the owners of state bonds . . . as long as banks borrow from the Bank of Japan at 0.5 percent interest and simply invest in public debt, the great bulk of interest payments on public debt operate practically as a subsidy to the banks" (Itoh 2000, 99).

The stagnation of Japanese capitalism during the 1990s was a direct response to systemic factors that were long-term and included a steady decline in the rate of profit for Japanese corporations, a massive buildup of both state and private-sector debt that attempted to address the crisis, and an imposition of regressive policy measures (from the 1980s through the present) that asked the middle and working classes to pay for the costs of further corporate subsidization.

In Japan, as in the U.S. and Western Europe, the period of the 1980s to the present has seen a neoliberal restructuring of corporate capitalism toward greater internationalization of production and state policies that have pushed the cost of capitalist restructuring on the middle and working classes. Specifically, the rate of exploitation of workers has steadily increased in Japan, as elsewhere in the core capitalist regions. This is due to a long-term process of capitalist crises that is reflected in capitalist investment decisions to cut wage costs by globalizing production. This intensified rate of exploitation is also assisted by state policy measures that have pushed down the social wage provided to Japanese workers in favor of increasing subsidies to Japanese corporations. In short, neoliberal policies have intensified in Japan and have served to increase the power of capital relative to labor both within the market and within government policy decisions.

The Japanese corporate structure, the keiretsu, has undergone significant changes from the 1980s to the present that have restructured the relationship between banks, corporations, and workers within Japanese capitalism. These changes have moved Japan toward a neoliberal capitalist framework that has reduced state constraints on corporate decision-making and made it easier for corporations to lower wage costs by relocating production abroad and by changing the terms of employee contracts. Japanese firms from the 1980s to the present have reduced their reliance on full-time employees with consistent lifetime wages and compensation benefits in favor of a highly differentiated compensation system. This restructuring of worker compensation has been accomplished by giving managers more discretion in adjusting the wages of regular, full-time workers depending on performance evaluation. This is a practice long reserved to managers, but the gap in discretionary pay has grown more extreme from the 1980s to the present. There has been a corresponding increase in the employment of contractual workers with limited employment contracts, part-time workers, and "dispatched" workers who are placed via an employment agency and therefore are more easily subject to the immediate (and disposable) needs of a company manager.

The Japanese state has facilitated the increased exploitation of the Japanese workforce by easing restrictions regarding the circumstances under which a business can change the employment status of the "regular" employee. The classification of "regular," "non-regular," and "dispatched" employees has long been regulated by a combination of company practices, government legislation, and the court system. "Regular" workers refer to workers who are hired for indefinite time periods and whose hiring is tied to the expectation of lifetime job guarantees, seniority benefits, and pension benefits. Large-scale manufacturing firms have had a higher percentage of "regular" employees than subcontractors, whose production is much more cost-constrained and contingent on demand from their supply network. As a result, subcontractors have always relied more on contractual and part-time workers than the larger firms. However, protections to "regular" workers had been codified in Japanese legislation starting in the 1950s and were further supported by court precedent, which had limited the replacement of "regular" workers by "non-regular" workers to a particular set of circumstances. Court rulings have stipulated that companies can only alter the status of "regular" workers under the following conditions:

> Business conditions had to necessitate retrenchment; the need for cutting back via outright dismissal as opposed to transfers or furloughs had to be clear; the selection of those for dismissal had to be fair and rational, and the procedure, including discussion with the union if present, had to be reasonable. In contrast, "non-regular" employees, typically hired on fixed contract, often in parttime status, were only protected from dismissal during the contract period. They had no protection when it ended. At the same time, labor laws from the 1950s placed some significant restrictions on the industries and contexts in which workers could be hired on time-limited contract, in particular when hired through third-party labor brokers. (Gordon 2015, 6)

In practice, Japanese corporations put pressure on Japan's subcontracting network by outsourcing production starting as early as the 1960s but intensifying in the 1970s and accelerating dramatically in the 1980s, as previously discussed. This contributed to greater reliance on wage differentiation among employees within a single firm, but especially within a very vulnerable subcontracting network. By the 1990s, the Japanese state accelerated these changes by passing laws easing regulations that had restricted the labor policies of Japanese firms. From 1996 through 2000, changes in labor law made it easier for Japanese firms to hire more "non-regular" employees, defined by short contracts, lower wages, and no social benefits. A further change in Japanese labor law was codified in 2003, which continued the trend of easing restrictions on Japanese employers. The total impact of these policy changes, combined with already shifting Japanese business practices, contributed to the following trends:

> The number of male non-regular employees nearly tripled from 1995 to 2013 (from 1.9 million to 5.4 million), and the number of non-regular male employees age 25 to 44 rose nearly five-fold (from 360,000 to 1,690,000). As a proportion of all male workers, non-regular employment rose from 7.4 percent in 1985 to 19.7 percent by 2012. The younger men in this status are the very people who in the past would have been starting and building careers as regular employees in medium to large scale corporations, with some realistic hope of building a long-term career in that organization. For commentators in the mass media, for the general public, for educators, and for labor bureaucrats, the fact that so many young men, the expected breadwinners and household heads of the nation, have been unable to enter the mainstream of regular employment constitutes a change with far reaching social and economic consequences. Their concern is bolstered by good evidence that non-regular male workers in their 20s and 30s were only half as likely to be married as regular male employees of the same age. (Gordon 2015, 16–17)

The patriarchal nature of the Japanese employment structure is evident in the preceding summary, as the biggest effect of recent labor changes in Japan is on young Japanese men, since women had long been subject to discrimination in the "regular" Japanese labor market. The neoliberal restructuring of the labor force, however, has made the Japanese labor system closer to the U.S. in the "flexibility" of the workforce as expressed in percentage of Japanese workers affected by shifts in GDP over a two-year period. From the 1950s through the early 1980s, only about 20 percent of Japanese workers' jobs were affected by changes in GDP, compared to a 100 percent metric for U.S. workers. By 2009, about 85 percent of Japanese workers' jobs were affected by changes in GDP, which was only 15 percent lower than the U.S. rate (Gordon 2015, 18). In other words, the flexibility of Japanese workers has intensified under the pressures of neoliberal restructuring, contrary to critiques of the Japanese labor sector as "inflexible" or "rigid."

Japanese corporations have steadily become more transnational over the past three decades, following trends that have characterized firms in the U.S. and the E.U. Corporations in each of these cases have responded to the competitive pressures of global capitalism by transnationalizing production in an effort to lower costs by seeking out cheap labor and greater access to foreign markets. At the same time, corporations have relied on their ties to capitalist states to subsidize the costs of their restructuring by lowering their taxation burdens, increasing their access to state credit, and reducing the costs of doing business by decreasing regulations, especially those governing employment practices. The results have contributed to increased corporate power, growing inequality, and accelerated transnationalization of production that has shifted the costs of restructuring from corporations to workers through the proliferation of subcontracting networks.

CONCLUSION

As this chapter has documented, transnational interest blocs were formed in the core states of the capitalist system through alliances between transnational corporations and states. State-capital cooperation created the conditions for the expansion of transnational production strategies. This included the promotion of neoliberal policies in the U.S., the E.U., and Japan that restructured capital-labor relations in a way that imposed greater costs on workers. The earliest stages of the internationalization of production, and the creation of an emerging transnational interest bloc, grouped transnational capitalist interests with their "home" states through corporate-led political associations that framed the terms for the internationalization of capital. The corporate groups coalesced in the Business Roundtable in the U.S., the European Roundtable in the E.U., and Keidanren in Japan, whose lobbying networks were crucial in providing the economic and political linkages between transnational capital and the state. The earliest manifestation of the successes of these business associations was the deepening of regional trade and investment agreements embodied by NAFTA and included in the formation and deepening of the European Union. In Southeast and East Asia, the Japanese state subsidized an internationalization of production for its own transnational firms, resulting in a substantial growth of cross-border subcontracting networks.

The next chapter examines how the transnational interest blocs identified in each of these three case studies have developed economic and political alliances in developing countries. Transnational firms that have relied on the U.S., Japan, and the E.U. to develop the conditions for transnationalization of production have also forged relationships with supplier networks that have become the basis for expanding their power and influence on a global scale. As these transnational alliances have deepened, transnational interest blocs have become very fluid in using their economic and political power to compete with other vested interests in developing countries, often successfully advancing their agendas within bilateral and regional investment agreements. At the same time, the rise of China has been crucial for the expansion of transnational interest blocs, as rival investors grapple for favorable position within the lucrative China market, while both cooperating and competing with interest blocs for power within the Chinese state and society.

NOTE

1. Part of this section is drawn from Ronald W. Cox, "Corporate Finance in US Foreign Policy," in *Corporate Power and Globalization in US Foreign Policy*, ed. Ronald W. Cox (London: Routledge, 2012), 17–25.

Chapter Three

Corporate Power and Global Value Chains

Corporations have relied on their instrumental and structural power to lobby governments, transform markets, and establish far-flung transnational production and supply networks in developing countries. In chapter two, I examined the relationship between transnational corporations and state actors in the U.S., the E.U., and Japan that pushed aggressively for neoliberal policies that favored the expansion of foreign direct investment, subcontracting, and access to foreign capital markets that had previously been restricted or closed. The U.S. Business Roundtable, the European Roundtable of Industrialists, and the Keidanren in Japan brought together the corporate leaders of transnational interest blocs committed to lowering the costs of production by pursuing strategies of internationalization, including the creation of global value chains linking corporate producers in the core capitalist countries to cheaper wage locations in developing countries. In this chapter, I will further examine how transnational capitalist interest blocs have promoted the internationalization of production by lobbying governments to deregulate their capital markets, which means easing or even eliminating restrictions on foreign investment. I will also examine the role of transnational firms in using regional trade and investment agreements, as well as bilateral investment treaties, to promote cross-border value chains and expand the power and privileges of corporations on a global scale.

To fully grasp how production has been steadily internationalized, it is essential to understand the long historical process whereby countries in the developed and the developing world deregulated their financial markets. Specifically, we need to examine the transition from a Bretton Woods era of managed or pegged exchange rates, which enabled countries to maintain capital controls (restrictions on foreign investment), to a deregulation of capital markets across much of the world economy. The most competitive global firms, whether in manufacturing, services, or banking, began to see the restrictions of the Bretton Woods system as a contributing factor to the long-term falling rate of profit that began in 1965 and lasted until 1982. As early as 1968, the U.S.-based Committee on Economic Development, consisting of the largest, most competitive global manufacturing and banking firms, began lobbying for a removal of capital controls within the U.S., as a prelude to removal of capital controls in foreign markets. This meant abandoning much of the corporate support for a Bretton Woods system that had pegged exchange rates within a narrow range to the dollar, which had been fixed in price at $35 per ounce of gold. Corporate elites increasingly favored a more integrated global financial marketplace that would lower the costs of capital movements across state borders.

Large-scale capitalist firms were increasingly looking for ways to lower their costs of production. By eliminating capital controls in domestic and foreign markets, access to foreign capital would be cheaper, less burdened by regulatory restrictions, and would provide potential sources of financing through foreign stock and bond markets that would enable an internationalization of production. Transnational interest blocs in the U.S., the E.U., and Japan favored the deregulation of capital markets, though such a process was uneven and involved political battles over the timing and the terms of such deregulation. In Eric Helleiner's classic work on the subject, he documents in a series of case studies the role of the most globally competitive fractions of capital in lobbying their home governments to get rid of capital controls (Helleiner 1996). The U.S. and Great Britain were the first states to do so in 1974, followed by the French in 1979, and most of the rest of the governments in Western Europe followed suit during the 1980s. The Japanese government eased restrictions on its own capital markets, reducing the cost of capital entry and exit, during the 1980s as part of the government support for a further internationalization of production of Japanese manufacturing and high-tech corporations in East and Southeast Asia.

Structurally, once the U.S. and the U.K. opened their capital markets, and other big market economies followed suit, there were pressures on smaller market and developing economies to do the same, or to risk capital flight to states that promised greater return on their investments. The debt crises in the developing world provided leverage for Northern governments and financial institutions such as the IMF to pressure governments to deregulate their capital markets as a precondition for foreign loans. The expansion of regional trade and investment agreements, as many as four hundred of them negotiated between 1990 and 2009, and bilateral investment agreements, as many as three thousand during this time, further contributed to accelerated global deregulation of capital markets (Rodrik 2018). To be sure, there were important exceptions, especially countries with the emerging market size and power of China, which has maintained controlled capital markets to the present day, a policy that was made possible by the attractiveness of that market for foreign direct investors, regardless of restrictions on capital movements. As I will explain later in this chapter, China became the epicenter of the new globalization by providing the largest platform for the internationalization of production, linking finished production in the China market to a range of supply networks throughout the rest of the world.

Corporations have been able to wield their influence with nation-states and with global institutions to accelerate the integration of production across the global economy. Corporate lobbying networks in the U.S., the E.U., and Japan favored deregulation of capital markets within their home states and also relied on their home states to promote the conditions for capital market deregulation in developing countries, either through bilateral investment agreements, the International Monetary Fund, or linkages with other blocs of investor partners (or potential partners) who wielded political and economic influence within developing countries. As corporations in the U.S., E.U., and Japan sought to expand their internationalization of production, the development of investment partnerships would become a crucial part of the process of production segmentation. Corporations in the core capitalist countries would maintain control over the most lucrative aspects of the production process: patents, trademarks, research and development, marketing, and distribution of the final product. At the same time, corporations would sell off production divisions that were less valuable in their home market, replacing those production divisions with a wide range of alternative production structures in foreign countries where production costs were considerably lower.

These alternative production arrangements were varied, depending on the sectoral strategies of parent firms, but included foreign direct investment, which exponentially expanded during the period of the new globalization, subcontracting, and license agreements with producers who have become specialists in original equipment manufacturing (OEM). The latter group of firms have consolidated their own market power in the new globalization and have grown as oligopolies within a complex structure of global production networks. The increasing complexity of these production arrangements has meant that the financial capital necessary to facilitate production has become much more dispersed across capital markets throughout the world. The key to understanding the power politics of these global value chains is to examine how corporations at the top of the value chains have increasingly financialized their ownership of the highest value-added assets. These dominant corporations rely on financial intermediaries, foreign production and supply networks, and foreign institutional investors to cooperate in the stages leading to final assembly of a product, which is then circumscribed, marketed, and distributed under auspices of the dominant corporation that owns the most valuable assets of this process.

The process whereby the dominant corporations have been able to secure the greatest rate of return within global value chains is best conceptualized as a pyramid structure. Just a few firms occupy the top of the pyramid in the global value chain production process within sectors of production. Their ability to extract the most value from the production process is a function of their effective utilization of their market power, their utilization of political power within and among nation-states that pursue policies that are favorable to capital accumulation, and their ability to expand the exploitation of labor on a global scale by politically mobilizing with their business partners in the developing world. In short, the power politics of global value chains involve the expansion of transnational interest bloc political coalitions within and across nation-states. While chapter two focused on the role of transnational interest blocs in establishing the neoliberal policies that would contribute to the conditions facilitating the internationalization of capital, here I examine the process by which dominant corporations, based mainly in the global North, restructured their corporate operations around a global segmentation of production. This process has involved a financialization of the leading Global 500 corporations, whose corporate boardrooms have become more oriented toward the interests of institutional financial investors and whose profits have increasingly been directed toward a higher percentage of corporate investment in "financialized" activities.

Corporate production strategies have been increasingly geared toward restructuring labor in their "home" markets of origin—a process documented in chapter two—toward a reorientation to foreign supply networks that are increasingly directed by lead corporate firms. These supply relationships are linked in a manner that allows the costs of production to be dispersed across thousands of actors, many of whom are highly constrained by tight cost margins. Original equipment manufacturers organize these supply networks to facilitate the integration of component parts across a range of distant locations. The extraction of value at the top of the value chain is tied to ownership of patent or trademark rights that are increasingly central to maximizing corporate profits within the supply chain. It is within this process of accumulation that financial activities are best understood: corporations at the top of global value chains leverage their financialization of legal, institutional, and knowledge assets within a system of production that distributes most of its value in branding, marketing, and distribution. This process of accumulation is tied closely to a services industry, including retail, where price markups are a significant contribution to the final value added. The relationship between corporate power and the expansion of a patent, copyright, and trademarks investment regime is crucial in understanding how corporations at the top of the value chain have leveraged their ownership of "financialized" assets (Morgan 2014).

When scholars write about financialization, they typically refer to any one or more of three trends within global political economy that coincide with the period I label "the new globalization." The first is the greater dependence of the global economy, and of national economies, on financial profits as a percentage of overall growth. The second is the growth in global capital flows that have exceeded the world's growth in trade and services. And, finally, nonfinancial corporations are diverting an increasing percentage of their profits into financial activities while reducing their capital investment in production (Milberg and Winkler 2013, 215). These three trends are closely linked in my analysis, though I will focus especially on the last trend. In recent decades, nonfinancial corporations based in the core capitalist countries (U.S., U.K., Germany, France, Japan) have increased their financial assets as a percentage of total fixed assets (Powell 2013, 89).

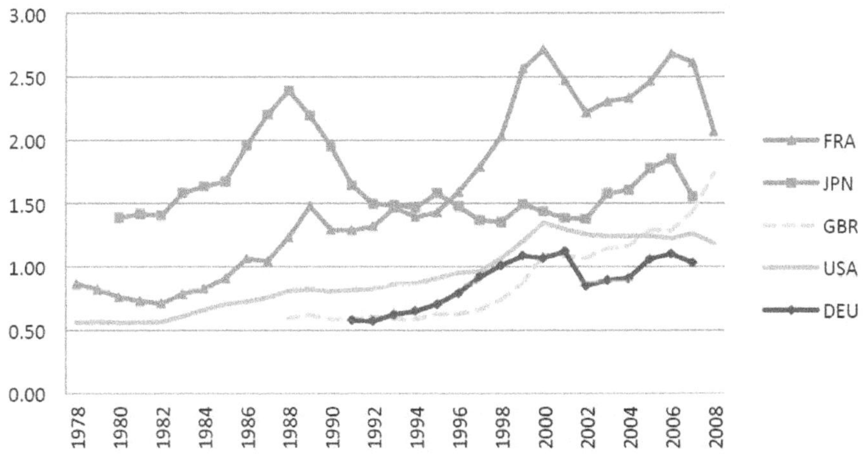

Figure 3.1. Nonfinancial Corporations' Total Financial Assets as a Share of Fixed Assets
Source: Powell 2013, 89.

The considerable variation in the above numbers indicates that not all nonfinancial corporations within each of the core capitalist countries are engaged in the same linear behavior. In general, however, what these country measurements have in common is a long-term movement toward greater financialization of investments by nonfinancial firms. This has meant that nonfinancial corporations have been restructuring their investments around three types of financial activities across the core capitalist economies. The first is investment in financial assets as a percentage of overall investment (captured in figure 3.1). The second is corporate buybacks of stocks coupled with increases in dividend payments. The third is a wave of cross-border mergers and acquisitions (M&As) where firms have sought to expand their global market position by restructuring their global operations around the most high-value activities. In fact, M&As have been used to increase the concentration of ownership of patents, trademarks, copyrights, R&D activities, and marketing and distribution networks while shedding lower-value activities involving production. See the breakdown in figure 3.2 of cross-border M&As compiled in a recent OECD study (Gestrin 2017, 1).

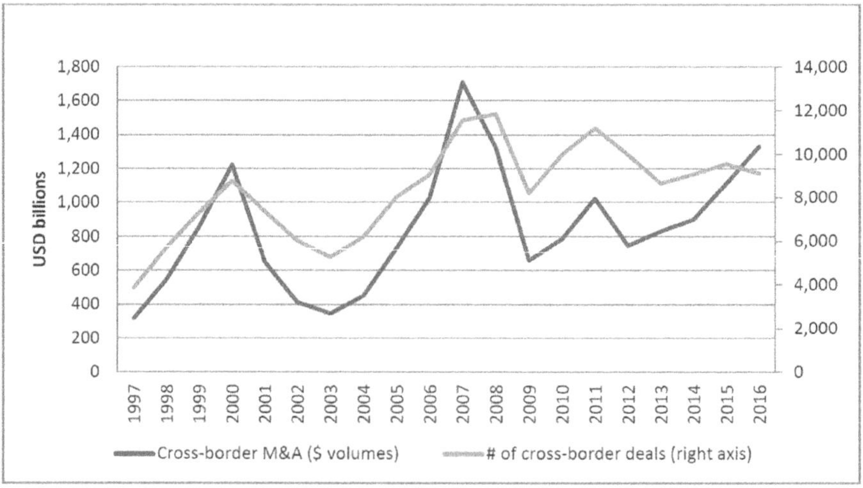

Figure 3.2. Cross-Border Mergers and Acquisitions
Source: Gestrin 2017, 1.

Nonfinancial corporations that are more engaged in global value chains as an overall percentage of their total revenues have been more likely to financialize their activities on a global scale, whether it be greater investments in financial assets, share buybacks, or an expansion of M&A activity (Milberg and Winkler 2013, 219–220). This is especially true for global high-technology firms, whose financialization of their own profits has accelerated considerably in recent decades. The extent of speculation by the leading global high-tech firms has been captured in a recent study of ownership of corporate bonds by economist Zoltan Pozsar. In the study, Pozsar found that the richest 10 percent of corporations measured by intellectual property value have been dramatically increasing their ownership of offshore corporate bonds in the past decade. That means that Apple, Microsoft, Cisco, Oracle, and Alphabet own 80 percent of the offshore corporate bond market, which comprises most of their offshore holdings of $700 billion in revenue, an increase from $100 billion of offshore holdings in 2008 (Foroohar 2018, 57).

These statistics illustrate the extent to which the new high-tech sector of global capitalism has financialized its profits in offshore accounts that comprise significant holding of corporate bonds. These purchases of corporate bonds were made possible by profits made from ownership of intellectual property rights. Corporations that want to escape the burdens of domestic taxation, while sheltering their profits in high-yielding financial activities, have increasingly turned to offshore platforms and the corporate bond market to maintain a rising flow of profits. At the same time, these firms have replicated the behavior of other nonfinancial counterparts in reducing their investments in capital production. Those investments increasingly fall on the middle to lower tier of the global value chain, where value extraction is determined by both market power (acceleration of corporate concentration at the top of the value chain pyramid) and political power (the ability of corporations at the top of the value chain to secure legal rights to patents, copyrights, R&D, trademarks, and distribution and marketing networks).

The control over the latter process has involved the political mobilization of corporations in transnational interest blocs that have worked with governments to secure investment agreements that protect intellectual property rights (IPRs). The dramatic increase of global investment agreements from the early 1990s to the present have been used to lock in favorable terms for corporate ownership of IPRs. Transnational corporations at the top of global value chains have utilized their political power to lock in favorable terms of treatment within these investment agreements, thereby promoting an investment landscape that has favored neoliberal measures extending IPRs and maximizing opportunities for the creation of global value chains in the developing world. As the corporations at the top of the pyramid of these value chains utilize tax havens to store profits from IPRs, they continue to rely on governments to support investment agreements that will facilitate the production of a finished product in low-cost locations. The next section of this chapter will examine the extent to which transnational interest blocs have succeeded in using foreign investment agreements to promote favorable conditions for the establishment of global value chains in the developing world. I will then examine some of the most important examples of how transnational interest bloc coalitions have shaped regional investment agreements led by the U.S., the E.U., and Japan, as well as the relationship between transnational firms and the China market.

TRANSNATIONAL CAPITAL AND GLOBAL INVESTMENT AGREEMENTS

Corporations in this new period of globalization have lobbied governments to promote favorable political conditions for the dispersal of production across state borders. Corporate lobbying networks aggressively supported neoliberal policies that lowered the costs of corporate relocation strategies in the U.S., the E.U., and Japan. These efforts coexisted with corporate strategies to reorganize production by linking corporations with subcontractors and supply networks in developing countries as an alternative to the higher costs of domestic production. The focus of the top corporations within global manufacturing and high-tech production became ownership of the highest value-added activities, specifically intellectual property rights. The consolidation of transnational corporate interest blocs as power brokers in global politics is most evident by the way that transnational capital has organized politically to promote investment protection of IPRs within global and regional trade agreements. Starting in the 1980s, transnational capitalist coalitions relied on lobbying networks linked to U.S., E.U., and Japanese government negotiators to promote a framework for the Uruguay Round of GATT that would lead to the adoption of Trade Related Intellectual Property Rights (TRIPS) as part of the creation of the World Trade Organization in 1994.

Corporate political mobilization in support of TRIPS began with the U.S.-based transnational corporation Pfizer, which led a mobilization of transnational corporations to lobby for the inclusion of strong protections for IPRs within the global trade organization. Pfizer was well connected to networks of transnational corporations in the U.S., Western Europe, and Japan and acted through domestic and global corporate organizations to mobilize corporate support for strong IPR policies in trade agreements. Pfizer was connected to several of the most important lobbying networks in the U.S. and used its position to promote the insertion of IPR rights within new global and regional trade agreements, which would soon become "investment" agreements whose contents focused much more heavily on protection of foreign investment rights and ownership guarantees than on reducing trade barriers. Pfizer executives used their position within the Business Roundtable and the National Foreign Trade Council in the U.S. to mobilize transnational corporate support for this IPR strategy. They also relied on their leadership on the Council of Competitiveness, established by President Reagan in the 1980s, and their leadership of the Intellectual Property Committee of the U.S. Council for International Business. But the key linkage with foreign transnational capital blocs in the E.U. and Japan came through the position of Pfizer's international president, Bob Neimeth, as chair of the U.S. side of the Business and Industry Advisory Committee to the OECD. Pfizer was joined by the most internationally competitive transnational firms based in the E.U. and Japan, which had already begun to advocate for an integration of IPR protection to a future trade/investment regime (Drahos 2003, 2–4).

This lobbying network represented the most significant political momentum linking the strategies of transnational interest blocs across the core countries of the capitalist global economy. The leading corporate backers of stronger intellectual property rights included firms that would occupy a central position within the new globalization, led by pharmaceutical and high-tech firms whose dependence on intellectual property rights value became a driving factor for a concerted corporate lobbying campaign. This meant that transnational firms increasingly joined together in global and regional coalitions to lobby for strong IPR protections within the WTO and within hundreds of new preferential investment agreements and thousands of new Bilateral Investment Agreements that would be established between the early 1990s and 2010. Transnational interest blocs worked closely with nation-states to advance their interests within regional investment agreements as a first step in what became a more expansive strategy of globalization. Transnational firms used their domestic "home" locations in the U.S., Western Europe, and Japan to advance favorable conditions for foreign direct investments in Mexico, Eastern Europe, and East Asia, respectively. The NAFTA agreement extended intellectual property rights protections to high-tech U.S.-based transnational capital, while the E.U. expansion did the same for high-tech and manufacturing firms that used Eastern European countries as a platform for global assembly strategies by the late 1990s and early 2000s. Similarly, Japanese high-tech and manufacturing firms relied on the Japanese state to negotiate IPR rights for Japanese foreign direct investors who were moving their production from Japan to East Asia.

Through this entire political and economic restructuring, high-tech firms that produced computer technology that was increasingly integrated into supply chain production became central to the politics of the new globalization. The ability of these dominant transnational firms to extract value added was directly connected to the exponential increase of information technology into global value chains, so that manufacturing firms became increasingly dependent on incorporating high-technology production processes into their value chain production. The revolution in global telecommunications and the increasing integration of high-tech infrastructure across the world economy is summarized in figure 3.3 (Baldwin 2011, 5).

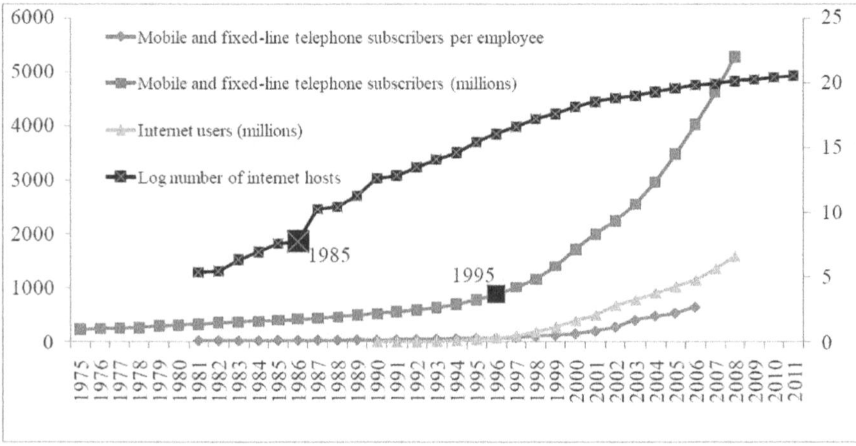

Figure 3.3. Growth of Internet Hosts and Phone Lines
Source: Baldwin 2011, 5.

The high-technology sector has long occupied a central position of power within the new globalization, where the most valuable manifestation of its power is the ownership of intellectual property rights that can be leveraged as value in the increasingly globalized system of production. However, for this system to work for firms that own intellectual property rights, the legal, political, and economic protection of IPR assets becomes a necessity to facilitate the establishment of global value chains. The ability of firms at the top of the value chain pyramid to extract disproportionately high value from production (even while not engaging directly in production themselves) is a primary characteristic of the new globalization. That means the political mobilization of transnational corporate interest blocs to lobby for greater intellectual property rights protection is central to the extraction of surplus value from value chains. It also means that corporations increasingly use mergers and acquisitions to take ownership of the most highly financialized aspects of production, namely acquisition of intellectual property rights that can then be used as leverage in market competition with other large-scale firms.

What started as a marriage between competing transnational blocs of capital and their respective home states in the U.S., the E.U., and Japan has become, especially over the past two decades, a much more globalized system of accumulation that has brought more developing countries into value chain production. This process has resulted in greater global corporate consolidation, through dramatic expansions of cross-border mergers and acquisitions (the largest on record just before the global financial crash of 2008), of high-value-added activities within the global economy. This process has strengthened the power of transnational corporate interest blocs on a global scale, whereby these blocs have inserted themselves as hegemonic or highly competitive fractions of capital within most nation-states in both the core and peripheral countries of the global economy. It is through this process of cross-border expansion of transnational interest bloc power that we can observe the political and economic linkages that tie the fortunes of the dominant transnational corporations at the top of the global production pyramid to the original equipment manufacturers and then the subcontractors and smaller-scale producers that occupy the middle-tier and lower rungs of the global value chains.

The politics of global value chain production ensure that workers embedded in production are located within a large-scale reserve army of labor that depresses bargaining power that would otherwise allow them to demand higher wages to compensate for their rising rates of productivity. Transnational corporations rely on state repression of labor through a value chain production process where smaller-scale producers are expected to control their tight marginal costs so that more value can be delivered to the top of the value chain. To control costs, labor organizing is often highly circumscribed (if not illegal outside narrow establishment institutions). Market competition within such a structure of production is relegated to the thousands of firms (and the greater number of workers) that are forced to compete to be subcontractors or licensed independent producers whose finished products will be inserted in a chain of production that involves thousands of intermediaries (financial and otherwise). The ability of these smaller-scale firms to maintain competitiveness often hinges on labor repression either by restricting or prohibiting legalized channels for independent worker representation and on the existence of a surplus population of workers that exceeds the supply needed for profitable production.

Economists have often defended foreign direct investment in developing countries by referencing the "backward and forward linkages" that such investments create, meaning that FDI has been assumed to be tied to an expansion of domestic supply networks that then contribute to economic growth and development. However, such spillover beneficial effects of the new globalized production structures are less apparent in a system where products are being produced in a global value chain that often bypasses much of the interior economies of developing countries. This is especially true given the establishment of export processing zones (EPZs), which have often been central to the consolidation of global value chains in smaller developing economies (Gibbon, Jones, and Thomsen 2008). These EPZs are highly disconnected from domestic production and exist as tax-free islands that are designed to facilitate global accumulation imperatives more than domestic development. In other words, inputs within this system often come from abroad, and the finished product, rather than contribute to more production locally, is geared toward a global value chain process that does not interact as much with complementary expansions of domestic manufacturing. As profits from this global value chain system are "extracted" from domestic economies and the finished products are marked up by the corporations that own the IPRs—and that market and brand the product—there is a greater gap between the value produced by workers and what they receive in wages. This growing gap between working-class productivity and the relative stagnation of working-class wages is a fundamental characteristic of the new globalization, as documented in recent IMF reports (Dao et al. 2017). According to conventional economic thought, workers' productivity rises should eventually equate to higher wages for workers as an exchange for the increased value of their factor production. Even when wages have risen, the gap between workers' productivity and wages has remained substantial, indicating that exploitation of workers has been intensifying if measured by wages in relation to productivity (Starosta 2010). Furthermore, as I will show extensively in chapter four, wages as a percentage of corporate revenues, as well as GDP, have been declining across both the North and South of the world economy.

Corporate interests that once concentrated their lobbying efforts much more closely toward their "home" states during the period of regulated capitalism have shifted toward a transnational interest bloc that links transnational firms to their corporate counterparts across the world. The consolidation of transnational corporate interest blocs is expressed through the rapid consolidation of a global investment regime that operates through structures of corporate-government-financial-supply networks that have achieved political and economic dominance during the period of neoliberal capitalism. The outlines of this investment regime have been forged by corporate lobbying networks that initially extended their influence on a regional scale through NAFTA, the expansion of the European Union to Eastern Europe, and Japanese expansion of corporate foreign direct investment in Asia. In each of these cases, corporations worked with powerful states in core capitalist countries to expand protection of investor rights as part of an aggressive effort toward the promotion of global value chains. Concomitantly, the corporate organizations most heavily involved in these regional campaigns have also worked together globally to forge investment regimes both multilaterally and bilaterally that would effectively change the characteristics of contemporary "trade" agreements.

U.S.-based transnational firms used their influence in NAFTA to push for investment protections, which expanded the rights of foreign investors to be free of domestic content laws, export requirements, government procurement restrictions, and restrictions on the movement of financial capital. Transnational corporations in the U.S. worked with business coalition partners in Mexico through groups such as the Mexican Council of Businessmen. The effectiveness of these lobbying networks was enhanced by long-standing corporate relationships with government bureaucracies in the U.S. and Mexico, including embedded institutional connections to ruling political parties and trade negotiating teams. Transnational interest blocs operated, as they have since NAFTA, inside a structure of hierarchal state and market power that has allowed transnational firms from the core capitalist countries to win concessions by taking advantage of a dependency relationship. But the dependency relationship is forged within a global system of class domination that allows transnational firms to enter foreign markets after having been extensively subsidized by their own governments, and after having consolidated market power within their sector of global production. The firms that won the most concessions in NAFTA, and in the ensuing regional investment agreements forged after NAFTA, were firms that occupied the upper tier of sectoral production within global capitalism. Their market power, combined with the structural advantages of their location within the core capitalist economies, allowed them to dominate the political economy of the NAFTA negotiations. The same structure of political and economic hegemony has produced a global investment regime that has radically expanded the scope of investment protections for powerful corporations since NAFTA (Baldwin 2011).

The incorporation of IPR provisions within multilateral, regional, and bilateral investment agreements has allowed for a steady "ratcheting up" of protection for corporate investors at the top of global value chains. Transnational interest blocs from the U.S., the E.U., and Japan viewed NAFTA as a useful starting point for a further incorporation of investment protections within the WTO. The missing ingredient in NAFTA was the incorporation of more robust protections for IPRs. To remedy this, transnational interest blocs led by high-tech and pharmaceutical sectors, but also including the most globally competitive manufacturing sectors, have worked with governments in the core capitalist states to develop the outlines of an IPR regime, both within the WTO and through the insertion of WTO-plus provisions within regional investment agreements and bilateral investment treaties. The interests of transnational interest blocs can be traced through content analysis of the expansion of WTO-plus agreements as manifested in four hundred regional investment agreements and over three thousand bilateral investment treaties that have been signed from 1990 through 2010. Bilateral investment treaties focus on a smaller subset of investment guarantees between states that fall short of the more elaborate set of negotiations characteristic of regional investment agreements. The latter commit participating nation-states to cooperate in a range of overlapping areas of trade and investment, subject to political ratification by states, making these agreements more time-consuming and more politically contentious and costly. Transnational firms and governments have utilized both measures to dramatically expand investment guarantees beyond those allowed in the WTO.

The moniker "WTO-plus" refers to the insertion of stronger provisions in regional investment agreements and bilateral treaties compared to TRIPS. As soon as transnational firms negotiated the inclusion of TRIPS provisions in the WTO, as part of the culmination of the Uruguay Round of GATT and the creation of the WTO in 1995, transnational capitalist groups from the U.S., the E.U., and Japan were frustrated by the inability to obtain stronger enforcement mechanisms to ensure that developing countries would provide maximum protection for investors across a range of policy issues. These included ensuring mechanisms that would allow for corporations to utilize measures designed to ensure quicker compliance and enforcement of TRIPS agreements, beyond what was provided for in the WTO.

The WTO standards, in fact, were the most extensive investment provisions ever included in trade agreements and superseded anything that had previously been proposed in multilateral forums. This meant that developing countries were obligated to enforce patent rights for at least ten years, extend copyright by at least fifty years, ensure that computer programs were granted the same status and protection as "literary works" and therefore would be protected by equivalent copyright laws, and restrict the ability of governments and "competitors" to license patented or copyrighted products by undertaking costly regulatory justification for the marketing of generic versions of a patented or copyrighted product. The exceptions were typically limited to national security and/or health emergency situations under which compulsory licensing procedures might be activated to ensure access to products deemed necessary on those emergency grounds.

In practice, developing countries, which were heavily dependent on foreign markets and were restricted in their financial ability to pursue compulsory licensing arrangements, often failed to mount effective challenges to the TRIPS provisions, even though such challenges were legal under the WTO. However, there was resistance among developing states to allowing for more stringent enforcement mechanisms within the auspices of the WTO, prompting transnational firms to rely on their "home" governments to pursue regional and bilateral agreements that would create quicker enforcement and compliance rules. This meant the establishment of investor-dispute-settlement measures that expedited the ability of corporations to sue governments for changing the terms or conditions of foreign direct investment agreements, for discriminating against foreign firms by differential treatment in trade and investment law compared to domestic competitors, for discriminating against foreign firms in government procurement policies, and for failing to extend or to honor the terms of the patent and copyright laws as specified in the investment agreement. The shift from "trade" to "investment" provisions reflected an orientation toward utilizing trade agreements to facilitate the creation of global value chains across the borders of states. Transnational corporate interest blocs structured these investment agreements by being involved directly in the negotiations between governments that wrote the rules governing access to foreign investment markets.

The power relationships embedded in these agreements favored the core capitalist states and core firms within these states. For the most part, the U.S., the E.U., and Japan negotiated investment agreements and treaties with partners in developing states that were running trade deficits with these larger states. At the same time, transnational corporations were able to offer investment "partnerships" with subcontracting firms by offering these firms opportunities to produce products that would have a guaranteed "market" position backed by the transnational firms' ownership rights, branding and marketing privileges, IPR rights, and links to retail and commercial networks that could not be tapped without the power of the lead firm. Most of the content of regional investment agreements has been devoted to expanding investment protections in areas of IPRs, competition policy, regulatory policy, procurement policy, and allowance of full capital mobility—allowing for easy entry and exit of capital funds tied to investment. The liberalization of foreign capital markets has been pursued by a coalition of transnational firms based in the core capitalist countries, their home governments, their investment partners in the host countries, and the government of the host country. These networks have been essential in providing for a steady expansion of strong investment provisions labeled "WTO-plus" in hundreds of investment agreements and thousands of bilateral investment treaties.

The relevance of regional investment agreements for facilitating global value chains is also apparent in an examination of the extent to which these agreements have resulted in the lowering of tariffs for imported goods, or intermediaries, used in production of component parts produced within global value chains. Transnational interest blocs have utilized regional investment agreements to expedite the move toward "zero tariffs" as applied to imported products used in value chain production. These products have become an increasingly important share of global trade and have been central to the effectiveness of global value chains as a cost-saving strategy that disburses production of a finished product across multiple state borders. Figure 3.4 indicates how several of the most prominent regional investment agreements have facilitated this trend during the period of the new globalization (Baldwin 2011, 13).

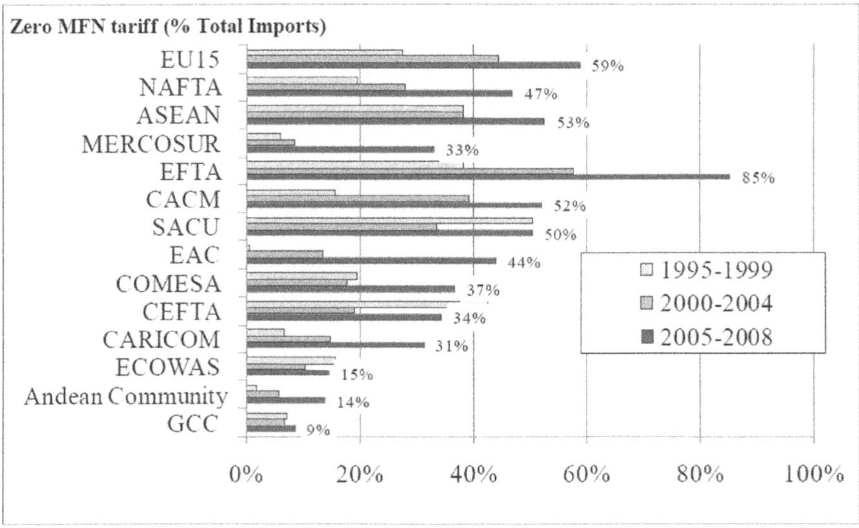

Figure 3.4. Share of Imports with Zero Most Favored Nation (MFN) Tariffs, Various RTAs, 1995–2008
Source: Baldwin 2011, 13.

As the terms of trade became more favorable to the expansion of global value chains, facilitated by regional investment agreements, bilateral investment agreements provided a range of additional investment provisions that extended protection for foreign investment partnerships. These included provisions prohibiting expropriation of foreign investment or at the very least quantification of the terms of compensation in the event that expropriation was initiated; assurances against discriminatory treatment; prohibition of performance requirements for investment; the ability to transfer investment-related funds by maintaining open capital markets; the ability of foreign firms to intervene to determine management structures as appropriate in firm-owned partnerships; and the ability of foreign investors to sue host governments that violate the terms of investment agreements—bypassing the WTO process in favor of arbitration panels outside the jurisdiction of the host country. The pervasiveness of bilateral investment treaties, and their relationship to the expansion of global value chains through the proliferation of these investment guarantees, is a crucial foundation for the new globalization. Figure 3.5 indicates how prominent bilateral investment agreements have become in recent decades (Baldwin 2011, 14).

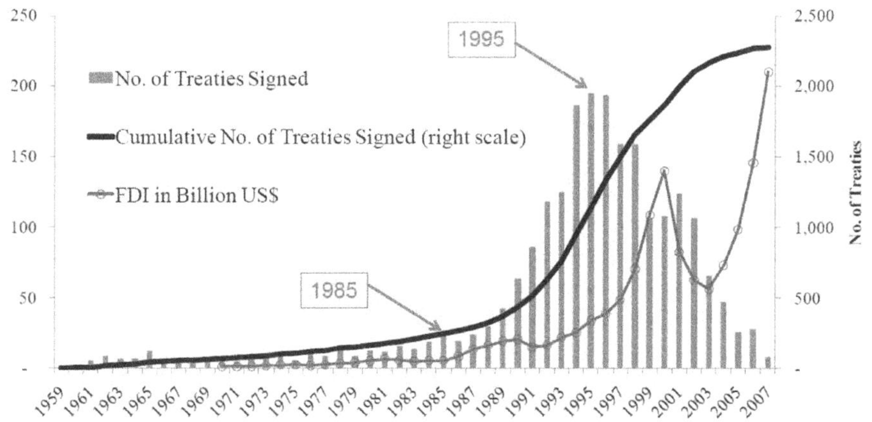

Figure 3.5. Explosion of Bilateral Investment Treaties
Source: Baldwin 2011, 14.

The earliest investment agreements were signed by core capitalist states with developing countries in nearby regional locations. These involved core states negotiating favorable investment deals for their transnational firms so that these firms would have low-cost access to developing country markets to produce goods within a global value chain. Examples of early BITS were those that were incorporated as adjuncts to broader regional investment agreements discussed in the previous chapter, which included bilateral investment agreements between the U.S. and Mexico that preceded the ratification of NAFTA; the E.U. expansion into Eastern Europe, which utilized bilateral investment agreements as a precondition for Eastern European membership in the EU; and Japan investment agreements with East Asia countries. In these cases, the investment agreements reduced the cost of intermediate inputs when traded between countries that were parties to these agreements. This low-cost trade in intermediate goods enabled the outsourcing of production within value chains that would produce a finished product that had previously been produced in the home market of the core capitalist country. The process of deepening and extending global value chains has involved extensive political and economic collaboration between corporate investors, states, subcontractors, and financial intermediaries, across the North-South divide. To illustrate how this process has worked, I will examine some of the most important recent examples of transnational interest bloc cooperation in the U.S.-CAFTA-DR regional investment agreement of 2004, the E.U.-CARIFORM regional investment agreement of 2008, Japan's move toward a regional investment agreement strategy from the late 1990s to the present, and the relationship between transnational capital and the crucially important China market.

U.S.-CAFTA-DR

The transnational interest bloc committed to the U.S.-CAFTA-DR agreement of 2004 had its origins in the alliances between the U.S. state, U.S.-based transnational capital, Caribbean Basin regimes, and Caribbean Basin business groups that developed in the 1980s.[1] During that decade the U.S. engaged in military, political, and economic intervention in an effort to transform the political economies of the region from import-substitution-industrialization toward export-led financial and production strategies. The U.S. Agency for International Development (USAID), the Export-Import Bank, and the World Bank provided loans to Caribbean Basin states and private industries to encourage a shift to export-processing zones that would be of central importance in establishing linkages between transnational firms and regional business interests. The U.S.-backed Caribbean Basin Initiative of 1983 contributed to the rapid growth of garment assembly enclaves in Central America and the Dominican Republic, alongside the growth of nontraditional agricultural exports (Paus 1988). By the late 1990s, 51 percent of Central American exports to the U.S. were concentrated in maquiladora production, mainly clothing, while 37 percent consisted of agricultural production, with a shift toward nontraditional exports (Robinson 2003, 65). At the same time new and powerful business groups emerged in the region that steered capital to these growing export industries, as well as to tourism, hospitality, real estate, and an assortment of light manufacturing industries.

The structural asymmetries of the U.S.-Central American and Dominican Republic relationship ensured that fractions of U.S.-based capital and their supporters in the U.S. state would have the upper hand in the negotiating process leading to the drafting and ratification of the U.S.-CAFTA-DR agreement. The U.S. Special Trade Representative pushed for a high level of secrecy in the negotiation of the agreement, while U.S.-based business interests made their preferences known in forums such as the Americas Business Council, whose recommendations were often inserted directly into the negotiated text of the agreement (Weissman 2004). The U.S. Special Trade Representative managed to include in the agreement a much wider range of provisions that spoke directly to the interests of U.S.-based transnational firms committed to making the agreement a model for future investment rules, dubbed WTO-plus because the provisions went well beyond what had been negotiated in multilateral forums. The fact that Central American economies were already structurally tied to export dependency on the U.S. market, and even more importantly interlinked in global commodity chains with U.S.-based corporate retailers, manufacturers, and distributors, made these governments more likely to support the agreement. The more robust civil society opposition in Costa Rica delayed ratification of the agreement there, while the more authoritarian political structures of the other Central American countries ensured that the opposition would be less effective.

The globalization of production and increased integration of the economies of the U.S., Central America, and the Dominican Republic have been uneven processes, reflected in the diverse networks of business support for U.S.-CAFTA-DR that have emerged among the member countries. El Salvador, for example, had the most far-reaching opening of financial markets in the region, beginning with the establishment of an exchange rate policy in 1993 that fixed the Salvadoran currency to the dollar, followed by the complete dollarization of the economy in 2001 (Towers and Borzutzky 2004). USAID and the Salvadoran political elites represented by the ARENA Party supported the process of the reprivatization of the financial sector from 1989 to 1994, leading to the development of the largest and most cohesive financial services sector within the Central American region. This encompasses Salvadoran financial groups that exercise control over a wide range of services, including insurance companies, stockbroker firms, pension administration funds, and foreign currency exchange houses (Segovia 2005).

The extent of the political power of these firms in El Salvador, entrenched within the authoritarian neoliberal structures of the Salvadoran state, and the lack of any effective organized opposition to these policies, was epitomized by the early ratification of the agreement by the El Salvadoran government, which approved the investment pact within a matter of days. The Salvadoran executive branch introduced the U.S.-CAFTA-DR agreement to the legislature only one week before the scheduled legislative vote, prompting a walk-out of the opposition party, the FMLN. The dominant ARENA Party then succeeded in waiving the requirement that a treaty pass with a two-thirds vote in favor of a simple majority. In addition, the vote took place at 3 a.m. with the National Assembly surrounded by riot police. Of the twenty-eight largest economic groups in Central America, ten are from El Salvador, indicating the strong concentration of political and economic power in the country (Segovia 2005). The ties between these groups, transnational capital, and the ARENA Party are robust, indicated by both the decision to dollarize the Salvadoran economy and to push through the investment agreements with no opportunity for political debate.

In Guatemala and Honduras the dominant groups in favor of the treaty are concentrated in agro-industry and manufacturing. The largest and most politically powerful business organization in Guatemala is the Co-ordinating Committee of Agricultural, Commercial, Industrial and Financial Organizations (CACIF), which aggressively supported CAFTA. Its members include the dominate agro-export conglomerates in the country, led by the Guatemalan

Sugar Association, as well as nontraditional agro-export industries that have grown in importance, and the maquila sector, whose export production has expanded dramatically (Krznaric 2006). In Nicaragua the ties between the financial services sector and the U.S. are extensive, having been created during the Sandinista period in an effort by Nicaraguan financial elites to escape the regulations imposed by the government. In the Dominican Republic, the leading business groups supporting the agreement are located in the fast-growing export-processing zones, which had seen a tenfold growth in employment over two decades. Dominican firms such as Grupo M, D'Clase Corporation, and Interamerican Products are closely tied to U.S. transnational firms as both importers of capital and suppliers of apparel to companies and department stores located in the U.S. (Sanchez-Ancochea 2008). In Costa Rica, U.S.-based high-tech firms and pharmaceutical producers, well established in export-processing zones, expected to benefit from provisions in the agreement that provided investment and property rights guarantees.

The U.S.-based pharmaceutical industry, using linkages established with foreign affiliates primarily in Costa Rica, joined with other transnational firms, including electronics, telecommunications, and financial services, to lobby for provisions that would extend many of the investment and intellectual property rights guarantees provided by NAFTA to Central America and the Dominican Republic. An investor-state provision, taken from NAFTA and adopted in other U.S. bilateral investment agreements, allows foreign corporations to file breach of contract suits against states that violate provisions of the agreement (Caliari 2005). The U.S.-CAFTA-DR agreement required an independent arbitrator to decide on the merit of such allegations, and to potentially offer a monetary award that includes an estimation of profits that would have been made by the corporation during the time that investment restrictions were imposed by the host government. In addition, U.S.-based pharmaceutical companies secured intellectual property rights provisions that go beyond what is allowed in the WTO. Under the agreement, pharmaceutical firms were able to protect the secrecy of data used to confirm a drug's safety for a five-year period after the drug had been approved for marketing anywhere in the world, even if the drug was not marketed for five years in Central America and the Dominican Republic. A firm could extend its secrecy guarantee for an additional five years from the time its drug was marketed in a member country for the first time, which prevented governments from using the data to approve applications for drug registration (Weissman 2004). This was intended to prevent generic versions of the good from being marketed in competition with foreign manufacturers, and it went beyond the more flexible provisions of the TRIPS agreement of the WTO, which allows countries some latitude in determining the circumstances for the release of test data for use in approving new drugs.

The investor provisions in the agreement extend to the financial services and telecommunications sectors, where U.S.-based firms successfully lobbied for inclusion of an easing of investment laws that will give greater access to U.S.-based transnational corporations. Banks and insurance firms secured full rights to establish subsidiaries, joint ventures, and branches in the region. Provisions target the restrictions that had existed in Central America, including barriers to foreign insurance companies in Guatemala; heavy regulation licensing of foreign professionals in Nicaragua; and numerous service monopolies in Costa Rica (Hornbeck 2006). The U.S. insisted that Costa Rica open its state-run telecommunication and insurance industries as a precondition for ratifying the agreement. This provision generated an outpouring of civil society opposition to the agreement in Costa Rica, led by labor unions, human rights organizations, and consumer welfare groups, which opposed what they considered to be the equivalent of structural adjustment shock therapy likely to raise unemployment rates and to increase prices. Costa Rica was the last party to this agreement to vote for ratification, but by a very narrow margin of just over 50 percent, reflecting the much more robust civil society in the country compared with the rest of Central America and the Dominican Republic.

Much of the U.S. agribusiness sector also lobbied for the agreement, together with commodity producers in Central America and the Dominican Republic who were already linked to a regionalized agribusiness commodity chain (Jurenas 2004). Although Central America and the Dominican Republic have become less dependent on traditional agricultural production, the rise of nontraditional agro-exports has been a trend that has integrated U.S.-based TNCs with suppliers in the region. As with textiles and garments, the U.S. state has played an important role historically in providing the institutional financing necessary to shift Central American production strategies away from traditional agricultural crops to nontraditional agricultural exports that were incorporated within a global food distribution network. William Robinson has documented this trend:

> As the NTAE [nontraditional agricultural enterprises] progresses, TNCs have come to exercise ever greater control, working their way "backward" from marketing to production. The industry is dominated by three giant food companies, Chiquita, formerly United Brands (and before that, United Fruit Company), runs numerous subsidiaries in the region, from its Chiquita Tropical Bananas Company in Costa Rica, to PATSA in Honduras and BASICO and BANACORP in Guatemala. Castle and Cook (which absorbed Standard Fruit in 1968) runs its own set of subsidiaries, as does Del Monte, which merged with and became

> an affiliate of RJ Reynolds in 1979. Del Monte has established its COAGRO subsidiary in Guatemala and its PINDECO in Costa Rica. Other TNCs with a significant share of the NTAE industry include Chestnut Hill Farms, Hanover Brands, Coca-Cola, PolyPack and Seaboard Corporation. (Robinson 2003, 187)

In addition to agribusiness interests, the top-tier lobbying network for transnational firms in the textile industry, representing more than $100 billion in annual textile production and sales, was actively involved in the negotiations and ratification of the U.S.-CAFTA-DR agreement, although these firms initially opposed it until they were able to secure investment guarantees that addressed their concerns about increased global competition from China. In fact, these firms and their lobbying organizations agreed to support U.S.-CAFTA-DR only after receiving assurances that the agreement would contain a provision that tariff-free status would be limited to yarn produced within the CAFTA-DR countries, alongside an additional provision that imposed quotas on a wide range of imports from China. The final agreement gave U.S. firms a competitive advantage over their Chinese competitors in the exportation of textiles, cotton, fiber, machinery, carpets and rugs, and fabrics to Central America and the Dominican Republic. Organizing themselves in a CAFTA-DR coalition of associations, these lobbying groups included the National Council of Textile Organizations, the American Fiber Manufacturers Association, the American Textile Machinery Association, the Carpet and Rug Institute, and the Association of the Nonwoven Fabrics Industry (Business Coalition 2006).

As these examples indicate, a transnational interest bloc secured favorable investment provisions in the U.S.-CAFTA-DR agreement. This interest bloc linked transnational capitalists with their subsidiaries and contractors in the Central American region. Transnational bloc formation operated differently depending on the political economy of the country. U.S.-based transnational capital enjoyed robust political and economic relationships with Salvadoran business groups and dominant political parties that had been established as early as the 1980s, which facilitated an early ratification of the agreement. The ability of a transnational interest bloc to ratify the agreement in Costa Rica was more complicated, given the vibrancy of civil society opposition networks that had to be overcome. Nonetheless, the final agreement reflected the interests of a transnational interest bloc whose power was articulated through the linkage between business organizations and states throughout the region. As we will see in the next section, a transnational interest bloc also exerted its power in the E.U.-CARIFORUM agreement, exhibiting similar characteristics to CAFTA-DR and to other regional investment agreements negotiated during this time frame.

E.U.-CARIFORUM

In 2000, the European Union signed the Contonou Agreement with 78 countries in the African, Caribbean, and Pacific Group of States (ACP). This treaty, which included the fifteen member states of the E.U. and mostly former European colonies, shifted the terms of previous trade and development agreements that had been negotiated from 1975 to 2000, known as the Lome Conventions. The Lome agreements "provided free access without reciprocity for almost all of the exports from the ACP countries to the E.U., and provided especially favorable terms for sugar, rum, bananas, rice, beef and veal" (Canterbury 2010, 96). In future negotiations, the E.U. would insist on reciprocal trade concessions (although least-developed countries would still be granted exceptions), investment and regulatory protections for transnational capitalist investors, and deregulation of financial and service markets in ACP countries. To facilitate these objectives, the E.U. established a process of negotiations that segmented the ACP countries into regional groupings of states that would negotiate separately with the E.U. The negotiating strategy adopted by the E.U. fragmented the ACP states into separate blocs and created new administrative and bureaucratic organizations through which negotiations would take place as part of Economic Partnership Agreements (EPAs). The E.U., through its Council of Ministers and the E.U. Commission, divided its negotiating partners into six separate groups, including the Caribbean Forum (CARIFORUM), the Pacific ACP (PACP), Central African, West African, Southern African Development Community (SADC), and East and Southern Africa (ESA) (van den Broek 2014, 37–39).

The E.U.-CARIFORUM investment agreement was concluded by 2008, establishing a precedent for an investment and regulatory agenda that would be adopted by the E.U. in future trade negotiations. The E.U. strategy for negotiating the CARIFORUM agreement was to require the Caribbean countries to bypass their regional organization CARICOM in favor of creating a new structure, CARIFORUM, for the purpose of negotiating the new investment agreement with the E.U. The negotiating process served to isolate CARIFORUM representatives from their own regional organizations, their home nation-states, civil society groups, and alliances with other ACP countries. At the same time, the E.U. negotiating structure privileged the interests of E.U.-based transnational corporations, whose influence with the E.U. Commission allowed them to set the agenda for the negotiations. A transnational interest bloc formed that brought together the negotiating teams established by the E.U. Commission, transnational capital, investment partners in the Caribbean, and Caribbean bureaucrats in CARIFORUM who favored a neoliberal trade strategy.

The E.U. Commission, working under the broad direction of the E.U. Council of Ministers, established advisory boards and task forces that negotiated the specific provisions of the E.U.-CARIFORUM investment agreement. These included transnational corporate interests that were able to influence the content of the negotiated provisions. On the CARIFORUM side were Caribbean bureaucrats who presided over new institutional arrangements that were created by the E.U. Commission. These included a joint CARIFORUM-EC Council established to deliberate over the policy impact of trade decisions; a CARIFORUM and EC Trade and Development Committee that facilitated the implementation of trade and investment policies; a joint CARIFORUM-EC Parliamentary Committee for political debate on relevant issues; and a CARIFORUM-EC Consultative Committee that enlisted private-sector groups as stakeholders in the negotiating process. Each of these newly created bureaucratic structures bypassed existing institutional mechanisms of CARICOM in favor of committees that had fewer ties to previous development approaches. This process signaled a break with the previous preferential trade arrangements of the Lome conventions in favor of a new approach that prioritized investment and regulatory policy changes in CARIFORUM countries as a precondition for continued favorable access to the E.U. market.

The structural power of the E.U. was evident in the negotiating process. The CARIFORUM countries entered the negotiations dependent on continued access to the E.U. market in order to fund mounting debt service obligations to foreign creditors. The previous Lome convention had established structural adjustment conditions for Caribbean countries that had tied eligibility to loans to a restructuring of domestic economies. This meant that most Caribbean trading partners were locked in to greater dependence on foreign direct investment in tourism and services as a way to finance their foreign debt obligations. Strong linkages had already been established between the functioning of the domestic Caribbean economies and access to foreign aid and investment. Foreign investment in hotels, travel agencies, cruise liners, and tourism-led development projects contributed to political and economic ties between foreign and domestic joint ventures in Caribbean economies. These ties allowed for the formation of transnational interest blocs in the negotiation of the E.U.-CARIFORUM investment agreement.

The transnational interest blocs that negotiated the agreement were led by E.U.-based transnational corporations whose interests were represented by corporate organizations with regular access to E.U. negotiating teams. The E.U. Commission relied on its Directorates General committees to carry out negotiations on behalf of E.U. interests. On the E.U. website, there were references to as many as thirteen negotiations with CARIFORUM that covered a range of investment-related issues. In each set of negotiations, corporate organizations within the E.U. were well represented, including prioritizing agenda items such as a strong set of provisions for protecting intellectual property rights. BusinessEurope was recognized by the E.U. negotiating team as a strategic partner in the negotiating process—indeed one of the four "official partners" listed by the E.U. Commission—that led the effort to incorporate intellectual property protections in the final agreement. Other working partners included the Eurochambers, part of the European Chambers of Commerce and Industry, which also lobbied for strong IP protection, and the European Services Forum, which included the largest European transnational corporations involved in finance, insurance, and telecommunications (van den Broek 2014, 55–57). Each of these corporate lobbies pushed for strong investment provisions that included protective policies in the area of IP, government procurement, competition policy, liberalization of financial markets, and limitations on any policy restrictions on foreign investments and profit repatriation requirements.

In order to fully grasp the broad reach and implications of the investment provisions that were included in the E.U.-CARIFORUM agreement of 2008, it is important to understand that these provisions go well beyond what was available to transnational capital in the multilateral process of the WTO. The ability of a transnational capitalist coalition, with disproportionate power within the E.U. bloc, to exert substantial influence over the terms of the final agreement is consistent with the dynamics of other regional investment agreements and bilateral investment treaties already discussed. There are several investment provisions that locked in Caribbean countries to liberalize their domestic market to facilitate greater flows of foreign capital. The deregulation of foreign capital flows was a crucial aspect of the agreement. For example, "article 123 on Capital Movements says the parties undertake to impose no restrictions on the free movement of capital relating to dircct investments and the liquidation and repatriation of these capitals and any profits stemming therefrom. Thus, the EPA, like most other North-South FTAs, facilitate the maximum opening, deregulation and liberalisation of financial flows" (Third World Network 2009, 27). There are only minimal exceptions allowed to countries that want to restrict capital flows, which can be done only after serious harm has been determined to be caused by capital flow liberalization (and therefore governments are able to act after the fact to check further destabilization, but not in advance of anticipated trends). The financial liberalization requirements also included provisions requiring Caribbean states to allow for the unrestricted and unregulated flows of new financial products, including derivatives, which had created destabilizing consequences for governments in the past, including contributing to the global financial crisis of 2008.

In addition to financial liberalization, Article 67 of the CARIFORUM-E.U. agreement committed Caribbean governments to foreign direct investment provisions that would

> not impose limitations on the number of commercial presences (in the form of quotas, monopolies, exclusive rights etc); on total value of transactions or assets; on total number of operations or quantity of output; on the participation of foreign capital in terms of maximum percentage of shareholding; and on requirements for specific types of commercial presence (subsidiary, branch) or joint ventures. This means that the foreign firm shall be allowed to have 100% ownership and be able to choose the nature of its corporate form. (Third World Network 2009, 28)

In addition, Article 68 included a "national treatment clause" that prohibited discrimination against foreign firms in government procurement policies. A Most Favored Nation (MFN) clause was written in Article 70 of the agreement, with the language stipulating that E.U. states would have to be given MFN treatment in any trade or investment agreement signed with another country or group of countries whose value of world trade is greater than 1 percent (Third World Network 2009, 28).

The ability of the E.U.-transnational capitalist coalition to advance its agenda is even more strongly supported when examining the language pertaining to IPRs in Article 132 of the agreement. BusinessEurope and the EuroChambers pushed for IPR protection that did not have the qualifying exceptions of the IPR rules established in the WTO TRIPS agreement. Instead, CARIFORUM countries were obligated to ensure "innovation and competitiveness" through an "adequate and effective level of protection and enforcement of intellectual property rights" (Third World Network 2009, 47). There was no corresponding language of exceptions to this requirement that CARIFORUM countries could invoke, such as ensuring access to medicine or pursuing development goals that might run counter to IPR protection such as reducing inequality or poverty. CARIFORUM countries that failed to honor their patent obligations would be subject to potential arbitration challenges by the aggrieved parties, with penalties possibly including increased tariffs on exports to the E.U.

Given the WTO-plus provisions in the agreement, there has been much scholarly debate and discussion about why CARIFORUM countries would agree to a treaty that seemed so lopsided in favor of the E.U. There are several factors that explain this. The first, not adequately developed or discussed in most of the scholarly literature, is that the CARIFORUM negotiators consisted of bureaucrats who shared the neoliberal ideology of the EU negotiators and were supportive of the open investment provisions of the agreement.

The stakeholders identified by CARIFORUM negotiators as having a "vital interest" in the success of the agreement were dominated by the investment partners of EU corporations in the tourism and services industries. Foreign investment in the region was increasingly linked to a political economy that had grown interconnected to global value chains that linked corporations owning cruise liners, foreign investors owning hotels and development resorts, and service industries whose very existence depended on maintaining and deepening existing value chain relationships. These tourist-services linkages were reinforced by a financial relationship that involved the presence of large-scale banks in the Caribbean whose future profits were tied to financing the development of a tourist-service economy increasingly in debt to private-sector lenders. The buildup of debt to finance an increasingly open economy based on the tourism-service sector was in large part a product of the previous restructuring of the Caribbean economies that had been encouraged by IMF and E.U.-backed structural adjustment programs (Melville 2002). The last Lome Convention resulted in structural adjustment policies that operated to reinforce dependency on a finance-tourism-service-debt economic structure that made Caribbean economies even more vulnerable to the closure of preferential access to the E.U. market.

The E.U. negotiators were able to use the threat of closing off preferential treatment to CARIFORUM countries as leverage in the negotiations. This is, in part, because the U.S. had successfully challenged the E.U. extension of preferential tariffs to its former colonies within the WTO. The U.S. government argued that the E.U. use of preferential tariffs discriminated against countries outside of these arrangements. The clash was rightly described as "banana wars," which pitted U.S.-based transnational banana producers (and other agribusiness corporations) against E.U. transnational agribusiness corporations that had benefited from preferential E.U. treatment due to their production locations within the former European colonies (Barkham 1999). The E.U. ultimately had to settle the U.S. claim, with the long-term result being the end to preferential treatment for its former colonies. Given that the CARIFORUM countries were about to be faced with greater competition in the global agricultural market, there was structural pressure for CARIFORUM negotiators to agree to a new deal with E.U. countries that would be based on reciprocal tariff reductions. However, the terms of the tariff reduction were considerably one-sided, as the E.U. had historically not insisted on equal trade access and now would be given such reciprocal access for the first time. A negotiated pact would allow for a gradual transition to these new requirements. More importantly, E.U. financial subsidies would continue to flow to CARIFORUM countries as a condition for reducing trade, regulatory, and investment barriers to E.U.

products. Given the structural dependency of CARIFORUM countries on the E.U. markets, the need for short-term E.U. financing to help address debt issues, and the embeddedness of the financial-tourism-services global value chain, negotiators were able to reach agreement (Heron 2011).

As we will see in the next section, transnational interest blocs also emerged in Japan's push for greater utilization of regional investment agreements. The final section will explore the dynamics of the China market, where U.S.-based transnational capital played a leading role in helping to secure most favored nation status for China, which helped pave the way for a dramatic increase in global value chains connected to the China market.

JAPANESE PTAs

Transnational capital based in Japan had joined Japanese allies in the most competitive sectors of the global economy to lobby for investment and IPR protections within the Uruguay Round of the General Agreement on Tariffs and Trade (GATT) and within the World Trade Organization (WTO). However, as with transnational interest blocs in the U.S. and the E.U., Japanese-based transnational firms in high technology, automobiles, electronics, and finance were frustrated by the slow pace of reforms within multilateral trade negotiations. As an alternative to these negotiations, these companies were looking for venues to gradually introduce substantive changes to trade rules that would allow for WTO-plus provisions. Within this context, Keidanren, the most cohesive and powerful corporate lobby for the globally competitive sectors of Japanese transnational capital, took advantage of opportunities to work with the Japanese Ministry of Economy, Trade, and Industry (METI) to advance proposals that would serve as guidelines for Japanese negotiation strategies in regional investment agreements.

The first such political opportunity emerged in response to two developments in the global trading regime: the passage of NAFTA and the failure of the Singapore agenda within the WTO. NAFTA had the effect of increasing the costs for many Japanese corporations doing business in the Mexican market, including electronics and automobile firms. NAFTA "phased out the duty drawback program in the maquiladora industry where the vast majority of Japanese electronics companies and parts makers operated," imposed "stiff rules of origin on automobiles that would force major readjustments in their supply chain to export competitively to the United States," imposed "major performance requirements on non-PTA [preferential trade agreement] car companies," and limited "access to the lucrative government procurement market to PTA companies" (Solis 2013, 100). Here we get a strong sense of why transnational investment blocs utilize regional investment agreements: to provide themselves market advantages relative to their transnational competitors. Transnational firms utilize their power within regional investment agreements to provide investment guarantees that disproportionately benefit their interests. In response, transnational firms from competing locations rely on their lobbying networks with their home states to prevent them from being "left behind" in securing similar investment provisions.

Keidanren represented the interests of transnational capitalists in Japan who favored liberalization of global investment and IPR rules but saw that the Singapore agenda in the WTO had been defeated. After having lobbied unsuccessfully for strengthened enforcement of IPR, investment rights, and procurement guarantees in the WTO, Keidanren became the vehicle for an aggressive corporate lobbying effort in Japan to negotiate strengthened investment provisions with foreign countries in regional investment agreements (Yoshimatsu 2005). Transnational firms represented in Keidanren understood that regional trade forums offered corporations more instrumental and structural flexibility in negotiating preferential investment deals that would allow for the insertion of much stronger measures of protection than could be attained in multilateral forums. These firms could then attempt to use the provisions enacted in regional investment agreements as leverage to expand investment protection within multilateral negotiations. As an important spillover effect, transnational firms in Japan wanted to keep pace with their transnational competitors in the U.S. and the E.U. by negotiating equivalent investment protections for Japanese-based transnational capital in regional investment agreements.

Japanese transnational corporations, led by Keidanren, had long preferred to work within multilateral trade venues such as the WTO, rather than regional investment agreements of the type being carved out by the U.S. and the E.U. This pattern changed in response to the NAFTA treaty. Japanese firms began to lobby the Mexican government for delaying or reversing the terms of the NAFTA treaty that reduced the competitive position of Japanese capital within the North American market. The Japanese Chamber of Commerce and Industry and the Japanese Maquiladora Association lobbied the Mexican Trade Ministry on behalf of Japanese auto and electronics firms. Officials within METI began to work with Keidanren in 1998 to develop the outlines of a preferential trade agreement, which I will refer to as a regional investment agreement, that would provide the framework for negotiating a set of investment protections for Japanese transnational investors in Mexico. Keidanren became the most important private-sector organization for developing an investment strategy that would guide the efforts of METI in the negotiations with Mexico.

Keidanren and METI hoped that the negotiations with Mexico could start as early as 1999, which was initially proposed, but sectoral conflict—a battle between rival transnational interest blocs—postponed the start of negotiations until 2002. Japanese firms in automobiles and electronics utilized their own lobbying initiatives, alongside the broader work of Keidanren, to emphasize how Mexico had diverted its trade and investment with Japan toward the U.S. and the E.U. after signing agreements with the latter two parties. Japanese auto firms found it difficult to meet the content requirements necessary to qualify for reduced tariffs for products traded within the North American market. Japanese exporters also faced higher tariff barriers than their competitors in the U.S. and the E.U. Japanese electronics producers faced a higher tariff rate (after the elimination of a duty-free drawback provision) on component parts exported from Japan to the Japanese affiliates within the maquiladora manufacturing enclave in Mexico. The total losses accruing to Japanese firms in automobiles and electronics were estimated to have risen to over $500 billion from the ratification of NAFTA through 1998, which led to concerted pressure from Japanese manufacturers in these sectors to reverse the trend. However, this transnational interest bloc—which linked Keidanren, METI, and a Japanese supply network inside Mexico linked to auto and electronics firms—was opposed by a rival transnational bloc in Japan dominated by agricultural and textile producers. The tensions between these competing blocs played out in the Japan-Mexico negotiation for an economic partnership agreement, which finally started in 2002 after being postponed by an inability to reach an agreement on the level of agricultural liberalization that would be part of the final agreement (Solis and Katada 2007).

The bureaucratic structure of the Japanese negotiating strategy accentuated the conflicts between transnational interest blocs in different sectors of Japanese industry. Japan utilized as many as four ministries to collaborate in trade negotiations, inviting considerable conflict between ministries with competing constituents in the private sector. These included METI, which took the lead in the negotiations; the Ministry of Foreign Affairs (MOFA), which emphasized overarching strategic interests for Japan; the Ministry of Agriculture, Forest, and Fisheries (MAFF), closely tied to the agricultural sector; and the Ministry of Finance, linked to the Japanese banking sector. The primary divisions emerged between METI and MAFF, with the latter insisting on minimizing the impact of any final agreement on specific sectors of Japanese agricultural production, especially those sectors designated the "five fingers": pork, chicken, beef, oranges, and orange juice (Solis and Katada 2007, 297). The final agreement, ratified in 2005, represented a compromise between the interests of Japanese manufacturing firms and these sectors of Japanese agriculture, which remained heavily protected, despite overall reductions in tariff barriers that were achieved in the final agreement.

As with the E.U.-CARIFORUM agreement, the Japan-Mexico EPA represented a successful lobbying strategy on the part of Japanese transnational investors, represented by Keidanren, which would be able to replicate this strategy across other Japanese EPAs. Keidanren had the necessary political and economic power to become the leading lobbying group for transnational capital. The organization had already established strong ties to METI, the Japanese bureaucracy that took the lead in the PTA negotiations. Keidanren consulted regularly with METI and produced position papers and policy proposals that provided the basis for investment provisions that were negotiated with Mexico. These provisions emphasized a gradual elimination of tariffs on automobile exports, including component parts, from Japan to Mexico over a seven-year period. Japanese electronics producers in Mexico were given back their ability to import component parts duty-free from Japan, which allowed their subsidiaries and investment partners in the maquiladora sector to compete effectively as producers in the North American market. And finally, the agreement leveled the playing field for Japanese firms to compete on equal terms with their U.S. and E.U. counterparts in government procurement contracts. The agreement did not cover intellectual property rights in a separate article, but it did commit signatories to a concerted effort to protect IPRs according to guidelines stipulated in the WTO, with enforcement provisions to be developed in accordance with the Madrid Agreement Concerning the International Registration of Marks. This essentially commits parties to the agreement to protect international registrations of patents and copyrights that have been registered in member jurisdictions and have attained recognition from the World Intellectual Property Organization in Geneva. Due to changes in the procedures associated with what was previously considered to be a weak registration system, more countries and regions joined the Madrid system after 2003, including the U.S., the E.U., and Japan.

In Mexico, the transnational interest bloc represented by Keidanren was supported by the Mexican Council of Businessmen, which also supported NAFTA for many of the same reasons. The most visible manifestation of this transnational interest bloc was the Mexico-Japan Business Committee. Transnational capital in Mexico had already become linked to global supply chains in autos and electronics, with a range of foreign transnational producers from the U.S., the E.U., and Japan establishing value chains in the Mexican economy that would allow for production for North American and foreign markets. These interests proved to be complementary in the negotiations that led to a final agreement (concluded by 2004 but subject to enforcement in 2005), with manufacturing firms on both sides endorsing the reduced tariffs on intermediate inputs that contributed to lowering the costs of production within value chains in Mexico. The Mexican Council of Businessmen also represented large-scale Mexican agricultural interests that were able to achieve some liberalization of agricultural exports to Japan, even if the final tariff schedule still offered protection for dominant agricultural sectors in Japan (Cokelet 2013).

As the U.S., the E.U., and Japan were all moving toward increasing their usage of regional investment agreements and bilateral investment treaties from 1990 through 2010, transnational firms also sought to establish easier access to the China market. This, more than any other set of trade developments, would dramatically shift, deepen, and expand the scope of global value chains, creating both greater global cooperation with domestic Chinese interests and more conflict about the terms of such investment liberalization.

TRANSNATIONAL CAPITAL AND THE CHINA MARKET

China is an important case study for an examination of the linkage between transnational corporations and states within global value chains.[2] This is true for several reasons. First, China is the second-largest recipient of foreign direct investment in the world, behind only the United States. Over the past three decades, the Chinese state has implemented policies that have expanded the role of foreign invested enterprises in the export sector of the Chinese economy. In 1979, Chinese laws limited foreign investors to joint ventures, and the first foreign direct investment in China was recorded in 1982. By 1986, China allowed wholly owned foreign enterprises within special economic zones but otherwise kept the expansion of FDI quite limited. The 1990s saw a steady expansion of FDI, with most foreign invested enterprises concentrated in the export sector of the economy. By the late 1990s, China had opened up the entire economy to FDI, although foreign firms remain concentrated in the southern and central coastal provinces. From 1995 to 2004, transnational corporations accounted for 30 percent of China's growth, and in 2003 and 2004, "this figure rose to over 40 percent" (Hart-Landsberg 2013, 4). Most significantly, by 2004, foreign invested enterprises produced 90 percent of computer exports from China, including components and peripherals, and 75 percent of the exports of telecommunications and electronics products (Hart-Landsberg 2013, 6).

The surge in information technology exports from China is the second factor that makes the country an important case study for transnational-state linkages. U.S.-based transnational firms in the high-tech sector occupy an increasingly pivotal role in global capitalism and in the proliferation of global supply networks. Firms in computers, telecommunications, electronics, and software have been central players in the transition from a Fordist system of capitalist production, characterized by the production of goods and services within nation-states, toward a global system of vertical production networks that disperses production of component parts across a range of countries and locations. The information technology sector has been the primary driving force in the restructuring of global capitalism. Advances in digital processing have enabled the exponential increases in cross-border financial speculation and the growth of global supply chains. The dramatic rise of Walmart as the leading U.S. multinational corporation would not have been possible without the integration of advanced communications technology that serves to link the retail giant with a global supply network that includes China as the most important foreign supply source. The integration of advanced technology within manufacturing, as early as 1988 in the U.S., allowed blue-collar workers to use just 40 percent of the workforce required to produce the same amount of goods in 1977 (Harris 2008, 5). At the same time, information technology firms have grown in size and profit margins relative to traditional manufacturing firms. By 1999 information technology firms in computer services and software, computers and office equipment, electronics, and telecommunication eclipsed finance, transportation, insurance, and energy as the most profitable sector within the global economy (Harris 2008, 22). From 2000 to 2009, China was the most important foreign location for the production of information technology products, indicating its centrality in the new accumulation system of global capitalism.

Among U.S. transnational firms, the leading lobbyists for expanding trade and investment opportunities with China are firms in the information technology and retail sectors, whose position within global capitalism has been strengthened by the dramatic expansion of foreign direct investment in the China market. Corporate influence is manifest in the expansion of lobbying networks that have worked with U.S. political elites for renewal of most-favored-nation status for China throughout the 1990s and for China's entry into the WTO in 2001. The changing political environment in China coincided with changes in the global production strategies of leading transnational corporations, reinforced by the rising political power of corporations within the U.S. Tax concessions offered to U.S.-based transnational firms were married to increasing political opportunities in China and East Asia to create global supply networks, especially in the information technology sectors. Transnational firms in these sectors have steadily increased their reliance on China and the East Asian supply chain for the production of everything from computer services and software, computer and office equipment, electronics, and telecommunications. Twenty-three of these information technology firms are based in the U.S., twelve in Europe, nine in Japan, with the developing world accounting for a very small percentage of firms at the top of the global value chain (Harris 2008, 20).

Aggregate trade statistics capture some aspects of the U.S.-China nexus that has been emerging in stages over the past three decades. Bilateral trade in 1979 was only $1 billion, but by 2009 U.S.-China trade totaled $366 billion, which made China the second-largest U.S. trading partner, behind only Canada. The trade deficit with China is the highest of any U.S. trading partner and is just over half of the overall U.S. trade deficit. China is the third-largest U.S. export market after Canada and Mexico and the largest source of U.S. imports. Yet in order to understand the political economy of China's export economy, we have to carefully look behind the aggregate trade statistics toward an examination of the transnational system of production that ties the two countries together. As late as 1998, foreign invested enterprises (FIEs) accounted for 73.7 percent of the value of all the information technology and computer exports from China. By 2008, that number had grown significantly, with FIEs accounting for 85.2 percent of this output (Scott 2011, 7).

The most explosive growth in the relationship between U.S. transnational corporations and Chinese exports occurred from 2000 to 2009. In 2000, Japan was the largest exporter of computer equipment to the U.S., and China was fourth. By 2009, China had eclipsed Japan by a large margin, with a 440 percent growth of Chinese computer exports from 2000 to 2009. During this decade, China went from a 12.1 percent share of U.S. imports of computers to a 58 percent share. The overwhelming majority of this trade came from producer networks in Taiwan, which engaged in foreign direct investment in China that accounted for about 75 percent of the computer equipment exports. The Taiwanese producer networks were part of a global supply chain that involved U.S. transnational firms signing original equipment manufacturing contracts with producers in Taiwan. The Taiwanese producers then engaged in foreign direct investment in the China market, which was then exported to foreign markets, helping to account for the explosive growth in computer equipment exports to the U.S. Figure 3.6 illustrates the emerging trend.

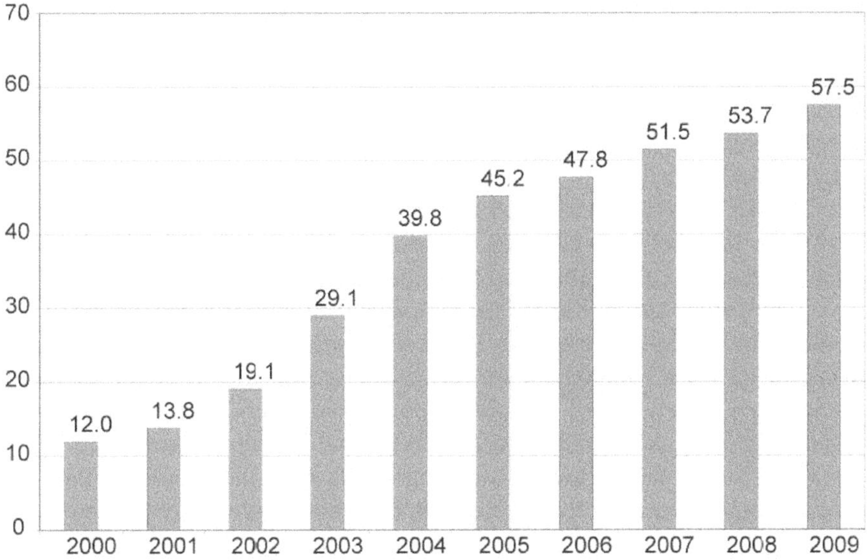

Figure 3.6. Share of Computer Exports from China (% basis)
Source: Congressional Research Service, data taken from USITC DataWeb (2010).

The political economy of U.S.-China trade continues to divide U.S. interest groups, with leading U.S.-based transnational corporations in high-tech manufacturing, information technology, and the retail sector lobbying for renewal of China's most-favored-nation status, which was accomplished without interruption between 1980 and 2001. These same firms lobbied successfully for China's membership in the WTO in 2001. There is a direct overlap between U.S. transnational firms at the top of global supply chain networks and the composition of the modern-day China lobby, whose goals have been articulated in concert with the policies of leading U.S. state bureaucracies and congressional lawmakers. In that sense, the pyramid of power extends from the market—increasingly characterized by the dominance of just a few firms at the top of global supply chains in manufacturing, information technology, and software—to the most powerful actors within the U.S. state. At the same time, sectors of industry linked to the U.S. Department of Defense and the U.S. military-industrial complex, as well as U.S. nationalists, consistently target China as a threat to U.S. strategic interests.

More recently, as I will explain in more depth in chapter five, there have emerged considerable tensions between transnational investors with stakes in the China market and recent shifts in Chinese investment requirements that have increased the obligations on foreign investors to share technology and to share ownership of investments with domestic Chinese firms. This has resulted in considerable conflict among blocs of investors in the China market, with transnational interest blocs tied to the U.S., the E.U., and Japan opposing Chinese state policies that have grown more restrictive in conditionalities required for foreign direct investment. Also, as political forces within the Chinese state have attempted to slow down the emphasis on export-led growth in favor of strengthening domestic demand, the value of the Chinese currency has been allowed to rise so that domestic demand incentives have increased. Concomitantly, the Chinese state has been more aggressive in requiring foreign investors to share investments with domestic Chinese firms, alongside technology sharing, which has increased tensions between foreign transnationals and competing power blocs in China. Transnational corporations across diverse sectors of the global economy continue to insist that China is increasing its long-standing violation of WTO policies through investment requirements that go beyond multilateral rules of engagement.

CONCLUSION

In this chapter I have examined how transnational interest blocs have led political coalitions in support of investment agreements designed to facilitate the expansion of global value chains. Transnational corporate lobbies, based in the U.S., the E.U., and Japan, and extending their influence through China, have negotiated a series of trade and investment deals that have expanded and deepened the prevalence and intensity of global value chains. The next chapter examines the political economy of value extraction within these global chains of production. In doing so, we will emphasize how corporate owners leverage their proprietary rights over high-value activities to super-exploit workers producing within those value chains.

NOTES

1. This section is taken from Ronald W. Cox, "Transnational Capital, the US State and Latin American Trade Agreements," *Third World Quarterly* 29, no. 8 (2008): 1535–1540.

2. This section is taken from Ronald W. Cox and Sylvan Lee, "The U.S.-China Nexus," in *Corporate Power and Globalization in U.S. Foreign Policy*, ed. Ronald W. Cox (New York: Routledge, 2012), 42–47.

Chapter Four

Labor in Global Value Chains[1]

Transnational corporations have increased their state and market power through the accumulation of surplus value within global value chains. As I have shown, the segmentation of production has been facilitated by corporate-state political alliances in the U.S., the E.U., and Japan. Transnational interest blocs pushed successfully for neoliberal policy measures and regional investment agreements that reduced the costs of segmented production across state borders. Governments, through networks of transnational corporate power that affected the direction of public policy, assisted their home transnational corporations in a manner that enabled the regionalization of global value chains, first in Japan-East Asia, next in the U.S.-North America, and finally in the E.U.-Eastern Europe. These early regional manifestations of global value chains saw the linkages between transnational firms based in the core countries and an emerging supply network in developing countries. Transnational interest blocs linked the interests of headquarter firms in the core capitalist states with contractors in developing countries that produced finished products through the exploitation of low-cost wage labor. The production of the finished product began with a regional focus, pivoting around transnational corporate interest blocs in core capitalist locations, but then expanded across a more dispersed and wider range of locations within the global economy by the late 1990s and early to mid-2000s. The wider segmentation of production across multiple developing states, producing a range of component parts for eventual assembly into a finished product, was achieved by mechanisms of both corporate market and political power. This chapter will examine the political economy of those power relationships, specifically how profits are distributed within global value chains.

Liberal accounts of global value chains assume a correspondence between the value of factors of production and the return to those factors in the form of profits and wages. In other words, corporations at the top of global value chains, headquarter firms, are assumed to earn disproportionate profits based on their ability to maximize wealth through factor ownership of high valued assets. These include ownership of research and development, technology, application of skill-based assets and knowledge in production, and integration of these high-value added factors into global value chains. In liberal accounts, headquarter firms are rewarded in the form of revenues and profits from ownership and management of these high valued assets. Workers, according to this logic, receive wages that correspond to their labor productivity. I argue here that this standard liberal account of factor value operates as an ideological veneer that conceals the way that power relationships determine the distribution of revenues within global value chains. Headquarter firms realize profits in global value chains by leveraging their oligopolistic market power to maximize the exploitation of workers. These firms use their size and market power to buy out competitors, to concentrate ownership of IPRs, to lobby for subsidies and investment protection from governments, and to divert revenues away from governments through tax havens and transfer pricing. They then convert their market and political power into a favorable bargaining relationship with foreign contractors, which exerts a downward pressure on production costs and most importantly wages, especially wages as a percentage of overall corporate revenues—which measures the extent to which exploitation is occurring (not higher or lower wages per se). Headquarter firms extract surplus value from workers by keeping wages well below increases in worker productivity.

The shift of manufacturing from the global North to the South, specifically through global value chains, is directly tied to the super-exploitation of workers within those value chains. Workers in the global South have become more important to the profits of headquarter firms in global manufacturing value chains over the past three decades. For example, workers in developing countries were producing 47.3 percent of the value of global manufacturing exports by 2015, a figure that has steadily increased from the mid-1980s to the present.

As I will show in this chapter, workers who are producing manufacturing goods in developing countries are primarily doing so as part of global value chains whose lead firms are based in Northern countries. Headquarter firms increasingly depend on expanding the ratio of worker productivity per capital investment in the global South. Transnational firms rely on two methods for accruing surplus value in global value chains. The first is foreign direct investment through subsidiaries. The second is arm's-length contracts with suppliers in the global South. This latter method has become increasingly important for transnational capitalist profits. By severing the transnational

	Exports	Output	Employment
Land-scarce regions			
Land-scarce OECD	1.1	4.5	-7.0
Other East Asia	13.4	14.1	1.1
China	45.5	15.8	5.5
India	16.1	15.0	0.0
Other South Asia	22.3	12.8	2.7
Land-abundant regions			
Land-abundant OECD	-5.8	-8.5	-8.1
Former Soviet sphere	-12.5	-5.0	-14.7
Latin America	-1.1	-12.5	-1.1
Middle East & N Africa	-10.8	-2.0	-0.5
Sub-Saharan Africa	-14.2	-1.5	-0.3
World	-0.8	-4.4	-1.8
Developing countries	14.9	8.7	1.7

Figure 4.1. Manufacturing Share Changes, 1985–2014 (percentage points)

Source: Wood 2017, table 8.

For exports and output, the shares are of manufacturing in the value-added content of all goods (manufacturing + primary). For employment, the shares are of formal manufacturing in economy-wide employment. "Developing" = non-OECD, non-FSS.

firm from the costs associated with foreign direct investment, the firm can maximize profits by pushing costs onto the independent contractor.

This system of arm's-length investment in global value chains is typically mediated by an extensive supply network, which includes original design manufacturers (ODM), which have emerged as an important corporate actor in global production strategies, especially after the recession of 2001 when transnational brand name corporations were looking to further reduce the costs associated with the various stages of production. As part of this process, transnational firms have contracted with ODMs to undertake "product design, development and manufacturing" as transnational firms maintain control of IPRs, branding rights, and marketing (Pratap 2014, 50). ODMs are large-scale firms that were initially based almost exclusively in the Northern capitalist countries but can increasingly be found in Asia, especially Taiwan and Singapore, where ODMs have been able to use their acquisition of technological knowledge to enter higher-value production activities independent of the contractual relationship with transnational brand name firms. The tension between the rising competitive power and independence of some former ODMs has led to increasing transnational competition among large-scale firms that were previously working with one another. At the same time, especially after the global recession of 2008, the Chinese state has become more aggressive in subsidizing its emerging high-tech sector in an attempt to achieve greater global competitiveness, which has contributed to recent trade disputes between the U.S. and China. Later in this chapter I will discuss in more detail how crisis periods in global capitalism, specifically the recessions of 2000–2001 and 2008, have affected the restructuring of global value chains and have intensified global competition around the reorganization of these chains.

In addition to the more recent expansion of ODMs, original equipment manufacturers (OEMs) have had a longer history within the global value chain process. Headquarter firms, or dominant transnational brand name corporations, contract with OEMs to supervise, manage, and coordinate production within an increasingly complex value chain network. OEMs are responsible for delivering a product according to specifications to either the ODM or the headquarter firm or retail corporation, depending on the relative complexity of the value chain. OEM firms, like ODMs, have grown larger and more concentrated in market size and power due to the logistical, financial, and organizational complexities of the contemporary global value chain. The ability of OEM firms to operate as large-scale "middlemen" in value chain production, sometimes complemented by ODM firms that design and source the finished product, has allowed headquarter firms to increase their specialization in core ownership activities that generate the most wealth from these value chains. As OEM firms have steadily increased their size, revenues, and distributional capacity, the logistics of finished production within the global value chain has become more concentrated and dependent on a large-scale contingent of global workers to ensure the finished production and delivery of the value chain product (Gereffi 2014).

Headquarter firms manage this process by maintaining control over the IPRs, branding, and marketing activities, while engaging in contractual arrangements with foreign contractors regarding the terms of product design, production, and delivery. OEM firms supervise the production process through a web of interdependent production networks, each tied to maximizing the extraction of surplus value from workers at every step of the production process. The gap between worker productivity/output and wages is central to the realization of profit in this system. And the concentration of market wealth and power at the top, and increasingly in the middle tier, of the value chain, has served a disciplinary function that pushes cost margins downward to small-scale producers and especially to workers. The lower tier of the global value chain is often divided into a three-tier supplier network. Firms in the first tier supply higher value-added components that are necessary to produce a finished product. The second tier includes local companies in the developing world that produce finished components. The third tier consists of "small local factories, informal sector units or home-based units, performing very low value adding, highly labor-intensive tasks" (Pratap 2014, 48–49).

The incorporation of just-in-time delivery mechanisms by the headquarter firm is evident in both supply- and demand-driven global value chains. Supply-driven chains are those that are led by dominant manufacturing firms whose control of high-value-added activities gives them a quasi-monopoly power within the value chain. These firms own the intellectual content of a product's production but increasingly do not engage in any actual production. The demand-driven firms are transnational retail giants such as Walmart, whose profits are closely tied to the labor of workers in the global South who produce goods stored on the corporation's shelves. Retail-driven value chains entirely omit the degree to which labor relationships of independent contractors allow the headquarter firm to reap disproportionate profits. Statistics of foreign direct investment therefore greatly underestimate the expansion of global value chains, and specifically where surplus value is coming from, by omitting from their calculations what has become a defining feature of production in global value chains: arm's-length contracts from headquarter firms to independent suppliers (Grinberg 2016).

Transnational corporate power within global value chains is partially derived from oligopolistic and quasi-monopolistic strategies that include mergers and acquisitions (M&A), buyouts of patent rights previously owned by other firms and/or subsidized through public institutions, and limits on competition through price fixing, transfer pricing, and intrafirm trading to lower costs of production. Cross-border mergers and acquisitions have been an important mechanism for increasing the concentration of corporate power within global value chains. The utilization of M&A strategies has enabled transnational corporations to gain greater control over the high-value activities that generate the most profits from global value chains; or at the very least, M&As are used to limit competition or to prevent competitors from acquiring valuable assets. Through the process of consolidating their control over high-valued activities in an increasingly global M&A process, transnational corporations have been able to use their ownership of intellectual property rights, their ownership of intermediate inputs in the production process—especially high-technology products and the skills underlying that technology—to extract concessions from contractors in developing countries who produce component parts across multiple platforms toward final assembly, distribution, sales, and marketing. Global value chains have steadily increased in importance, as measured by the percentage of manufacturing goods produced in these chains (Pratap 2014, 35–42).

These value chains are defined by the entirety of networked processes that enter and exit the value chains. That includes the IPRs, R&D, intermediate goods that serve as "inputs" in the assembly of component parts and the finished product, and the marketing, distribution, and sale of the finished product. Throughout this segmentation of production, thousands of actors are working across multiple countries to produce a product whose final assembly and sales will reflect the value added in production from various locations. Who reaps the benefits from this value-added process is a function of power, specifically the ability to turn ownership rights into surplus value through investment agreements negotiated across these global platforms. As we saw in the previous chapter, transnational corporations have built-in economic and political advantages in extracting surplus value from these investment agreements.

First, the sheer size, scale, and asset ownership accrued to the firms at the top of the global value chain pyramid provide them with maximum leverage in both economic and political negotiation with their supplier networks. Part of this is due to straightforward market logic: a firm that has control of knowledge and informational assets and has leveraged those assets into brand ownership and marketing relationships with powerful retail chains can utilize this capital to put pressure on competing supply networks for favorable production deals. Hundreds of potential suppliers compete to secure a favorable location within global value chain production, thereby driving down the costs of producing component parts. The tight cost margins experienced by the supplier firms are passed along to their own societies in the forms of super-exploitation of wage labor, quick turnaround of production, and environmental costs that are often deregulated out of existence for the sake of satisfying the contractual demands of the "headquarter" firm. Part of what allows transnational corporations to dominate pyramids of value chain production is the fact that they start with a dominant structural market position, which they then leverage in negotiations with competing suppliers. These suppliers exist in a world of cutthroat capitalism, while the dominant transnational firms compete as oligopolies that attempt to restrict entry into the high-valued activities of the global capitalist economy.

Second, transnational firms leverage their ownership or control of intermediate products that are used as forward "inputs" in production within global value chains. The highest value-added inputs that have enabled global value chains to achieve sustained growth as a percentage of overall manufacturing production are concentrated in high-technology products. Transnational firms that own these high-technology products are well positioned to accrue surplus value through their ownership rights. This means that the ability of transnational manufacturing firms to control the knowledge, techniques, skills, and utilization of intermediate goods that are imported as "inputs" in global value chains is crucial for determining the flow of profits within the value chain pyramid. As economists and social scientists have observed in studying global value chains, traditional trade statistics do not capture how value is distributed within these chains. Exports of finished goods do not tell us anything about who owns the highest value-added intermediate products that serve as "inputs" into the production of the finished good. We can correct for this deficiency in traditional trade statistics by looking at measurements of "input-output" components within global value chain production. What such measurements reveal is how ownership of the most valuable "inputs" of production, high-value intermediate goods, is crucial in explaining how surplus value is extracted within value chains.

Surplus value is as integral to capitalist production today as it was in the mid-nineteenth century when Marx observed industrial workers surrendering their labor, beyond subsistence levels, to capitalists in the form of profits. Since then, capitalists have devised a variety of mechanisms to reward wealth instead of work. To fully gauge the power of monopolists, financiers, and shareholders, one has only to look at the distribution of surplus value to these owners of production. The rampant inequality in the global economy is a symptom of decades of unproductive profits accruing to the wealthiest. By segmenting production across a wide range of supplier networks, headquarter firms have effectively marginalized labor from collectively bargaining a share in rising corporate profits, thus also neutralizing their political power. The development of global value chains (GVCs) is therefore partially understood as a purposive act to disperse competition among a vast network of suppliers and contract labor. Being able to drive down costs, while utilizing monopoly pricing mechanisms, has allowed managers of GVCs to extract surplus value from industrial production undertaken by contractors on terms that are highly favorable to dominant sectors of capital (Aguiar de Medeiros and Trebat 2016). By identifying the relevant actors and their impact on policymaking, the first three chapters have detailed a framework to help us understand how production networks are governed and coordinated. This chapter builds on the previous but pays particular attention to the operation of GVCs in developing countries and their evolution of novel mechanisms for surplus value extractions, particularly trade in intermediate inputs.

GLOBAL VALUE CHAINS AND INTERMEDIATE INPUTS IN DEVELOPING COUNTRIES

Researchers have struggled to accurately measure the value added in global value chains. This has become a greater challenge due to the ability of headquarter firms to extract payments from their ownership of intellectual property rights in a variety of ways, most of which are not captured by traditional trade statistics. This has led scholars to utilize more fine-tuned methods of tracking value-added in traded goods. Such methods have included using input-output statistics to better track the increased importance of intermediate goods as a percentage of total global exports. Intermediate goods are those exports and imports that are used in the production of products across state borders. Transnational corporations derive their highest profit margins from their ownership of high-technology and capital-intensive products that serve as intermediate inputs in production. These inputs are either incorporated by a subsidiary of a transnational corporation through foreign direct investment or sold through a contractual relationship with an independent production network that includes multiple suppliers. The latter method has grown increasingly important in global production trends. Through analyzing input-output tables, we have a better grasp of ownership of high-value activities within global value chains, and therefore where value is being added within the value chain.

Using input-output statistics within global value chains provided by the OECD-WTO database on trade in value added, there are several conclusions that scholars have contributed to understanding the political economy of global value chains during the period of the new globalization. First, there has been a steady deepening of global value chains as measured by an increase in intermediate goods as a percentage of overall trade in finished goods, which was at its peak during the period from 2001 to 2008, which represented the highest period of complex cross-border segmentation, dispersal, and breadth of global value chains.

CONTRIBUTION TO THE TRADE IN GLOBAL MANUFACTURING BY TRADE TYPE, 1995–2015

This pattern tracks closely the rise of regional and bilateral investment agreements and the ascendancy of China as the apex of capitalist global production platforms, all of which accelerated the growth of intermediate inputs as part of global value chain expansion. However, periodic global capitalist crises have slowed the growth of intermediate inputs over time relative to

Percent

	Contribution to growth of total manufacturing trade			Contribution to decline in total manufacturing trade		
Trade type	1995–2000	2001–08	2009–14	2000–01	2008–09	2014–15
Trade in intermediate goods	45.3	52.0	50.2	79.0	55.4	47.0
Trade in final goods	54.7	48.0	49.8	21.0	44.6	53.0

Figure 4.2. Contribution to the Trade in Global Manufacturing by Trade Type, 1995–2015
Source: Degain, Meng, and Wang 2017, 39.

total manufacturing trade. In the aftermath of the capitalist crisis of 2008, transnational corporations reorganized their global value chains, a process that involved a consolidation of production and distribution networks across fewer global countries and territories—a transition whose political and economic manifestations will be the subject of the last chapter of this book. This has meant that global value chains, especially within the last five years of global production trends, have experienced a transition away from spatial deepening and territorial breadth toward more intensification around key locations within the global economy. In the period following the global capitalist crisis of 2008, there has been a consolidation of ownership of high-valued activities at the top of the global value chain—more global mergers and acquisitions, as well as a greater level of consolidation of ownership of original equipment manufacturers who dominate the contractual work of organization and logistics within global value chains (*The Economist* 2016).

Long after the global financial crisis, there remains a high concentration of profits and high-valued activities within the global value chain architecture. That is illustrated by the statistics regarding who is capturing the largest gains from value chain production. A 2015 OECD study finds that just six OECD countries capture 33 percent of the value from global chains, including the U.S. with 8.2 percent, Germany with 7.7 percent, Japan with 4.6 percent, South Korea with 4.2 percent, the U.K. with 3.8 percent, and France with 3.6 percent (Aguiar de Medeiros and Trabat 2016, 13). These statistics are misleading, namely because the value captured by transnational corporations is conflated with "states" within whose territories they carry out their market capture of profits. In other words, the value captured within global value chains is distributed within a global class structure of accumulation in which corporate profits are increasingly delinked from income flows to societies or to states within whose territories they operate.

The input-output data in global trade statistics is consistent with the locational advantages of transnational corporations that own the highest-value-added intermediate products that serve as inputs in global value chains. The ability of transnational firms to leverage their ownership of intermediate products is reflected in a rising percentage of profits going to transnational corporations and a lower percentage of wages going to manufacturing workers in developing countries. In fact, there has been a dramatic relocation of manufacturing production in the past two decades from the North to the South, especially in China and East and Southeast Asia. This is indicated by rising manufacturing production, and increasing manufacturing productivity, by Asian workers located in the highest value-added manufacturing activities, including high-technology and computer sectors. Despite the higher rates of production and productivity, the domestic value added by those manufacturing exports has actually been trending downward over the past two decades.

This is because of the ability of transnational corporations to use their market and political power to extract high surplus value from the value chain by adding the most valuable productive inputs and/or by charging more rent for those inputs. One way this is accomplished is through transnational corporations selling access to technology and intermediate products on favorable terms, given the hyper-competition that exists among competing supply networks within global value chains (GVCs) (Quentin and Campling 2018, 36–38). The other way is through the suppression of wages in developing countries relative to corporate revenues. Wages have declined relative to increasing production and productivity in manufacturing exports that comprise the component parts in global value chains (Selwyn 2016, 14–17; Smith 2016, 133–166). The result of market concentration at the top of the global value chain and hyper-competition within the middle and lower tiers of the value chain is skewed distribution of profits at the top.

Within global value chains, developing countries usually situate themselves within a network of backward and forward linkages. Backward linkages are foreign inputs that are used for export production. Forward linkages are inputs provided to foreign partners for export production. Level of development, location, size of domestic market and industrial sector, as well as quality of infrastructure and institutions are all determinants of the scale and scope of GVC participation. GVCs still operate in proximity to primary commercial hubs in Europe (Germany), North America (the United States), and Asia (Japan). Asia, Africa, Latin America, and the Middle East participate primarily through agriculture, processed foods, plastics and rubber, textile, metal products, electrical and electronic equipment, and motor vehicles. Asia tends to participate in the highest value-added activities within global value chains, including but not limited to electronic equipment, computer products, and automobiles, while Africa, Latin America, and the Middle East are more competitive in agriculture and foodstuff and lighter manufacturing products. Yet there are significant variations between regions and among developing countries.

Intermediate inputs sit between primary inputs and final products as the goods and services (energy, raw materials, semi-finished goods, components, machinery, intellectual property, etc.) used up in the production of other goods for final consumption. Of the indicators of global value chains, the increased trade in intermediate inputs is potentially the most telling. According to a 2012 OECD study, more than 50 percent of global manufactured imports are in intermediate inputs, and over 70 percent service imports are in intermediate services (OECD 2012). The OECD-WTO Trade in Value-Added (TiVA) database provides an intuitive, and ultimately more accurate, way to measure foreign trade and GVCs. Simply put, it measures trade in intermediaries. More importantly, we can now measure to what extent, and in what sectors, developing countries are embedded in GVCs. The data also allows for a better determination of both backward *and* forward GVC participation.

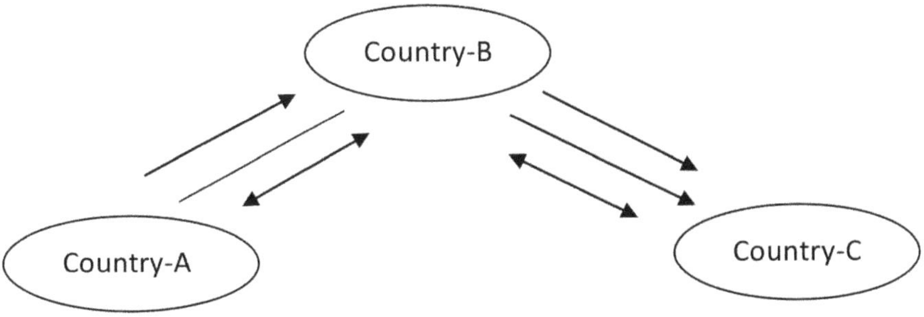

Figure 4.3. Trade in Value-Added (VA) and Global Value Chains (GVCs)
Source: Ransford Edwards

Figure 4.3 represents a simplified illustration of Global Value Chain (GVC) participation. The upper, terminating rays: Country-A → Country-B or Country-B → Country-C signify domestic value-added sent to a consumer economy. Resembling conventional trade, this measure captures content of final or intermediate goods consumed by the importing country. An example of domestic value-added sent to third economies is captured in the second set of lines where Country-A provides intermediary inputs to its foreign partner, Country-B, which, in turn, consumes that input in the making of a final good exported to Country-C. In this value chain, Country-A is said to have "forward linkages," while Country-B's participation is through "backward linkages," or the sourcing of foreign inputs for the use in final goods for export. There also exists a recursive trade pattern highlighted by the third set of lines. In this model, intermediates are exported overseas for processing and assembly, then reimported as a final good or for further export. This was the staple of vertical production networks embodied in regional and bilateral trade and investment agreements discussed in the previous chapter.

With 1995 as the benchmark, the general trend has been less of a reliance on conventional trade and increased participation via forward and backward trade networks. For instance, for the sample of south and southeastern Asian countries in figure 4.4, there is a consistent decrease in the amount of domestic value-added sent to consumer economies. For all sampled countries, in 1995, the average domestic value added of gross exports was 65 percent. In 2011, that number was 50 percent—an average decline of 23 percent. During that period, all countries, except for Cambodia, increased their participation in forward global value chain trade. Led by the Philippines (+114 percent) and Brunei (+102 percent), he overall trend was greater involvement in the provision of intermediaries

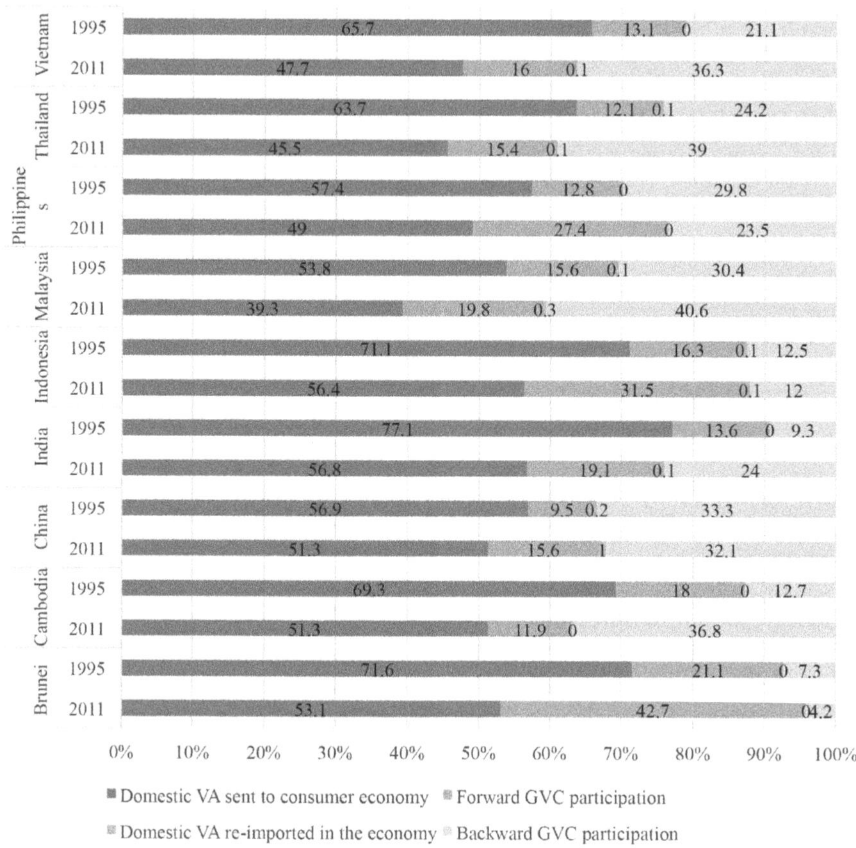

Figure 4.4.
Source: Banga 2013, 17.

for foreign countries, which further process these inputs into final products. In terms of backward linkages, the results have been more mixed. While the overall percentage of change (+49 percent) favored increased coordination with suppliers of intermediary goods and services, led by Cambodia (+189.8 percent) and India (+158.1 percent), several countries regressed in this form of trade, namely Brunei (–42.5 percent), the Philippines (–21.1 percent), Indonesia (–4 percent), and China (–3.6 percent). The drastic relocation of manufacturing production to China and the further peripheralization of East and Southeast Asia is borne out in the prior data. However, the depreciating shares of domestic value-added are tending to offset gains in gross manufacturing production and worker productivity. Traditionally, through active collective bargaining, workers were able to translate increased productivity into higher wages and better working conditions. However, transnational corporate alliances have used their political power to legitimize their management of value chains and are thereby better positioned to extract surplus value from the global value chains.

Similar to FDI statistics obscuring the veracity of global value chains, trade data—particularly that related to the hegemonic model of export-led growth—have increasingly concealed the disaggregation of trade dictated by GVCs. Increased specialization along value chains has adversely affected developing countries at the lower strata via two related mechanisms. First, specialization prohibits diversification, thereby "trapping" these countries into low-value-added activities. Second, productive proficiencies work to increase the reliance on intermediate inputs imported from upstream suppliers. The impact has been both a ceiling being placed on industrial upgrading and the erosion of domestic value-added as a share of industrial exports.

Taken together, developing countries are increasingly reliant on trade within global value chains in order to acquire value from the segmented production that leads to the final production, marketing, and distribution of a product. Nowhere is this more evident than in the everyday consumer goods that dominate our lives, including apparel, coffee, and the plethora of smart electronic devices within our current orbit. These value chains also play a significant role in organizing less omnipresent goods such as industrial equipment, business services, transportation and storage, and electrical machinery. As states and transnational corporations work together in transnational interest blocs, corporate actors have emerged as hegemonic global power brokers in social and labor relationships.

The next section will focus on the class dynamics of global value chains by analyzing the concentration of transnational corporate power at the top of the chain and the super-exploitation of workers at the bottom. I will conclude the final chapter by discussing the contemporary crisis of the new globalization by looking at the efforts of transnational interest blocs to reshape global value chains in the midst of a crisis in the rate of profit.

TRANSNATIONAL CORPORATE POWER AND WORKER EXPLOITATION

The most extensive study of the distribution of value within global value chains was done by Timmer et al. (2013), who examined as many as 560 global value chains in 14 manufacturing categories across 40 countries. The breadth and scope of this study were unique in several aspects, which is worthy of further discussion here. First, the authors' methods of analyzing the value distribution within GVCs was part of a recognition among scholars that traditional statistical measurements such as GDP fail to capture how and where value is created within the new globalization. Instead of analyzing the global economy based on state-centric measurements that aggregate production trends within countries, or exports and imports between countries, newer statistical tools are needed to analyze the way that value is produced and captured within global value chains. The researchers used factors of production, including capital, high-skilled labor, and less-skilled labor, to examine the distribution of value within a wide range of tasks associated with global value chains. This framework has the advantage of integrating all of the tasks associated with manufacturing, including service tasks that facilitate the organization and logistics of production as well as the sale and distribution of the final product. The objective was to analyze statistical data pertaining to changes within the distribution of value in global value chains from 1995 to 2008.

The findings are instructive in identifying an increasing share of income in GVCs going to owners of capital and to relatively high-skilled workers within the production process, while less-skilled workers have seen a steady decline in income from GVCs. Timmer and his coauthors used the World Input Output Database (WIOD) for accessing data on trade in intermediate inputs as a series of production tasks carried out across forty countries that together accounted for 85 percent of global production at the time of the study. The countries included all twenty-seven EU countries and thirteen other major economies (Australia, Brazil, Canada, China, India, Indonesia, Japan, Mexico, Russia, South Korea, Taiwan, Turkey, and the United States). The disaggregation of global value chains was achieved by examining the range of tasks associated with the trade and processing of intermediate inputs in the production of finished goods. The factor categories used in this study are commonplace within neoclassical economic theory, which divides factor production along the lines of capital, high-skilled labor, and low-skilled labor used in production. In this way, the power relationships involved in the ownership of capital and in the capital-labor relationship are heavily muted in favor of treating each of these factors separately by identifying their (separate) relative contribution to the finished task.

Despite these limitations, this study is one of the very few, and probably the best to date, to extrapolate the WIOD databases to tease out information pertaining to value flows across tasks of production within global value chains over a lengthy time period (1995–2008). The study relied on the methodology incorporated within the WIOD data, which is based on two sets of measurements: National Accounting Statistics (NAS) and value-added accounts of production activity that divide production workers into three categories: low-skilled (corresponding to below secondary schooling), medium-skilled (secondary schooling and above but below college degree), and high-skilled (college degree). The authors used a number of statistical adjustments to these datasets, including pairing the NAS data with a UN COMTRADE database, to create data for three types of traded goods: intermediate use, final consumption use, or investment use. The finished dataset allows for a disaggregation of tasks of production across a wide range of intermediate, investment, and finished goods production within global value chains. Such a segmentation of the data, when combined with an analysis of the value-added production tasks undertaken by capital and various categories of labor, provides us with an overview of some of the most important recent trends in global value chain production.

One of those trends is the increasing importance of the foreign value added share within global value chains from 1995 to 2008.

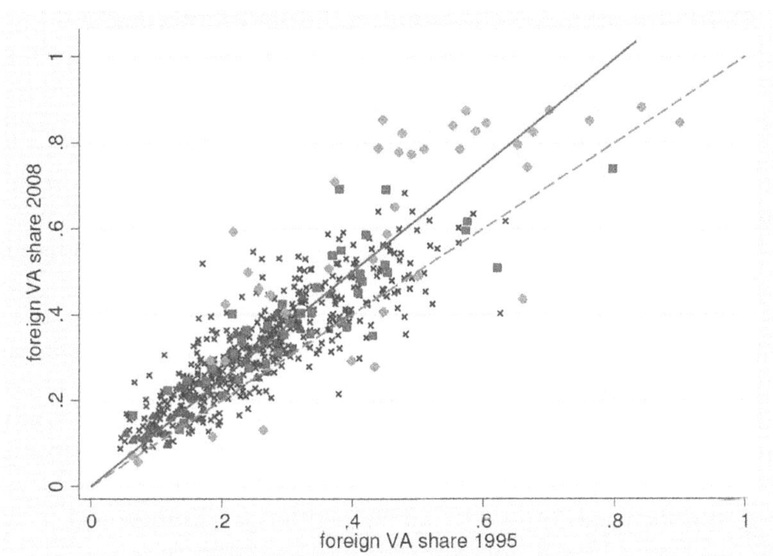

Notes: Each dot represents the share of foreign value added in final output of manufacturing sector in a country in 1995 and 2008, as a ratio of final output. This share is calculated according to equation in the main text. Observations have been included for 558 manufactures GVCs, identified by 14 industries of completion in 40 countries. Triangles indicate food manufacturing (ISIC rev 3 industries 15 and 16), squares electrical equipment (30-33) and diamonds petroleum refining (23) GVCs. All other GVCs are represented by crosses. The dashed line is the 45 degree line. The solid line has been obtained by OLS regression through the origin with slope coefficient of 1.20.
Source: Author's calculations based on World Input-Output Database, April 2013.

Figure 4.5.
Source: Timmer, et al. 2013, 30.

The trends captured in figure 4.5 indicate the extent to which foreign inputs are becoming more important as a percentage of value added within GVCs. This correlates well with the growing power of transnational capitalist firms, based disproportionately in the rich core of the capitalist global economy, to provide high value-added inputs to production (capital-intensive products, R&D, patents, copyrights—tangible as well as intangible capital) across the widely dispersed tasks embedded within GVCs. The ability of headquarter firms in core capitalist locations to leverage the ownership of these high-valued assets has increased as the relative importance of foreign inputs to production has expanded and intensified. Headquarter or parent firms establish economic and political leverage due to their market power and favorable geographic location in the negotiation of GVC governance. Through this power relationship, headquarter firms are able to use their quasi-monopoly power to charge high prices for access to their high-value assets, which competing contractors are forced to pay in the form of licensing fees and contractual rights to use these assets in the production process. As we saw in chapter three, regional investment agreements have become central arenas for establishing the terms whereby headquarter firms and their home governments are able to use their structural market and political power to negotiate favorable contracts from the host governments and the contractors, subcontractors, and/or subsidiaries involved in GVC production.

The increasing flow of foreign inputs from relatively wealthy locations within global capitalism provides a snapshot of which regions and interests are accruing the largest gains from the steady expansion of GVCs. The earliest expansion of GVCs was heavily concentrated around regional locations, with U.S.-based transnationals expanding their foreign investments and contractual relationships in NAFTA and Central America, while the E.U.-based transnationals expanded rapidly into Eastern Europe, and Japan expanded into East Asia, creating a regionally oriented expansion of GVCs whose governance was closely linked to earlier histories of market power and political power. With the steady rise of China as an increasingly important global power, the production platform of the global economy has expanded well beyond regional orientations. China is emerging as an important site for both foreign transnational accumulation of profits and domestic value-added advances in high-end manufacturing production. This development is causing heightened competition between transnational interest blocs looking to expand further into the China market on terms that are favorable relative to their competition. Figure 4.6 illustrates how various regions compare with each other in value added.

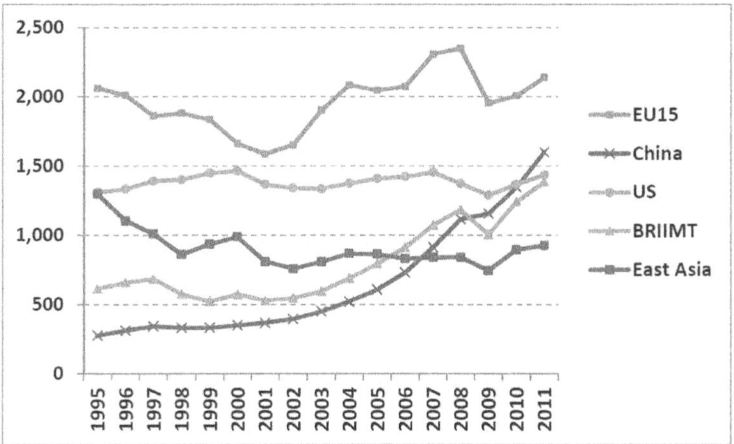

Notes: East Asia includes Japan, South Korea and Taiwan. BRIIMT includes Brazil, Russia, India, Indonesia, Mexico and Turkey. EU15 includes all European countries that joined the European Union before 2004. Value added in national currencies converted to US$ with official exchange rates and deflated to 1995 prices with the US CPI.

Figure 4.6. Value Added by Region in Global Production of Manufactures (billions of 1995 U.S. dollars)
Source: Timmer et al. 2013, 32.

Figure 4.4 provides a regional and country breakdown of value added with GVCs over an extensive time frame (1995–2011). However, there are significant limitations to this method of grouping value-added flows. The first is that country and regional snapshots understate the extent to which value extraction from GVCs is narrowly concentrated around ownership of high-value assets by transnational firms. Transnational corporations do not necessarily keep their value added in the form of profit inside their home country. Instead, these firms have increased their propensity to financialize their profits in tax havens, or to divert their profits in financial investments, neither of which are captured in this study. This study does capture the value added through licensing fees and contractual costs that are paid to owners of high-value assets by their subcontractors or through their subsidiaries, namely by identifying the location where the value is recorded as having been received. But this misses the extent to which transnational firms are able to increasingly redirect profits to foreign tax havens or through financial speculative investments, which are not captured by this dataset. This dataset also ignores the way that headquarter firms acquire more value through merger and acquisition strategies whereby transnational corporations buy out competitors solely for control of high-value activities, which increasingly is a cross-border process that facilitates a transfer of value added from one location to another. Therefore, this picture of value added understates the extent to which transnational corporations at the top of global value chains are able to extract value from labor to capital.

However, Timmer and his coauthors do use the WIOD database to trace the extent to which value is flowing to capital versus labor over the timeline of this investigation.

Notes: Value added to global output of final manufacturing goods. Value added by labour is measured as wages and salaries and other employer costs, and includes an imputation for self-employed workers. Capital compensation is residually defined as non-labour value added such that the labour and capital shares add up to one. High-skilled workers are defined as having college education or above.

Figure 4.7. Value Added by Labor and Capital (Share of Global Final Manufacturers Output)

Source: Timmer et al. 2013, 31.

Figure 4.7 captures the disproportionate flow of value added to capital and "high-skilled" labor, but the assumption is that these factors of production generate returns on their investment that is commensurate with the productive value that they add to the various stages of production within global value chains. So "less-skilled" workers are thought to add less value to the production process than the capital-intensive goods and the skilled workers who manage the incorporation of those goods in the production process. The problem with this formulation, a problem embedded within neoclassical economic assumptions, is that it eviscerates the social relations of production in favor of a simple "factor" exchange. If capital and "high-skilled" workers are getting more value over time than "less-skilled" workers, it must be because their market worth is being reflected in the prices returned to them within the factor allocations of goods and services. In other words, neoclassical economists assume a correspondence between factor value and rates of market return that are supposedly reflected in prices. Timmer and his coauthors seem very aware of this problem and do in fact suggest that concentration of wealth at the top of the global value chain may in fact be creating a power imbalance that favors an increasing transfer of wealth from less-skilled workers to owners of production.

During the period that is the subject of Timmer's study, transnational capital was increasing its exploitation of "low-skilled" labor by adding hundreds of millions of workers to GVCs through an expansion of foreign direct investment or, more commonly, through an expansion of subcontracting production through arm's-length contracts that pushed more of the costs of those contracts downward to producers at the low end of the GVC. This increasing reliance on a low-wage super-exploitable labor force represented a major shift from manufacturing production from the North to the South. In other words, the wages paid to "less-skilled" workers were held down by a wide range of factors not accounted for in the traditional factor models of value added. One of these factors is the structural power of transnational firms to mark up the prices of products at the top of the GVC due to their dominant market position as oligopolies. The markup is the difference between the wages paid to workers in developing countries, disproportionately in Asia, and the surplus value accruing to transnational firms and their branding, marketing, and sales managerial workforce at the top of the GVC. The classification of this workforce in the Timmer study, as "high-skilled" workers, conflates the position of those workers who are exploited in high-end production activities with managers and mid-level corporate bureaucrats whose positions are better described as managerial. The dispersion of value from "less-skilled" workers does in fact decline relative to those that own capital and those that manage the capital assets. But the ability to extract surplus value from the GVC is very much dependent on the social relations of production embedded within the system.

The investment behavior of transnational capital during the new globalization indicates that investments in manufacturing production in the global South have become more central to the accumulation strategy of transnational corporations. This is captured by examining investment flows from transnational corporations to developing countries in recent decades. By 2013, "FDI flows to developing countries surpassed those to developed countries for the first time" (Smith 2016, 72). This trend was especially pronounced when examining the longer-term shift toward manufacturing FDI in the global South, which from 2010 to 2012 totaled $151 billion and surpassed the $145 billion received by developed countries (Smith 2016, 72). These statistics represent a long-term shift of transnational capital accumulation strategies that is only partially captured by FDI statistics. As previously discussed, transnational capital has moved toward arm's-length contracts with foreign suppliers, which are concentrated in developing countries and have contributed to the long-term growth of the industrial workforce in those countries. Second, the data on FDI investment only counts full-time employment in FDI subsidiaries and therefore omits employees of subcontracting firms as well as temporary and casual workers. Datasets that include these additional workers indicate the extent to which developing countries have become more central to the global accumulation strategies of transnational capital. The dramatic expansion of the industrial workforce in the global South is notable in figure 4.8.

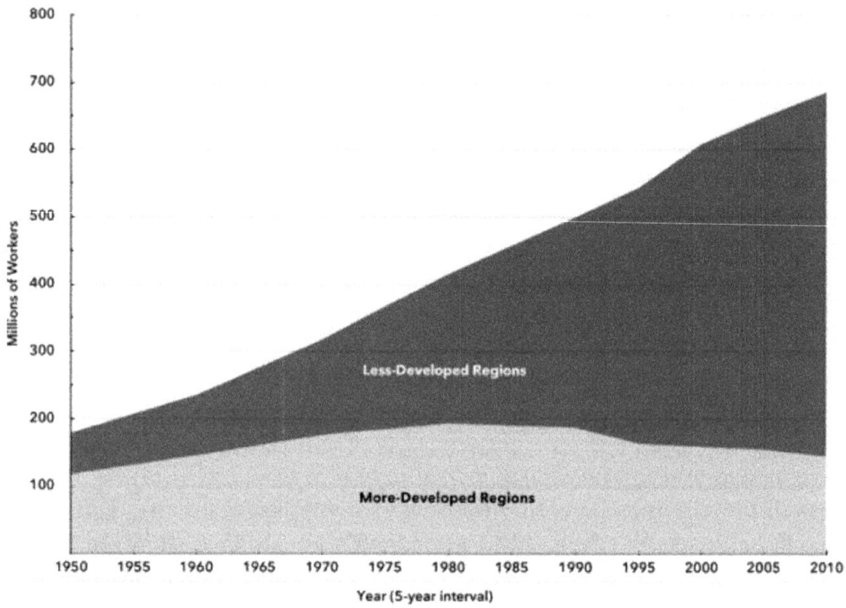

Figure 4.8. Imperialism and the Law of Value
Source: Smith 2011, 20.

Exports from developing countries have increased dramatically, both as a percentage of their total exports and as a percentage of world manufactured exports. The exports of developing countries are increasingly used as manufacturing inputs for transnational corporations in Japan, the U.S., and the E.U. Figures 4.9 and 4.10 illustrate these trends.

Figure 4.9. Developing Economies' Trade in Manufactures
Source: UNCTAD 2013.

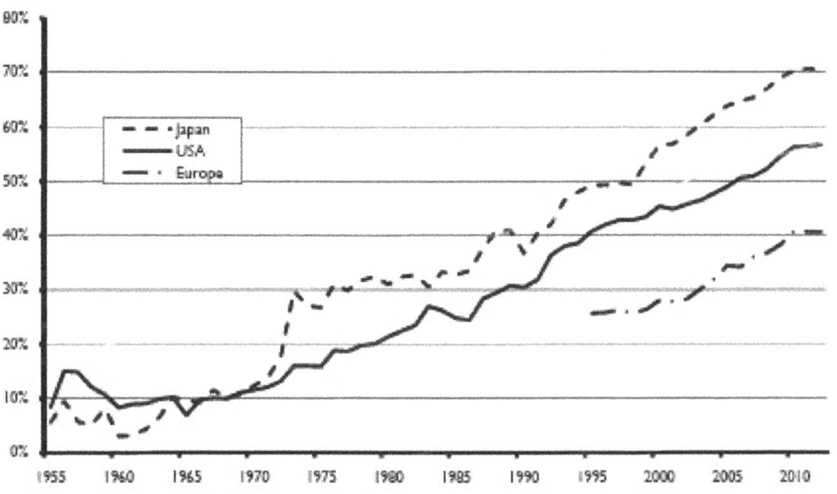

Figure 4.10. Developing Nations' Share of Developed Nations' Manufactured Imports
Source: UNCTAD 2013.

Figures 4.9 and 4.10 illustrate the growing importance of manufacturing exports, especially intermediate goods used in global value chains, from developing countries. However, despite the dramatic increases in manufacturing exports, developing countries have not experienced a corresponding increase in manufacturing value added.

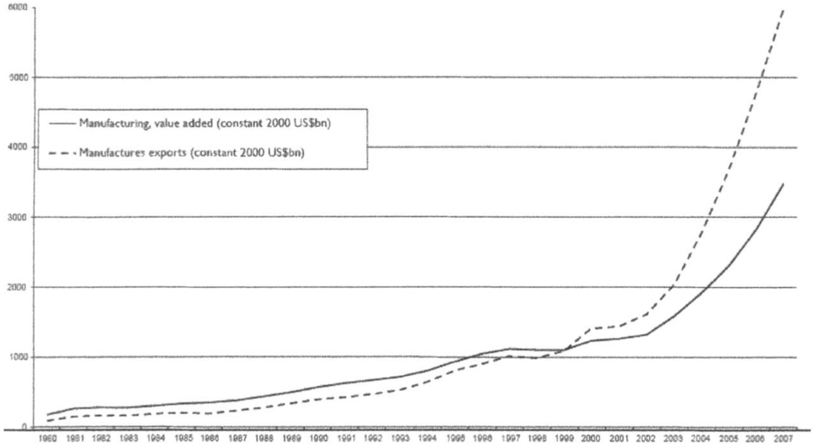

Figure 4.11. MVA vs. Manufactured Exports, 1980–2007
Source: World Development Indicators

Extrapolating from figure 4.11, the gains from rising manufacturing exports are increasingly being captured by transnational corporations at the top of global value chains, as measured by value-added statistics. As a recent study noted, 55 percent of the value in global value chains is captured by the twenty-one wealthiest OECD countries, which includes the U.S., Japan, South Korea, Canada, Australia, Taiwan, and the fifteen pre-2004 members of the E.U. (Aguiar de Medeiros and Trabat 2016, 13). Other scholars, notably Banga (2013) have calculated that 67 percent of the value captured in global value chains goes to the OECD.

Transnational corporations' investments in developing countries, especially Asia, whether in FDI or arm's-length contracts, have proven to be more profitable per worker employed than comparable investments in developed countries. In fact, there is a significant discrepancy between the types of FDI investments carried out by transnational firms in the North versus those in the South. The so-called "N-N" investments that involve FDI across developed countries are heavily skewed toward mergers and acquisitions or transfers of ownership of an existing firm. The value that is being acquired is ownership rights of high-end activities such as intellectual property rights; branding, marketing, and advertising functions; and financial services activities. As John Smith has noted,

> In 2007, for example, developed economies received 89% of the $1.64 trillion in M&A FDI, more than half of which occurred in financial services . . . on the other hand, developing nations received 69 percent of total greenfield investment between 2008 and 2013, accentuating a pattern that was clearly established in the five years before the outbreak of the global economic crisis—between 2003 and 2007, developing nations attracted 59 percent of global greenfield FDI flows. (Smith 2016, 72–73)

Greenfield investments in developing countries have been used to expand manufacturing production, whereas M&A investments in developed countries privilege control over high-value activities, including financial assets, that are increasingly used to maintain oligopolisitic power within the global market and within global value chains.

The global M&A statistics illustrate a tendency of transnational capital in developed countries to further concentrate ownership around the financialization of high-value assets. The diversion of profits into share buybacks, tax havens, and acquisitions of intellectual property rights are illustrative of these trends. The skewed distribution of income away from labor and toward capital is a global phenomenon and is captured by rising inequality between rich and poor within both developed and developing countries. To fully understand these patterns, however, we have to move beyond a focus on GDP statistics, because they conceal the extent to which global value chains have been a primary vehicle for transfer of wealth from workers to capitalists. As Timmer's analysis of factor allocation within global value chains illustrates, regardless of capital intensity or labor intensity of the sector of production analyzed, the value added has increasingly been captured by capital and "high-skilled labor," while for most workers the share of value has declined. This is true in both Northern and Southern countries, as the deindustrialization of Northern labor has been accompanied by a steady and long-term shift in the reliance on Southern low-wage labor to take its place. At the same time, capital's share of income is increasing and labor's share is declining across both the North and the South (Ness 2015).

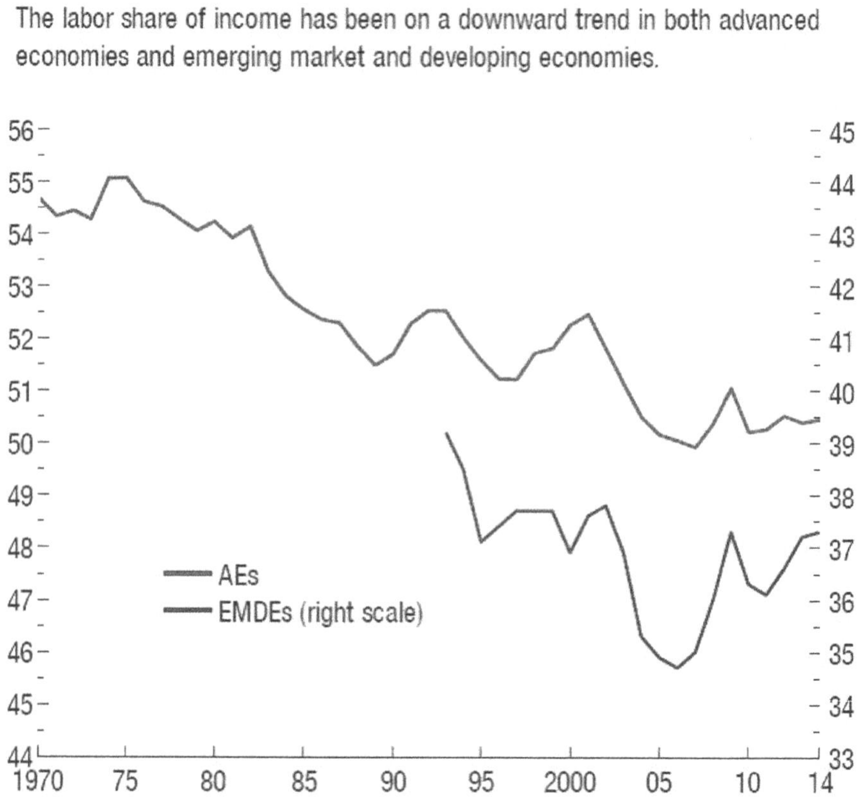

Figure 4.12. Evolution of the Labor Share of Income

Source: CEIC database; Karabarbounis and Neiman 2014; national authorities; Organization for Economic Co-operation and Development; and IMF staff calculations.

The extent to which labor's share of income correlates with the proliferation of global value chains is illustrated by a recent IMF study, which, unlike the Timmer study that used two categories, divided labor into high skill, middle skill, and low skill (Dao, Das, Koczan, and Lian 2017). The authors of the study concluded that global value chains were a strong contributing factor toward a reduction of wages in developed and developing countries, a process that they referenced (in keeping with previous scholarly literature) as a "hollowing out" of the middle-income working class. Within this system of measurement, much like Timmer's, the "high-skilled" labor category is better described as a managerial elite rather than a "working class," given the strong overlap of this group with managerial staff and salaried positions within both developed and developing countries. The extent to which the managerial elite and salaried professionals represent an upper tier that connects the interests of actors within the transnational interest bloc across state borders deserves further reflection. The fact that the most lucrative benefits of global value chains are flowing to capital and upper-tier managers in both developed and developing countries is suggestive that the owners and managers of global value chains are reaping the biggest rewards, accelerated by lower corporate taxes in both developed and developing countries and lower union densities.

While increases in high-skill and decreases in low-skill labor shares are driven predominantly by common shifts to skill supply across countries (through higher educational attainment, for example), technological change and global value chain integration exert strong negative impacts on middle-skill labor shares, consistent with the hollowing-out hypothesis.

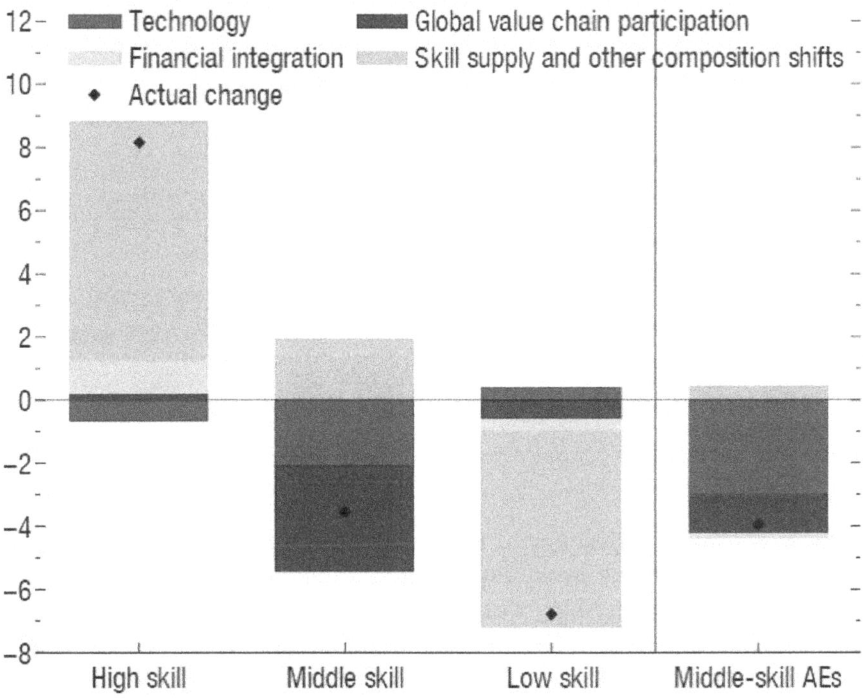

Figure 4.13.

Sources: World Input-Output Database and IMF staff calculations.

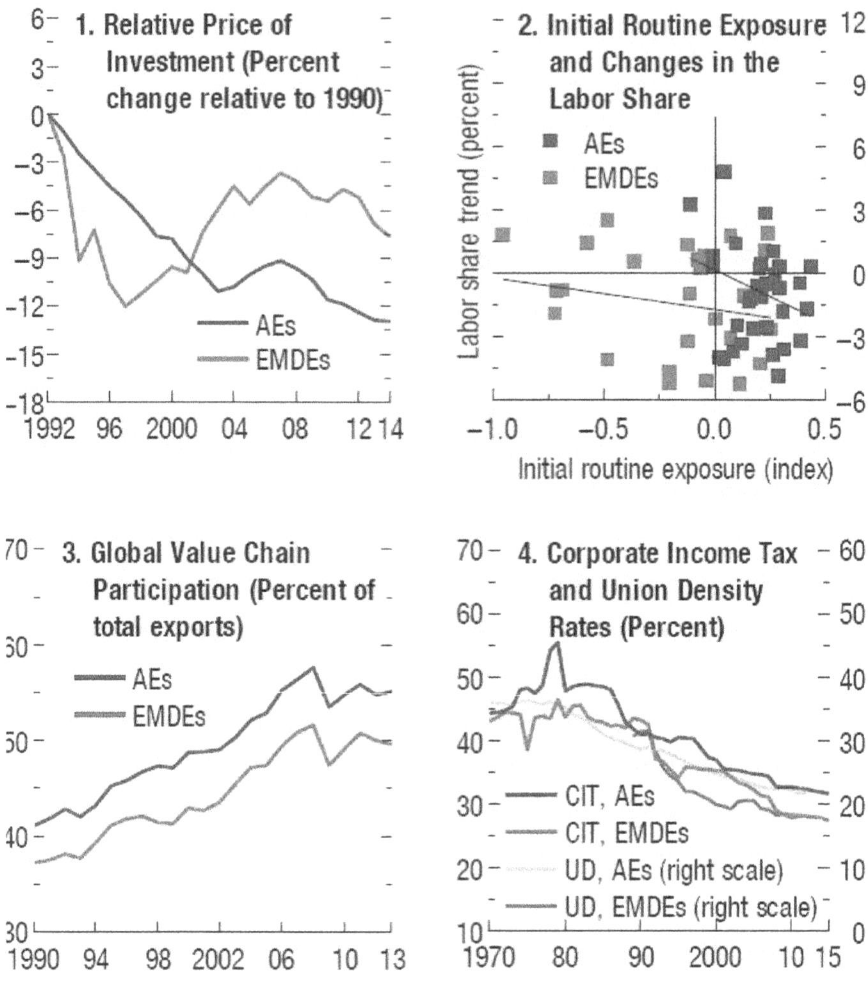

Figure 4.14.

Sources: Autor and Dorn 2014; Eora Multi-Region Input-Output database.

Examining the implications of figures 4.12 and 4.13, there is a very close relationship between the steady expansion of global value chains and a greater concentration of ownership, wealth, and power within global capitalism. Transnational corporations have been able to leverage their control over high-value assets to increase profits and to force down wages within the global value chain. Within this global structure of accumulation, transnational firms have been able to utilize the capital mobility of their increasingly intangible and financialized assets to reduce their taxation obligations. The expanded reliance of transnational corporations on production within global value chains closely tracks global trends of increased inequality, declining wages as a percentage of national and global income, and financialization of assets toward tax havens and shelters that drain societies of needed revenues. These trends constitute the architecture or political economy of global value chains as a system of transnational interest bloc power that has shaped the new globalization.

THE SHIFTING ARCHITECTURE OF GLOBAL VALUE CHAINS

Transnational interest blocs have linked transnational corporations with their contractors, supply networks, and governments in both the global North and South to promote favorable political and economic conditions for the growth of global value chains. In this system of segmented production, transnational corporations have shifted their mechanisms for extracting surplus value by relying increasingly on the super-exploitation of workers in developing countries. The working class in the global South has expanded exponentially over the past two decades while their wages have fallen as a percentage of industry profits (across a wide range of global industries) and as a percentage of GDP in the vast majority of developed and developing countries. The gap between productivity and wages is hidden beneath a veil of subcontracting relationships that have become increasingly central to transnational corporate profits. The sale of intermediate goods from a tier of global suppliers to an original equipment manufacturer to a brand name transnational corporation masks the extent to which labor is undervalued in the production process through a pricing system that effectively dispenses with worker health and safety, environmental regulations, and wages that allow for worker reproduction.

A recent study used data from the International Labor Organization to examine the gap in wages between industrial workers in OECD and non-OECD countries. The study examined the wages of workers engaged in goods production in OECD countries versus those of workers engaged in export goods production (of intermediate manufactured goods) in non-OECD countries. The findings indicated that OECD industrial workers received eleven times the wages of non-OECD industrial workers, as of 2010 estimates. However, the productivity of OECD workers was found to be just 2.9 times the productivity of non-OECD workers, a significant gap compared to the 11:1 wage differential. When the researcher examined the impact of this wage differential, the conclusion was that wages were priced so far below productivity in non-OECD goods exports that $4.9 trillion was effectively transferred to the Northern countries in the form of unequal exchange (the differential between the productivity [value] of non-OECD exports to the OECD and what the OECD countries paid for those exports) (Cope 2012, 230–246).

Of course, the value is not being transferred between "countries," nor does the unequal exchange flow back primarily to the workers in the Northern countries. Instead, the beneficiaries of the wage gap are transnational corporations at the top of the global value chain, whose increasing reliance on subcontractors in the developing world pushes the cost of production down toward those workers and firms that can least afford to bear those costs. As a result, workers in Southern states can be said to be "super-exploited," referring to the process by which the value added in production by these workers lags well behind productivity and, most importantly, makes it difficult for workers to utilize their wages to reproduce their labor power. This latter point is especially true when considering the increasing reliance on part-time workers in the developing world, the increasing propensity toward gender discrimination through the use of women workers who earn less than men in segmented labor markets, and the pool of contract workers who essentially earn piece-rate wages. This has meant that workers in developing countries need supplemental sources of income to satisfy basic needs. This includes a continued reliance on agricultural subsistence production, unpaid domestic labor, and extended family members' additional income sources, often from self-employment, the black market, or remittances from immigrant labor, where possible.

This super-exploitation of Southern workers is possible due to the intensified competition at the bottom of the global value chain between firms operating at tight-cost margins and underemployed and part-time workers competing with each other as part of a large reserve army of labor—lacking the ready ability to migrate without paying exorbitant costs. These factors are exacerbated by a political and economic power structure, in both developed and developing countries, that has been captured by transnational interest blocs that have effectively pushed neoliberal policies weakening the bargaining power of labor while reducing taxes on corporations and the rich. Further accentuating these trends is a globalized accumulation structure that has allowed for an exponential expansion of global capital flows while maintaining severe restrictions on flows of labor across state borders. The relative ease of capital flight is easily contrasted with restrictive immigration policies, which have proven to be costly and risky for those workers who manage to circumvent the obstacles inhibiting relocation, as immigrants who manage to make the journey to a foreign country often remain vulnerable to deportation and super-exploitation.

In addition to an increased reliance on low-cost labor in developing countries, transnational corporations have undertaken several strategies within global value chains that are responsive to the periodic structural crises of capitalism. The first phase of transnational corporate utilization of global value chains began during the mid- to late 1980s, when transnational firms accelerated their FDI and later their increasing reliance on subcontracting through original equipment manufacturers (OEMs) to counter the effects of a long-term profit rate crisis that had lasted from 1965 to 1982. In response to this crisis of profitability, corporations supported regional restructuring close to the home market of the headquarter or parent firm, including U.S.-NAFTA, E.U.–Eastern Europe, and Japan–East and Southeast Asia. In the U.S., this involved considerable corporate restructuring, as transnational firms sold off corporate divisions to replace in-house production networks with outsourced production from overseas contractors. E.U. firms relied increasingly on foreign producers in Eastern Europe in lieu of domestic expansion of production. Japanese firms shifted toward a greater reliance on supply networks in East and Southeast Asia.

During the high-tech bust that led to the recession of 2000–2001, there was a second phase of transnational corporate restructuring of global value chains in response to new crisis conditions. In his tracking of falling rates of profit within capitalist crises of accumulation, Michael Roberts (2016) has argued that transnational corporations were experiencing another falling rate of profit as early as 1998, and that the 2000–2001 recession exacerbated these trends. Stock market valuations, especially in the high-tech sectors of the global economy, were well above asset values, creating the perfect storm of circumstances for a capitalist production crisis. In response to these crisis dynamics, high-tech firms in computers and electronics led the way in creating more complex value chains. This meant that transnational corporations increased their investments in intangible assets such as intellectual property rights and branding, marketing, and distribution networks while shedding direct investment in foreign plants and equipment. There was less reliance on FDI and more reliance on foreign contractors to assume a greater percentage of the costs of foreign production operations. Transnational corporations were also producing less in-house high-value-added inputs to production and increasing their reliance on large-scale producers to add further complexity to the global value chain.

The most tangible expression of this was the increasing utilization of original design manufacturers (ODMs) as corporate investment partners that would be responsible for creating and incorporating the highest value-added components in the production process. These firms were initially located almost exclusively in the core capitalist countries but have since shifted toward foreign locations, especially East Asian locations, where ODMs have become more prominent in the current phase of global value chains. The increasing complexity of this second phase of global value chain restructuring is epitomized by an exponential increase in high-tech production in China, in addition to a broader outsourcing of overall production to East and Southeast Asia. This deepening of value chain production created greater South-South linkages, especially in Asia, which was the dominant location for the highest value-added manufacturing in this phase of value chain restructuring. This meant an increase in the sheer number and variety of suppliers, including an expansion and greater dispersal of lower-tier suppliers producing the cheapest component parts all the way to original equipment manufacturers to original design manufacturers (Pratap 2014, 83–112).

The increasingly segmented division of global production was part of a transnational corporate effort to further reduce costs and to place increasing emphasis on ownership of IPRs, research and development, and branding rights while relinguishing even more involvement in the production process. Increasingly, especially in the high-tech and electronics sector, this meant shedding direct control over producing high-value inputs to production in favor of the increasing finacialization of assets—relocating IPR assets to foreign tax havens and increasing speculative financial activities in lieu of investing in production. There was an increased emphasis on contractual relationships with a wider range of parties. This increasing complexity of actors, locations, and division of labor within global value chains added to the risks associated with this expansion. It also would enable potential competitors to more easily acquire the technology necessary to upgrade their competitive position versus the dominant transnational corporations. This has become especially true in China, where transnational corporations in the high-tech computer and electronics sectors emerged after the 2008 global capitalist crisis in a more competitive position relative to transnational capital based in the U.S. and the E.U. The greater complexity of production proved especially vulnerable to the recession of 2008, which was followed by yet another strategic shift by transnational capital in response to another global capitalist crisis.

The next chapter will examine the effects of the capitalist crisis of 2008 on competition within global value chains. The 2008 crisis has contributed to a very recent crisis in global value chains, including intensified competition among transnational interest blocs, the rise of nationalist and far-right political parties and movements, and a challenge to state capacity and legitimacy in the U.S. and Western Europe. In this context, I will examine the opportunities for workers' movements to more effectively challenge the highly concentrated wealth and power of dominant transnational capitalist firms.

NOTE

1. Ransford Edwards contributed to the research in this chapter.

Chapter Five

The Crisis of Neoliberal Capitalism

Transnational firms have consolidated their market power and their political privilege by intensifying the exploitation of workers within global value chains. Corporations established the architecture of global value chains by consolidating their ownership of high-value activities while pushing costs of production downward in the supply network. These changes occurred over several decades spanning what many commentators have called "neoliberal capitalism." The shift toward neoliberal capitalist strategies of accumulation was a response on the part of large-scale capitalist firms to a steady decline in the rate of profit from 1965 to 1982. Transnational capitalists used both market and political mechanisms in an attempt to overcome the long-term tendency within capitalism of the rate of profit to fall. In response to long-term crisis, the most globally competitive and powerful capitalist firms utilized political and economic strategies that further concentrated wealth and power within global capitalism. During the neoliberal capitalist period, the wealthiest one percent have increased their consolidation of wealth and market power so that by 2016, "just one percent of humanity owned over half of the world's wealth" (Oxfam Briefing Paper 2016).

The race among dominant transnational corporations to achieve a monopoly or quasi-monopoly position by acquiring the latest technological advances is a defining characteristic of the latest phase in the "new globalization." This phase accelerated after the global capitalist crisis of 2008, which has resulted in several trends that have been driven by a systemic crisis in neoliberal capitalism. The first is the stagnation of global value chains reflected by global trade statistics, as the volume of global trade dramatically fell in the aftermath of the 2008 capitalist recession and has failed to rebound to pre-crisis levels (Timmer et al. 2016). The biggest factor behind the global trade slowdown has been the stagnation of trade within global value chains, which has intensified after 2014 after having rebounded from 2011 to 2014 (Constantinescu, Matoo, and Ruta 2015). In response, transnational corporations are reducing the complexity of global value chains (incorporating fewer suppliers) in favor of greater capital intensity and greater consolidation of those value chains around the most important global markets (Degain, Meng, and Wang 2017). As part of this process, transnational corporations have reorganized their global capitalist employees more rigidly around two categories: production supervisors and managers that oversee the logistical and supply operations of the global value chains and are relatively well paid, and workers who produce within these chains at wages that continue to stagnate and decline relative to capitalist revenues (Timmer et al. 2013).

Second, the gap between the profits of the dominant transnational corporations and the wages of the global capitalist workforce has grown wider, as more wealth is concentrated at the top. This has resulted in a further "hollowing out" of the industrial workforce in the core capitalist states, often expressed as a shrinking "middle class," alongside the increased exploitation of the global working class (Milanovic 2016). These class tensions have resulted in further deligitimacy of capitalist governments in the West, contributing to the rise of Donald Trump in the U.S. and other quasi-fascist political figures and parties in Western Europe. The increased class tension is a long-term by-product of the contradictions of a neoliberal capitalist political project that has steadily increased the power of transnational interest blocs while reducing the political influence of workers and ordinary citizens, whose political marginalization and alienation have steadily increased. As I will show later in this chapter, the political and economic power of transnational corporations has served to deligitimize the governing institutions of core global capitalist states, creating a political crisis that has heightened tensions based on class, race, and nationality.

Third, the global value chains that were previously dominated by North-South linkages, with the dominant transnational corporations concentrated in the Northern states, have increasingly been challenged by the dramatic rise of China and the policies of the Chinese state, particularly in the area of high technology, which has helped to shift global value chains a bit more in a South-South direction, with countries of the global South, led by China, reorienting global value chains (to some extent) toward production, marketing, and consumption within the global South (Horner and Nadvi 2018). The Chinese state has enacted policies that have contributed to a greater emphasis on domestic production and accumulation and to more stringent requirements for foreign transnationals investing in high-technology manufacturing in China in an attempt to assert greater control over these value chains.

The heightened competition among transnational interest blocs in the China market reflects the current contradictions within global capitalism. The Chinese state has long been an important player in mediating the political and economic conditions necessary to help transform and expand global capitalism into a vast global value chain network. Indeed, as many scholars have documented, China has become the epicenter of global production activities, which includes high-value activities centered around production of computers, electronics, telecommunications, or, taken as a single category: information technology products. The battle over the extraction of surplus value from the China market is at the center of the latest crisis of neoliberal capitalism. Competition among transnational interest blocs within the China market has intensified under the current dynamics of global capitalist accumulation. The key battles revolve around how surplus value will be extracted from contemporary global value chains.

In order to understand the current phase of the neoliberal capitalist crisis, several aspects have to be addressed. The first involves the increasing power of information technology corporations within the architecture of contemporary global capitalism. This is not entirely novel, but it is taking new and accelerated dimensions after the global capitalist crisis of 2008. Prior to the 2008 crisis, information technology firms were already central to capitalist accumulation due to the importance of high technology in enabling the integration of global value chain production. Firms that owned information technology were in a favorable position to leverage their ownership as global capitalist production expanded. The most globally competitive manufacturers depended on information technology to segment production across countries and regional locations. Dominant transnational retail corporations likewise depended on the high-tech revolution in information technology to facilitate just-in-time global network deliveries and distribution. The increasing power of information technology corporations within neoliberal capitalism has always exceeded their actual contribution to GDP and their actual contribution to employment, which until recently has remained relatively small within core capitalist economies.

Second, there has been a steady exponential growth of the information technology sector during the period of neoliberal capitalism, with "investment in the IT sector [jumping] from $17 billion in the 1970s to $175 billion in 1990, then to $496 billion in 2000. It then dipped following the turn-of-the-century dot-com bust, only to climb up to new heights after 2008, surpassing $700 billion as 2017 drew to a close" (Robinson 2018, 6). By 2017, of the six transnational corporations with the highest market capitalization, five were high-tech firms (Apple, Google, Microsoft, Amazon, and Facebook) and the sixth was a financial investment firm (Berkshire Hathaway), which has considerable investments in high-tech companies. The growth in market size and power of these tech giants is directly linked to the rising importance of ownership and control of data processing in contemporary capitalism. The capitalist crisis of 2008 has led to a further concentration of investments in high-tech corporations whose ownership of data collection, storage, processing, and infrastructure has become more central to capitalist accumulation strategies. Transnational corporations in manufacturing and services that are looking to expand market access and market share are increasing their investments in data processing, which means that more financial capital is flowing toward information technology firms. Institutional investors looking toward the most profitable activities to steer investment funds have targeted information technology companies above other sectors of capital, further contributing to their exponential growth in market capitalization.

Third, information technology firms have steered a very high percentage of their revenues toward offshore financialized assets and tax havens, in an effort to shield their profits from taxation and to maximize their financial portfolio options. Increasingly, IT corporations are purchasing bonds floated by transnational corporations in other sectors of the global economy as a way to hedge their enormous financial assets across a range of financial investments. In effect, these IT firms are becoming the new investment banks by purchasing bonds issued by a wide range of transnational corporations that have been borrowing money (and leveraging their own assets) to help compensate for a long stagnation in global markets following the 2008 capitalist crisis (Foroohar 2018). Global overcapacity in production, including production embedded within global value chains, has steered more investment capital toward information technology and IT services in an attempt to restore a higher rate of profit in capitalist production activities.

Transnational corporations across a wide range of sectors see investments in information technology, especially in digital communications and data, as central to advancing their competitiveness and restoring profit margins in the midst of heightened global competition. This retooling of investment priorities has resulted in a slowing and reorientation of global value chains, especially from 2014 to the present, when investment in global value chain production has stagnated. Transnational firms that were previously committed to an expansion of value chain production have turned increasingly toward investments in information technology, which potentially could be used to further revolutionize capitalist production relationships. This means that transnational firms are looking toward increased investment in high technology to reduce reliance on low-cost labor in global value chains. Transnational corporate investments in automated production processes involve greater reliance on digitization, data infrastructure, and roboticization to leverage ownership assets toward higher-value activities. This process has already involved expanded mergers, acquisitions, and concentration of capital within the information technology sector during the most recent phase of global capitalist competition after the 2008 capitalist crisis. Information technology firms have emerged as central players in the global competition for ownership of "capitalist platforms" that can be utilized as rents during the transition to what some have described as the fourth industrial capitalist revolution. As more transnational capitalist firms look to expand their reliance on digitization and automation processes, the ability of information technology firms to consolidate ownership of the global data infrastructure is increasingly central to the accumulation imperatives of the new global capitalist architecture.

Nick Srnicek, in a 2017 book called *Platform Capitalism*, analyzed how high-tech corporations are increasingly monopolizing their control over global "platforms" that provide data services that other transnational corporations increasingly depend on. The rapid growth of the high-tech service sector within the global economy is a product of a structural shift in global capitalism toward acquisition of revolutionary technological processes. The production, buying, and selling of goods and services in the global capitalist marketplace is increasingly tied to processes of automation, artificial intelligence, roboticization, and cloud infrastructure systems that facilitate business transactions. High-technology transnational corporations are the dominant global players in consolidating ownership over these activities. As I have noted, Apple, Google, Microsoft, Amazon, and Facebook have the highest market capitalization among transnational corporations, apart from Berkshire Hathaway. These corporations, alongside Cisco and Oracle, also have been in the lead when it comes to cash hoarding and shifting their revenues to tax havens, especially after the global capitalist crisis of 2008.

	Reserves (billions of USD)	Amount held offshore (billions of USD)	Amount held offshore (percent)
Apple	215.7	200.1	92.8
Microsoft	102.6	96.3	93.9
Google	73.1	42.9	58.7
Cisco	60.4	56.5	93.5
Oracle	50.8	46.8	92.1
Amazon	49.6	18.3	36.9
Facebook	15.8	1.8	11.4
Total	568.0	462.7	81.5

Figure 5.1.

Source: Srnicek 2017, 31.

The centrality of these high-technology firms to the latest trends in capitalist global restructuring needs to be understood in a broader context. First, high-technology firms derive the highest percentage of their profits from their intellectual property rights, which can be easily financialized and therefore more easily shifted to tax haven locations. Second, the sheer magnitude of their revenue streams and the importance of their activities to other capitalist sectors gives them structural power beyond their market value. High-technology firms, not limited to those in figure 5.1, and large-scale transnational manufacturing corporations are increasingly moving to acquire technological leadership across multiple global capitalist platforms. These include a wide range of capitalist "platforms" that are being revolutionized by the incorporation of new technological processes, including cloud and industrial platforms.

For example, Amazon Warehouse Services has emerged as the leading transnational corporation in renting out "cloud computing services, which include on-demand services for servers, storage and computing power, software development tools and operating systems, and ready-made applications" (Srnicek 2017, 61). Google, Microsoft, and IBM are competing to offer related services. Google is "selling its machine-learning processes"; Microsoft is building "an artificial intelligence platform that gives businesses the software development tools to build their own bots"; and IBM "is moving to make quantum cloud computing a reality" (Srnicek 2017, 62). In the area of industrial platforms, General Electric, Siemens, Microsoft, and Intel are competing aggressively to own the technology that allows dominant firms to position "themselves as the intermediary between factories, consumers and app developers . . . to monitor much of how global manufacturing operates, from the smallest actuator to the largest factory," and to "draw upon these data to further solidify their monopoly position" (Srnicek 2017, 69).

During the period from 2000 to 2008, transnational investors from the U.S., the E.U., and Japan dominated the high-tech FDI sector in China. In the aftermath of the 2008 global crisis, the Chinese state implemented a more aggressive strategy toward foreign transnationals in the high-tech sector by increasing requirements for joint technology sharing and the transfer of intellectual property rights. Though Chinese state-owned and private sector firms remain well behind the leading transnational firms in leading technologies such as semiconductors, the Chinese Communist Party has been attempting to reverse what it sees as a history of almost complete deference to U.S.-based transnational corporations. A Communist Party–linked newsmagazine "singled out" the "Eight Guardian Warriors"—Apple, Cisco, Google, IBM, Intel, Microsoft, Oracle, and Qualcomm—in a critical report that said these firms "had been able to drive right into China . . . whereas Huawei and another

Chinese equipment maker ZTE had been kept out of the United States (Zhong and Mozur 2018). In an effort to reorient the Chinese economy toward more favorable acquisition of high technology, the Chinese state has attempted to increase the magnitude, scope, and depth of technology restrictions and technology-sharing requirements for foreign transnationals. These measures have included "banning government offices from installing the most recent version of Microsoft Windows," removing Cisco, Apple, and Intel products "from state lists that officials use as guides when buying equipment," and fining Qualcomm "with a $975 million fine for anticompetitive behavior" (Zhong and Mozur 2018).

The political pressure led more U.S.-based transnationals to agree to link their foreign investments to Chinese partners, including "Advanced Micro Devices, Intel and Qualcomm," which "began working with Chinese organizations in microchips, which China imports in huge quantities to put into smartphones, computers and other electronics" (Zhong and Mozur 2018).

However, despite the attempts by the Chinese state to steer more technology agreements toward private and state-owned firms in China, the reality is that the U.S.-based technology giants continue to benefit heavily from their presence in the China market. These firms have every reason to oppose a trade war with China, given the stakes of their investment. They prefer a strategy of cooperation and selective negotiation in setting the terms of foreign direct investment, rather than the economic nationalist strategy that is preferred by some of the hard-line officials within the Trump administration. As recently as 2017, Apple continued to be a dominant foreign investor in China, generating $18 billion in revenue from investments there, which represented 20 percent of its total sales. Boeing's China sales totaled $12 billion in 2017, "almost 13% of its overall revenue" (La Monica, CNN Markets Now, March 22, 2018). Intel, Texas Instruments, Nvidia, Micron and Qualcomm maintain a signficant presence in the China market, with "manufacturing plants there and Chinese tech companies that use their processors" (La Monica 2018). Nike "sold $1.2 billion of sneakers and athletic apparel in China," according to its last quarterly report of 2017. General Motors announced that it had sold "a record high 4 million vehicles in 2017 . . . fueled by strong demand for Cadillac and Buick brands" (La Monica 2018).

The embeddedness of transnational corporations in the China market remains a key characteristic of the new globalization—one that has not been altered by the recent moves of the Chinese state to deepen the ties between these foreign transnationals and Chinese companies. However, as the competition has intensified for acquisition of the most high-value products in the latest phase of global capitalism, the range of actors clashing over terms of access to the China market has increased. The election of Donald Trump as U.S. president has further strained U.S.-China relations, as the Trump administration is forcefully threatening a trade war against China and other countries if these trading and investment partners fail to change their behavior toward the U.S. As of this writing, the escalation of tariffs between the U.S. and China is intensifying the levels of conflict among competing transnational interest blocs that are being forced to adjust to the nationalist policies of the Trump administration.

The tension between the U.S. and China over the terms of access to the China market is being filtered between competing transnational blocs of state and private-sector actors. U.S.-based high-tech and manufacturing firms that are already well positioned within the China market oppose the use of protectionist tactics against China. They prefer instead a more strategic approach to foreign competition and leverage in the China market that involves more U.S. subsidies to the high-tech sector and more aggressive state support for acquisition and retention of the latest technological innovations within future trade and investment agreements. In January of 2017, just before Donald Trump took office, the CEOs (and former CEOs) of high-tech firms, along with a prominent U.S. defense contractor, were enlisted by the Obama administration to write a report about the best way to preserve the U.S. leadership role in semiconductors, chipmaking, robotics, and the move toward 5G technologies (President's Council of Advisors 2017). The participants included Microsoft, Qualcomm, the J. P. Morgan Chase Institute, and Northrup Grumman, as well as groups with close links to private-sector and security interests such as Kissinger Associates, among others. The overall orientation of the report was a recommendation to avoid using protectionism to challenge China's attempts to steer technology toward Chinese state and private-sector firms. Instead, the authors of the report advocated more aggressive, proactive steps that should be taken to help maintain a U.S. lead, which included pressuring China toward greater enforcement of intellectual property rights, fewer restrictions on technology sharing in the China market, and greater use of diplomatic negotiating channels, including trade and investment agreements, to support U.S.-based capitalists in maintaining their lead in high-technology ownership. Essentially, these are identical to the strategies I have documented throughout this book. But this report added a nationalistic twist that framed the entire discussion around U.S. "security objectives," equating the ability of U.S.-based transnational capitalists to maintain their lead in high technology to enhanced U.S. "security." The way that security interests are framed always goes through the most powerful private sector-actors, indicating the extent to which the definitions of national security are heavily shaped and directed by who has the most private-sector power and influence.

The Trump administration partly finds itself in power as a result of the effective use of nationalism, xenophobia, racism, and China bashing that derives from an exaggeration of Chinese "threats" to U.S. national security. Trump's campaign heightened the nationalist rhetoric by appealing to U.S. "white" workers, telling them that he would fight for their jobs by aggressively preempting China from continuing its practices of "undercutting" U.S. businesses and investors. In taking this stance, Trump was staking out a political narrative that was heavily driven by electoral considerations—he managed to win in part by successfully appealing to significant numbers of white working-class voters in key midwestern swing states, though the extent of this "working-class" vote has been exaggerated (Davis 2017). These appeals were being driven by right-wing nationalists within his administration who had long viewed China as a threat to "national security" whose trade and investment policies had to be stopped by strong U.S. actions so that protectionist measures would if necessary be utilized to grant further privileges to U.S. traders and investors in the China market. The U.S. military-industrial complex has typically trafficked in this elevation of the "China threat" to enhance its own bureaucratic and private-sector interests. Nationalists within the Trump administration, specifically U.S. Trade Representative Robert Lighthizer and trade advisor Peter Navarro, are spearheading a strategy of protectionism to advance what they perceive to be "U.S. interests" in China, and to some extent they have the support of the military-industrial-security-intelligence complex, as well as some U.S. business sectors, especially sections of the steel industry in the Midwest, that view China as a competitive threat. These hard-line nationalists view trade and investment negotiations as an win-or-lose proposition that pits U.S. corporations and the U.S. state against the Chinese state (Beshudi 2018).

However, there are divisions within the Trump administration on how to tactically approach the issue of increasing access, privilege, and profits for U.S. firms in the China market. As I have shown, leading U.S. firms in the information technology and manufacturing sector currently make significant amounts of profits from their location in global value chains in China. They are long-standing partners with Chinese private capital and the Chinese state across diverse sectors of the Chinese economy. These actors, represented by powerful U.S. business associations such as the Business Roundtable, have close allies in the Trump administration, such as U.S. Treasury Secretary Steven Mnuchin and Director of the National Economic Council Lawrence Kudlow. Their preferred strategy is to broker a U.S.-China deal that will commit China to easing restrictions on joint venture requirements and technology sharing, while providing more open-ended access to U.S. traders and investors, especially in the information technology sector (*Economic Times*

2018). The tension in the Trump administration lies between the nationalist/protectionist strategy of the hard-liners and the internationalist preference for negotiation with China. Trump internationalists share the concerns of U.S. high-technology and manufacturing firms that a trade war would be too destructive to risk, even as a negotiating tactic, while nationalists advocate a trade war as a "national security" necessity.

In order to understand the particular roots of Trump's ideological nationalism, we have to locate the emergence of the Trumpian political coalition within the broader currents of the crisis of contemporary capitalism. Indeed, it would be a mistake to see Trump or his far-right counterparts in Europe as an aberration.

THE CRISIS OF CAPITALIST DEMOCRACY

The rise of Donald Trump as president of the United States is a strong manifestation of the crisis of capitalist democracy under neoliberalism. Trump exists side by side with the rise of far-right xenophobic movements in Europe that have begun to effectively contest elections over the past decade. These reactionary movements, despite their populist rhetoric, have used the scapegoating of minorities and immigrants as a tool to further advance neoliberal corporate policies by camaflouging those policies under the veneer of populist nationalism. Trump, like his reactionary counterparts in Europe, which include a range of far-right parties, built his electoral appeal around the fundamentally racist program of defending the interests of "whites" against immigrants and minorities, whose very existence was equated with threats to the health and safety of "law-abiding" Americans. In his speeches, Trump sent code words to "white" Americans indicating that he understood their grievances in "having been bypassed, ignored and forgotten" in contemporary U.S. politics and that his administration would support their interests through a dramatic expansion of "law and order" policies that would include increased policing, deportation, and criminalization of the immigrant population as well as a "take the gloves off" approach to police conduct in inner cities. The appeals to "whiteness" coexisted with the use of explicitly class-based language designed to draw a wedge between white workers and minority members of the working class. Yet contrary to the rhetoric that emphasized solidarity with the "white working class," Trump's actual campaign contributions came overwhelmingly from corporate interests during the last two months of the campaign. According to extensive documentation of Federal Election Campaign data unearthed by Thomas Ferguson, Paul Jorgensen, and Jie Chen

Trump received his largest campaign donations from hedge fund investors, steel corporations, casinos, and some Silicon Valley firms (Ferguson, Jorgensen, and Chen 2018).

The fact that corporate interests would ultimately gravitate toward Trump in the last couple of months of the campaign, and would continue working with him to advance their agenda, is indicative of their own search for lowest-common-denominator solutions to implement a continuation and acceleration of their policy preferences. In all likelihood, Trump was not their first choice, but corporations saw in his election victory an opportunity to advance key components of their neoliberal agenda, which would include the most dramatic and extensive tax cuts for corporations in U.S. legislative history, even surpassing the earlier "supply side" tax cuts pushed by presidents Ronald Reagan and George W. Bush (Gittleson 2018). The tax cuts were promoted alongside a systematic slashing of U.S. government regulation of big business, often undertaken via executive orders by President Trump. The administration during its first year alone "has succeeded . . . in bringing the regulatory system to a near halt," mainly through a dramatic restriction of any new regulatory action that could be pursued by regulatory agencies (Vinik 2018). Trump has also issued executive orders weakening existing regulations in finance, the environment, workplace health and safety, consumer protection, federal employment, and an extensive set of business investment practices.

The deregulation agenda has mostly been welcomed and celebrated in the business and corporate press, and among corporate interest groups that have worked closely with Trump on deregulation and tax cut issues. At the same time, the Trump administration is aggressively implementing a domestic policing, surveillance, and criminalization program that targets immigrants, low-income communities, and minorities as part of the self-described "law and order campaign." This exists side by side with a dramatic escalation of the military budget and a dramatic expansion of the use of U.S. drone strikes and military operations, justified by reference to the ongoing "war on terror." The fact that not all corporate interests are supportive of Trump's attacks on immigrants and minorities is hardly surprising. Among corporate executives, there is more discomfort regarding Trump's use of racist rhetoric than there is over actual policy choices—especially when it comes to corporate tax cuts and deregulation, which these transnational corporations have endorsed. The institutionalization of the far right within the ranks of the Republican Party and the long history of the Democratic Party endorsing and implementing neoliberal policies are at the root of the increasing deligitimacy of U.S. capitalist institutions, including Congress and the presidency itself. The historical patterns of growing deligitimization have anticipated Trump and his contemporaries in Europe.

In the primary elections to select presidential nominees, the dominant corporate donors to the Republican and Democratic Parties were incapable of stopping Trump and were even blissfully unaware of the extent to which his appeals would ultimately be successful. Their inability to steer the usual list of preferred candidates to the office of the presidency is itself a product of a systemic crisis of political legitimacy, wrought by decades of polarization of incomes under neoliberal capitalism. Capitalist democracies during the period of regulated capitalism (1945–1979) gained legitimacy by the appearance of the separation of capitalist ownership rights in the marketplace from the political institutions that govern capitalism. During this period, Social Democratic parties in Western Europe, and to a lesser extent the Democratic Party in the U.S., paid some amount of attention to labor unions and mass constituents in formulating their policy agendas. The era of neoliberalism (1980 to the present) has broken any such appearances, with the dominant political parties, regardless of party label, moving rightward to embrace many of the same economic policy agendas. This includes support by both center-left and center-right parties for the central components of what is often referred to as "neoliberalism": reduction in social welfare spending, support for privatization of essential public services, deregulation of health and safety regulations, erosion of antitrust laws, reduced taxes on the wealthiest citizens, and the globalization of markets on terms negotiated by corporate elites.

This pursuit of neoliberal economic policy agendas on the part of mainstream political parties has coincided with lower voter turnout and dramatic reductions in public legitimacy—reflecting a rise in public distrust of governments and a belief that governments are run by the wealthy for the wealthy—and the emergence of third parties in Europe that are often dominated by the far right of the spectrum, including xenophobic and openly racist and fascistic parties. Instead of capitalist crises leading to the emergence of left-wing alternatives, which has been seen to a certain extent in Greece and Spain, the current strength of far-right parties has eclipsed the ability of a coherent left to mount an effective counterattack. The inability of capitalist economic crises to generate the emergence of mass movements on the left is a puzzle worthy of further reflection. Left-wing scholars and activists have grappled with this question over the past two decades and have managed to develop some theories as to why a left based in working-class constituencies has not emerged to challenge the neoliberal consensus of policy-making elites. A full explanation is complex and cannot be reduced to only one variable.

The emergence of a transnational global capitalism in which production is increasingly dispersed across the borders of states has fractured the ability of workers to defend themselves at the nation-state level. As I have argued in this book, the interest of transnational capital has been thoroughly globalized and protected through as a many as four hundred investment agreements signed between capitalist states during the 1990s and 2000s (Gathii 2011). At the same time, workers are restricted from moving across borders, which are increasingly policed and militarized. Those who have been allowed to cross the borders of nation-states face high levels of marginalization, policing, and criminalization, further solidifying the structural power of capital, both economically and politically (Chomsky 2014). Right-wing forces have been able to take advantage of these circumstances to wax nostalgic about the "loss of national heritage" in appeals to groups of white workers who are willing to accept such claims, generating increasing levels of support for quasi-fascist groups. Meanwhile, the parties in power of the center-left and center-right are quick to use immigrant labor as a scapegoat for broader societal problems, further lending legitimacy to far-right hate groups and repeating historical patterns.

While important, the impact of structural global factors in explaining the drift of parties to the right of the political spectrum is not sufficient in explaining the lack of a clear left alternative. The institutional features of governance in an age of neoliberal capitalism need to be inserted into the equation to fully grapple with the politics of the right turn. But for skeptics, it is first necessary to show that this right turn does exist across a range of states with diverse institutional and class histories. Fortunately, scholars have a tool to measure such shifts in policy preferences over time. It is known as the Mapping Policy Preferences database, and it examines the extent to which political parties of differing labels have adopted similar neoliberal policies while in positions of power in Western Europe and North America (Mudge 2011). From the 1990s to the present, the trends from this database are quite clear: regardless of institutional differences or levels of commitment to social democracy, the trajectories of Social Democratic parties in Europe and the Democratic Party in the U.S. show remarkable convergence in their support of neoliberal policies. That means that ostensibly center-left parties have moved to embrace many of the tenets of neoliberal orthodoxy in supporting reductions in welfare spending, privatization of social services, "competition policy" that has served as a justification for greater liberalization of markets on terms highly favorable to corporate interests, and reductions in the tax and regulatory obligations of the upper-income strata of their populations.

The extent to which center-left political parties have turned in favor of neoliberalism, even in Scandinavian countries with a longer commitment to Keynesian redistribution, requires some amount of explanation. The first part of the equation is the greater structural and instrumental power of capitalist political organizations, which were central in promoting neoliberal policies at the highest levels of policymaking, as I demonstrated in chapter two of this book. This is not strictly a matter of lobbying, although there have been expansive networks of corporate lobbying in the U.S., Canada, and Western Europe, led by the Business Roundtable in the U.S. and the International Chambers of Commerce and the European Roundtable of Industrialists in Europe (Murray and Scott 2012). The most powerful corporate groups can minimize overt lobbying by exerting a more profound influence on policy-making through the process of agenda-setting, which entails the establishment of policy foundations funded by transnational corporate actors that can establish the parameters within which policy debates occur. For example, the policy technocrats within the European Union are advised by a network of well-connected policy foundations that do the bidding of their corporate donors, whose interests are often cloaked in the garb of technocratic problem-solving "solutions" to policy dilemmas. Many of the deregulatory and market liberalization policies in the European Union owe their existence to a well-established network of policy associations with deep ties to transnational capital (Cronin 2013). Similarly, corporate networks have been directly involved in the negotiation of the bilateral investment agreements led by the European Union and the U.S. that have helped establish the terms for the globalization of production, including corporate supply chains that have weakened the ability of labor unions to counter the negative effects of "free trade."

The second part of the puzzle is also significant: the professionalization of party hierarchies in the institutionalized discourse of neoliberalism has made their policy orientation closer to each other than their rhetoric or oppositional discourse would appear. Even in the U.S., where the scholarly literature of American politics has emphasized the "polarization" of political parties, the polarization has occurred within an overarching agenda of neoliberalism. It was the Clinton administration, after all, that not only embraced but implemented many of the neoliberal policies supported by the Reagan administration in the 1980s: a move toward balanced budgets that saw an increase in reductions of federal social welfare expenditures in the neoliberal era, an emphasis on criminalization and policing in federal justice policies, and a further deregulation of the banking sector that reached its height in wide bipartisan support for the elimination of the Glass-Steagall Act, which eliminated the already weakened barriers separating commercial and investment banking (Meeropol 1998). While the Clinton administration did support the increases in tax rates for the upper 2 percent of taxpayers, the increase was not enough to offset its support for corporate restructuring and tax loopholes that furthered the neoliberal globalization agenda, not to mention its support and leadership in passing NAFTA, which became the model of corporate-backed investment agreements over the next twenty years. In other words, the regressivity of the Reagan era was codified and solidified by a Clinton administration that talked of a "third way" whose rhetoric was designed to bypass association with traditional conservative or liberal policy proposals, but in fact gave ideological cover to neoliberal policy measures. Given the history of Democratic convergence with the neoliberal policy agenda, which actually started with Democratic president Jimmy Carter, there is clearly a cavernous gap between political scientists' contention that the parties are "polarized" and the rather overwhelming evidence that both parties have pursued neoliberal policy agendas.

The extent to which Republican and Democratic Party elites diverge from one another is often expressed in social issues such as religion versus secularism, abortion rights versus "pro-life," nativism versus legal immigration, and individual property rights such as gun ownership, all of which are rarely if ever discussed in the public arena within the larger context of corporate power and class privilege but instead are more narrowly conceptualized as a cultural war of identity pitting those that "think like us" against those that "oppose our values." This liberal framing of these identity and cultural issues contributes to a retreat from addressing class power and privilege in favor of "identity" markers and has greatly contributed to the party polarization that does exist, even if it's not polarization around neoliberalism, which both parties have endorsed (Krasa and Polborn 2013).

In Western Europe, where a different set of technocratic institutional politics prevails, the party elites position themselves differently, as purveyors of a technocratic "wisdom" that comes from a regulatory and institutional structure increasingly insulated from public opinion. Indeed, the very establishment of a European Union around a European Central Bank that takes its cue from the German Bundesbank indicates the extent to which the European project is a corporate project, with roots of support from the most powerful corporate actors in Europe, not the least of which is the European Roundtable of Industrialists. But instead of the crass lobbying embedded in U.S. politics, the technocrats at the center of the regulatory apparatus of the E.U. legitimize the crafting of E.U. policies in the language of codified rule-making that is designed to insulate European elites from the more "narrow" concerns of citizens within the nation-states of Europe.

The result has been a predictable gap between an E.U. elite that emphasizes a common European project, and European citizens who feel that this project is being forced down their collective throats. With Social Democrats tied to the corporatist agenda of the E.U., with its top-down structure and its promise of social benefits and redistribution to the masses (which masks the neoliberalism at the heart of actual E.U. policies), the double-speak between what

Social Democrats say about the benefits of the E.U. and how ordinary workers experience the actual neoliberal policies on the ground becomes harder to sustain. The result is an E.U. bureaucracy that is increasingly delegitimized, as evident by the negative votes on the E.U. Constitution in France and the Netherlands in 2005, while other votes were either canceled or postponed as E.U. technocrats worked to move around public opposition to save their political project. The recent appointments of E.U. technocrats in place of actual governing officials to preside over the implementation of austerity policies in the indebted states of Greece and Italy speak volumes about the replacement of citizenship with corporate technocracy (Streeck 2014, 97–164).

The rise of the European far right needs to be viewed in this historical context, with strong similarities to the rise of Donald Trump in the U.S. In both Europe and the U.S., the far right had long found a home within the more conservative establishment parties. Corporate interests have often bankrolled the far right as bulwarks against policy measures that they oppose, especially high levels of taxation on the wealthy and income redistribution. In Europe, far-right political parties, which recently improved their electoral performance, have much older histories within mainstream political parties. The leadership of the United Kingdom Independence Party emerged from the British Liberal Party. The founder, Alan Sked, "was also an early member of Margaret Thatcher's Bruges Group, founded on the basis of a speech she gave in 1988 arguing that the Tories had not successfully rolled back the frontiers of the state in Britain, only to see them re-imposed at a European level" (Afonso and Rennwald 2017). The Dutch far-right nationalist Geert Wilders began as "a protégé of liberal politician Frits Bolkestein, a proponent of Reaganomics who went on to push for a radical deregulation of the European labor market as European Union commissioner" (Afonso and Rennwald 2017). Jean-Marie Le Pen, the far-right nationalist of France and the founder of the French National Front, "was first elected to Parliament in 1956 for the party of Pierre Poujade, who championed a tax insurgency on behalf of small shopkeepers against the so-called 'fiscal Gestapo'" (Afonso and Rennwald 2017).

The roots of the radical right are in middle-class, white nationalist currents, with a disproportionate representation of small-business owners whose cost margins are tighter than those of their corporate counterparts. The extent to which the far right has been able to attract working-class voters has been limited by their opposition to the very social programs that have been supported by the working class. However, given the context of the rise of neoliberalism and the shrinking of the social welfare state, the far right has attempted to broaden its appeal to white working-class voters by a combination of racist messaging, anti-immigration policies, and verbal support for a preservation of some aspects of the social welfare state—at least in the case of the far right in Britain, France, and Denmark. In the case of the Tea Party in the U.S., there has been more consistent opposition to government spending and regulation, policy positions that have resulted in some factions of the Tea Party movement receiving generous corporate funding. The move of Tea Party supporters to vote for Donald Trump, against the preferences of the Republican Party strategists, indicates that once unleashed, far-right nationalist movements cannot be easily contained and controlled.

In recent decades, the far-right parties in Europe have overtaken many of their Social Democratic Party counterparts in gaining support from white workers who have grown disillusioned with Social Democratic Party policies, especially the embrace of neoliberalism, which has coincided with broader patterns of inequality and reductions in working-class living standards. The Danish People's Party, the Party of Freedom (Netherlands), the Front National (France), the Northern League (Italy), the Austrian Freedom Party, and the Swiss People's Party have all seen a growing working-class support base that has come at the direct expense of Social Democratic Parties. A recent study by Alexandre Afonso and Line Rennwald traces this movement of workers to far-right nationalist parties to an explicit shift in the rhetoric of far-right parties toward support for an expansion of social welfare measures, redistribution of wealth, increased credits for people on low incomes, and increased pensions. However, this rhetorical shift has been contradicted by the actual policy positions that far-right parties adopt when in power. This has led Afonso and Rennwald to conclude that "voters cannot be tricked indefinitely," a conclusion that has been demonstrated by the experience of the far-right government that recently ruled Austria, which lost two-thirds of its seats after its "conservative cabinet committed to implementing wide-ranging austerity," a policy position that went directly against its campaign appeals to white workers (Afonso and Rennwald 2017).

The tension between far-right parties using populist rhetoric to attract working-class voters is rooted in the fact that far-right coalitions have historically been dominated by small-business factions that feel most threatened by the rising costs of regulations and taxation measures, and by corporate coalitions that attempt to use far-right political movements to advance parts of their policy agenda. As transnational corporations provided aggressive support for attacks on the social welfare state, the rise of far-right political organizations provided ideological ammunition for those attacks and could serve at times as allies of broader capitalist interests.

However, the capitalist crisis of 2008 encouraged the far right to elevate its racist, misogynistic, and xenophobic rhetoric to a broader public platform in order to take advantage of the increasing illegitimacy of mainstream political parties and institutions. The passage of the Brexit Amendment in the United Kingdom rode the coattails of a conservative nationalist critique of the E.U. that had divided the Conservative Party since the days of Margaret Thatcher. In fact it was the conservative prime minister who pushed for British citizens to be able to vote for whether or not to stay in the E.U., with the conservative leadership being convinced that Brexit would be defeated in the process. Much to the astonishment of the British establishment, a combination of small-business support for Brexit alongside the growing resentments of sections of the white working class against the British immigrant population resulted in victory for the pro-Brexit side. Though corporate interests in Britain favored staying in the E.U., there was a section of British capitalists, closely linked to corporate supporters of Donald Trump, who saw Brexit as a way of defeating the global factions of the ruling class and thereby contributing to the "deconstruction" agenda favored by far-right quasi-fascists like Steve Bannon in the U.S. The pro-Brexit vote was championed by right-wing corporate libertarian Robert Mercer, a hedge fund billionaire who was Trump's biggest campaign donor and whose family had been instrumental in bringing Steve Bannon into the Trump campaign when it had been floundering. The Mercer family heavily funded the ultra-right-wing publication *Breitbart News*, which was directed under the editorial leadership of Bannon.

The tension between the long-standing transnational corporate support for pro-corporate investment agreements and the rise of far-right factions endorsing policies of protectionism need to be better understood, especially given the rise of Trump and the triumph of Brexit in the U.K. First, the rise of the far right should be seen as part of the crisis of neoliberal capitalist legitimacy. The inability of powerful transnational capitalists to fully direct and control who gets elected and on what terms is becoming an increased reality at the core of the capitalist system in the U.S. and in Europe. Second, the relationship between transnational capital, the Trump administration, and the European far right is much closer than it may appear on specific issues. Transnational capitalists have worked with the Trump administration to support the corporate tax cut and the deregulationist agenda of the administration, which was seen by much of the U.S. business establishment as a welcome continuation of neoliberal corporate policies. Likewise, both Trump and the far-right parties in Europe use racist attacks, criminalization of immigration, and attacks on lower-income communities as tools to oppose the interests of the broader working class. The lengths to which the far right goes to demonize minorities and immigrants only further divides, cripples, and weakens an effective countermobilization of workers and the poor against the system. This orientation of the far right mirrors the tendencies built in to the capitalist sytem: decades of transnational capitalist attacks against the working class have contributed to the very existence and legitimacy of far-right groups, as workers have turned against one another based on deeply embedded histories of racial and national distinctions.

The key question becomes: how does the working class overcome its divisions and unite to push back against decades of defeats within global capitalism? This will require thinking strategically and mobilizing collectively. The increasing consolidation of global value chains may give the working class a new opportunity to unite in gaining more power against the owners of global capitalist enterprises. The creation of key logistical nodes that facilitate the final assembly and delivery of global products to their destinations has actually served to concentrate workers in strategic locations within the global capitalist system. At those nodes the working class may be able to use their leverage to force substantive changes in the way the system is organized.

WORKING-CLASS POWER IN GLOBAL VALUE CHAINS

A recent International Labor Office Report concluded that 20 percent of the global workforce is employed in value chains (ILO 2015). Transnational corporations increased the portion of their workforce employed by corporate subsidiaries (through foreign direct investment) by twenty-one million in 1990 to seventy-one million in 2015 (Mosley 2017, 154). The number of workers employed in global value chains is significantly higher than this figure, given that transnational firms have increasingly relied on subcontracting through original equipment manufacturers who in turn contract with lower-tier supply chain firms. As a result, workers in developing countries now account for a majority of workers employed in global manufacturing. The terms of such employment have grown more precarious as global value chains have become more complex and differentiated. Transnational firms push down the costs to low-tier suppliers, which then squeeze the wages paid to workers, who are underpaid relative to their productivity and often lack an adequate social safety net; this increases the level of vulnerability and pracarity in employment. The segmentation of production across countries lends itself to a "divide and conquer strategy" whereby the headquarter firm, whether a supply firm or a demand firm, is able to force competition among low-tier businesses within the supply network, further encouraging poor working conditions.

Given these circumstances, how do workers effectively fight back in an effort to increase wages and promote better working conditions? The answer is complicated by the fact that capitalism is a global system with imperatives toward maximization of surplus value by capitalist owners. The ability of workers to effectively fight for reforms is always threatened by the logic of the system, which has proven malleable in reversing short-term gains by workers to facilitate the imperatives of profit. That being said, the transnational corporations that benefit the most from global value chains remain vulnerable to value chain disruption, especially given the increasing consolidation of value chains that has been occuring within global production over the past decade. Gary Gereffi has identified the long-term trends of consolidation that have been accelerated since the global capitalist crisis of 2008. The 2008 crisis has encouraged a greater consolidation of ownership at the top of global value chains, as headquarter firms have accelerated their mergers and acquisitions in an effort to further concentrate ownership of high-value activities—which is especially apparent in the concentration of power and privilege within the global information technology sector, as examined in the previous section. But such consolidation has also been apparent in the concentration of ownership within other sectors of global manufacturing, as well as the intermediate parts of the supply chain, which includes the original design and equipment manufacturers. As Gereffi has noted, "the question increasingly posed by the transnational lead firms of GVCs is 'how can we rationalize our supply chains from 350–500 suppliers to 25–50 suppliers" (Gereffi 2014, 15).

In 1980, "the world's 1,000 largest companies . . . represented about 30 percent of the GDP of the OECD countries. By 2010, that figure rose to 72 percent" (White 2017). Within this global concentration of corporate power, there has been a further level of corporate concentration within the major sectors of global value chains. In the automobile sector, just sixteen car manufacturers "sell more than 1 million vehicles per year, but those cars are built from parts supplied by just ten major component makers, meaning that auto assemblers are now reliant on a small cadre of mega suppliers who each sell parts to rival assemblers" (Lee and Gereffi 2015, 322). The rise of mega-suppliers has meant greater levels of concentration among just a few dominant firms in coordinating the production of component parts for final assembly of automobiles. The auto manufacturers as headquarter firms still have disproportionate power in these relationships, due to their ability to "determine when, where and at what price they will sell fully assembled vehicles to customers around the world" (Lee and Gereffi 2015, 322). However, the auto manufacturers have been able to use information technology to reorient the value chain process by redirecting production toward a more consolidated supply chain network that is more capital-intensive and located closer to larger markets where cars are sold.

For the big three U.S.-based auto manufacturers—Ford, GM, and Chrysler—there has been a dramatic consolidation of suppliers from 1990 to 2010, mirroring the trend in other manufacturing sectors. The market power of headquarter firms exerted such pressure on original equipment manufacturers and lower-tier suppliers to force a combination of bankruptcies and mergers at the lower tiers of the supply chain. "The number of supplier firms declined by 80 percent from 1990 to 2010, particularly in the 1990s as many tier 3 suppliers either went bust, exited the parts business or merged with others to defend or gain market share" (Moody 2017, 51). The result has not been a reduction in working-class positions in U.S. auto manufacturing, which some observers may have assumed to be the case. Instead, the U.S.-based auto manufacturing sector has employed roughly the same number of workers to facilitate the transition to a more consolidated automobile manufacturing process, a figure that totaled 733,000 by 2015, only slightly less than the 770,000 recorded in 2000. To be sure, there has been clear evidence of increased exploitation of this U.S. workforce, as workers are categorized into different classifications, allowing manufacturers to take advantage of a workforce that is considerably less costly, but more productive, than it used to be. This process mirrors the trends that we have discussed in previous chapters pertaining to Germany, the E.U., and Japan, where multitiered classification of workers has resulted in overall lower wages despite higher productivity.

In the sector of mobile phone production, just a few headquarter firms/brands dominate the contracting of production across a few countries. "The five leading firms account for more than half of global markets in mobile phones (56 percent), smartphones (60 percent), contract manufacturing (75 percent) and smartphone operating systems (99 percent). Two leading firms control a big portion of each market, such as Apple and Samsung in smartphones, which give rise to oligopolistic market structures" (Lee and Gereffi 2015, 326). This concentration of ownership is complemented by the consolidation of production locations, "with just five large exporters, China, South Korea, Hong Kong, Vietnam and the U.S., commanding 74 percent of the world's exports in 2012, with China alone representing half of them" (Lee and Gereffi 2015, 326). This increased concentration and consolidation has resulted in a growth in size and power of original equipment manufacturers such as Foxconn, whose profits have soared given their dominant location as an OEM within the center of burgeoning supply networks. Corporate market power serves to block upgrading by new competitors from locations that are outside the arc of centralized corporate power. This structure of corporate power and privilege also results in the concentration of corporate networks within logistical nodes of production that pivot around key countries in regional locations where demand is growing fastest, which is led by China and East Asia, and in Africa is dominated by the centrality of South African capital within value chain linkages to the African continent. In South America, Brazilian firms have emerged as leaders of agri-commodity value chains whose links to Europe and to China have led to further concentration of corporate power and privilege in Brazil, including the active involvement of Brazilian agribusiness corporations in what has been described as a parliamentary "coup" against the Labor Party president, Dilma Rousseff. The coup has paved the way for greater agribusiness consolidation of agricultural land in the Brazilian countryside (Vigna 2018).

In fact, there has been a concentration of corporate power in global agribusiness that has also been accelerated by the utilization by headquarter firms of big data. For decades agribusiness corporations have accelerated the pace and scope of cross-border mergers and acquisitions, which have further consolidated the global agri-food sector.

> Since 2015, the "biggest year ever for mergers and acquisitions," a number of high-profile deals have come onto the table in a range of agri-food sectors—often with a view to linking different nodes in the chain. These include the $130 billion merger between U.S. agro-chemical giants, Dow and DuPont, Bayer's $66 billion buyout of Monsanto, ChemChina's acquisition of Syngenta for $43 billion and its planned merger with Sinochem in 2018. (Mooney 2017)

As explained by Pat Mooney:

> Financialization—ie the increasingly powerful role of financial actors, motives and trends in shaping global economic activity—has become a major driver of corporate consolidation across various sectors as investors demand higher and short-term payouts. However, beyond the physical (e.g. drones) and scientific (gene editing) technologies behind agri-food sector consolidation, information technology (IT) comes out as the newest and most powerful driver. Big Data connects inputs—seeds, fertilizers and chemicals—to farm equipment and retailers to consumers in unprecedented ways. A significant horizontal and vertical restructuring is underway across food systems. (Mooney 2017)

This pattern of concentration of capital and the consolidation of manufacturing production is occurring across all manufacturing sectors and agricultural sectors, driven by the headquarter firms' acquisition of information technology as a tool to rationalize supply chain management. This has meant a logistical shift of production toward a more concentrated supplier network, a more consolidated and centralized working class located at key logistical nodes within the global value chain delivery system, and heightened exploitation of workers both in the core of the capitalist system and in developing countries. In core locations, decades of transnational capitalist attacks on workers unions, reduced health and safety protections, less regulatory supervision, and increased utilization of a multitiered and differentiated (non-union) workforce has increased exploitation of workers. In developing countries, super-exploitation occurs, which, as detailed in chapter four, goes uncaptured by traditional development statistics, which undercount the gap between productivity and wages that is a structural and instrumental product of often unchecked corporate and state power within developing countries, where enforcement of laws regulating worker pay, safety, health, and overall working conditions is low to nonexistent.

Under these circumstances, how do workers begin to fight back to tilt the balance away from rising and largely unaccountable corporate power? The place to start is by mapping a strategic orientation to corporate power in global value chains. This means identifying the transnational headquarter firm's location at the top of these value chains, connecting the profits that flow to that firm from supplier networks and examining the key logistical "choke points" that are essential to ensure "just in time" delivery of component parts as they are being assembled into finished vehicles or as they are being processed and delivered to market locations. The increased concentration and consolidation of global value chains has meant that transnational firms and their supply networks are more tightly interconnected than ever before. This provides opportunities for developing worker strategies targeted at disrupting the most valuable distribution points within the value chain process. These distribution points are typically located in the largest global markets of the U.S., the E.U., Japan, China, and other select locations within East Asia. The opportunities, however, for effective utilization of labor pressure vary by sector and are necessarily differentiated given the opportunities (or lack thereof) of cross-border worker solidarity, either through unions or independent worker actions that may involve wildcat strikes, work stoppages, etc.

Building transnational union networks that strategically plan effective actions based on a clear assessment of power relationships within global value chains is a key organizing tool.

> The Global Union of Foodworkers has been particularly effective in building such networks and forcing management at such global corporations as Coca Cola and Unilever into regular negotiations. In the construction industry, the Global Union Building and Woodworkers International (BWI) has networked unions in conjunction with major sports events such as World Soccer Cup and the Olympics, bringing public attention to bear on working conditions at construction sites in such countries as South Africa, Brazil and Qatar. And the

> Global Union IndustriALL coordinates a number of transnational union networks in various sectors. (Fichter 2015)

These models are important starting points, but they are limited in scope and scale and are hardly sufficient at this stage to tackle the enormity of the balance of power held by transnational firms.

Namely, the above efforts are focused on gaining leverage with headquarter firms in global value chains by selectively mobilizing workers and orienting them toward a marketing campaign that then highlights the complicity of brand-name corporations in value chain exploitation. If successful, these firms will agree to make concessions that may make a marginal difference in securing higher pay for workers employed by lower-tier suppliers. The long-term leverage for workers, however, can only be realized by a more concerted effort to target the increasingly centralized logistical nodes of the value chain. Corporations make their profits by ensuring timely assembly and delivery of their product to the most important market locations—brand-name capture and market power are increasingly financialized at the very top of the value chain cluster. In order to get the attention of these firms, and to shift the power toward workers at the bargaining table, including the global union structures referenced above, more militant actions are needed at key nodes within the value chain. That's why strategic examination of value chains remains such a valuable resource in helping workers organize their collective efforts to disrupt production and force a greater amount of profits to be diverted as wages.

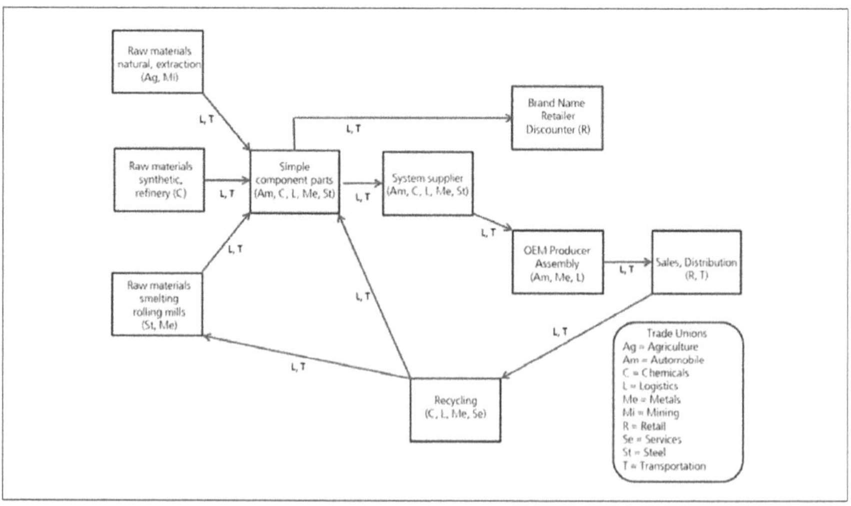

Figure 5.2. Global Value Chain Model and Trade Unions
Source: Fichter 2015, 6.

This process of increasing worker leverage must utilize a multipronged offensive that involves global worker solidarity that can be used to develop strategic plans for organizing workers within global value chains, as well as acknowledging the diverse circumstances confronting workers in different value chain locations—which means developing the most effective political strategies for confronting power in countries where governments exercise the most extreme repression and prohibition against a wide range of working-class actions. And, finally, worker coordination of political and economic actions has to be undertaken in a way that maximizes leverage against the most powerful headquarter firms at the top of the global value chain, where market leverage is the greatest.

A targeted campaign that involves both political and economic power objectives is essential. That means workers must privilege broader alliance networks that give them the most opportunity to advance their interests as a class, and not tie their fortunes to institutional structures of power and privilege that will easily sacrifice short-term reforms for a return to more exploitation. A crucial part of this strategy is identifying alliance networks between working-class organizations, left political organizations, and grass-roots organizations representing the most exploited and marginalized. It also means developing programs that tie economic struggles to political struggles that are able to produce victories against capital on multiple fronts. Thus far, the institutional capture of the reform process by business unions, liberal NGO networks, and "corporate social responsibility" advocates promises window-dressing reforms that do nothing to change power relationships and indeed have proven useful in limiting and controlling opposition and dissent. Alternative grassroots networks have to be built in order to develop effective strategies for change.

CONCLUSION

Transnational corporate power within global value chains has been a by-product of features that have long been inherent to global capitalism. The first is a built-in tendency of capitalism toward falling rates of profit that lead to structural crises within the system. The second is the increased concentration of capitalist ownership as a response to the falling rates of profit and the imperatives of capitalist accumulation. The third is an inherent tendency of capitalist owners of production to look to foreign markets and increased exploitation of workers as "solutions" to capitalist crises. I have explained these long-term dynamics of capitalist crises in relationship to the expansive growth of global value chains. Within these value chains, transnational firms have steadily attempted to usurp a higher percentage of control over high-valued activities and to force the costs of operations downward on workers, societies, and those that are most vulnerable. The growing concentration and consolidation of corporate power that have characterized neoliberal capitalism are nothing new. Instead, the latest period of capitalist restructuring represents a deepening effort on the part of transnational capitalist interest blocs to mitigate crises through increased market access and increased exploitation.

In the latter part of this chapter I suggested a reinforcement, deepening, and intensification of worker cross-border mobilizations that are necessary to shift the balance of power from capitalists to workers, both in core capitalist countries and in developing countries. Just as transnational capital has organized itself globally, workers and the disenfranchised have to organize themselves across state borders to realize the goals of long-term emancipation. A significant part of the effectiveness of this process is being aware of the extent to which transnational firms at the top of global value chains use market and political strategies to usurp value from workers, societies, and communities.

The research agenda that I have outlined in this book has implications for both theory and practice in better understanding power relationships and in suggesting how to build effective strategies for contesting corporate power. The final chapter offers further reflections of the urgency of a class-centered analytical framework for better understanding international relations and political economy. I will also contrast the theoretical framework that I have used in this book with other theories and approaches used in the field of international relations. Finally, I will argue for a synthesis between theory and political strategy, or a praxis that can help guide social movement activists in challenging corporate power.

Chapter Six

Transnational Interest Blocs in Theory and Praxis

Throughout this book, I have documented how transnational corporations have used their economic and political power within states and within markets to shape the contours of the neoliberal era of global capitalism, essentially the period from 1980 to the present. As chapter five documented, the neoliberal era is deep in crisis, which has led to a fracturing of ruling coalitions and a rise of far-right political movements that have gained momentum and, in some cases, have been elevated to positions of political power. Transnational corporations throughout the neoliberal period have attempted to overcome periodic declines in the rate of profit by directly influencing state policies so that corporations and the rich pay fewer taxes, face less oversight and regulation, and are able to increase the levels of exploitation of workers both domestically and globally. This has resulted in a steady decline of public legitimacy for governments in the U.S., the European Union, and Japan, countries that represent the very center of global ownership and accumulation of profits for the most dominant transnational firms. As these firms continue to demand a further "deconstruction" of the social welfare state, the capitalist democratic institutions that gained legitimacy with social welfare policies are viewed as less legitimate. This has led to the latest crisis of the capitalist state, discussed in the previous chapter.

The usefulness of the transnational interest bloc theory is that it puts class analysis at the front and center of international relations in a way that can explain these major global trends of political economy. Unlike other analytical frameworks, realism and liberalism, that separate states from markets in an artificial and unproductive way, the theory of transnational interest blocs locates political and economic power within a class framework that examines the ways that corporate power shapes political and market outcomes. This involves an analysis of both instrumental and structural power wielded by corporations. Instrumentally, firms come together across sectors to act as an interest bloc that forms to advance the interests of a dominant class fraction. This interest bloc furthers its agenda through incorporation and representation within the political apparatus of the nation-state, as well as providing elite leadership within regional and global institutions. The ability of transnational corporations to work together as a class fraction (a cohesive political body that expresses the interest of corporations across various sectors of production) is evident when examining the extent to which transnational interest blocs formed in the U.S., the E.U., and Japan around the most competitive and dynamic transnational firms. As previous chapters have documented, these interest blocs were represented by the Business Roundtable in the U.S., the European Roundtable of Industrialists in the E.U., and Keidanren in Japan. Structurally, the ability of transnational corporations to move investments to a wide range of different locations, increasingly on a large scale through global value chains and subcontracting with foreign producers, puts pressure on states to adjust their policies if they want access to such investments. Each of the prominent transnational interest bloc organizations in the core regions of the global economy have used both their instrumental and structural power to advance their preferred neoliberal policies in the U.S., the E.U., and Japan.

The fact that these corporate organizations were pursuing many of the same policy goals and objectives, albeit in different contexts and facing different obstacles, indicates that the global system of capitalism operates through the interests of the dominant capitalist classes, regardless of societal and institutional context. These dominant fractions of transnational interest blocs unite transnational firms as a class when it comes to supporting broad neoliberal policies that transfer the cost of capitalism from the rich to the working class and the poor, as well as trade agreements that privilege the ownership rights of dominant investors, and global institutional arrangements that advance the interests of the richest and most powerful owners of capital. In this way, the interests of these dominant corporations transcend the institutional and strategic parameters that are typically the focus of liberal and realist analyses, respectively (Wolff and Resnick 2012).

The instrumental power of capitalists to secure the policies that they prefer is mediated in a range of societal contexts, with different institutional histories and state-society relationships. These relationships have been determined in large part by the history of class struggle and the extent to which non-business groups were able to effectively use the state to secure concessions from the dominant classes. In capitalist states with stronger histories of advanced social welfare policies and working-class incorporation in the political process, the ascendance of transnational interest blocs has not proceeded at the same pace as in societies that have had histories of relatively weak social welfare states. During the so-called "golden age" of capitalism, the social democratic welfare state, especially robust in much of Western Europe, was made possible by a configuration of class relationships that allowed workers a partial seat at the table. In other words, while never the dominant political and economic power broker within global capitalism, the working class was able to elevate its ability to have its interests represented politically as a subordinate actor to business interests during the period of managed capitalism, from 1945 to 1980. While this period is easy to over-romanticize, the socioeconomic policies associated with social democracy produced a lower income gap between rich and poor than any other period of capitalist history. However, the contemporary period of neoliberal capitalism is reverting to the much more common history of capitalism: a radical redistribution of profits and revenues from the bottom to the upper one percent of global capitalism (and even more of this concentrated income has gone to a smaller fraction of that upper one percent, as documented in studies of global inequality) (Milanovic 2016). The neoliberal capitalist period has been globalized, ultimately affecting all capitalist states to varying degrees, regardless of their previous histories.

In the neoliberal period, global capitalist competition has intensified as capitalist firms have grown larger in size and socioeconomic power through cross-border mergers and acquisitions, expansion of transnational production across state borders, and heightened global super-exploitation of workers throughout the global value chain. This heightened global competition has been mediated by states and has involved frequent shifts in capitalist relations of production on a global scale as capitalist firms look to consolidate ownership of the highest value-added assets within the global production and distribution. As these shifts occur, transnational interest bloc competition has intensified between fractions of capital that are trying to position themselves as owners of the most lucrative technological innovations within global capitalism. China has emerged as the center of contemporary capitalist interest bloc competition, with the Chinese state simultaneously providing subsidies and market access to a wide range of transnational firms, but increasingly trying to direct the accumulation process in a way that will benefit the strategic and economic interests of those interest blocs that have the most political and economic power within the Chinese state. The Trump administration, representing both national ideologues in the U.S. that see China as a "security threat" and firms that have felt most threatened by the rise of China, have embarked on an aggressive and unilateralist set of tariffs, which have escalated against a range of trading partners, especially China, but also the E.U., Canada, and Mexico.

In explaining this crisis moment in neoliberal capitalism, liberal and realist frameworks focus their analysis on the stability of institutions (liberals) or the security interests of states (realists). Liberals argue that the contemporary crises of liberal institutions are a product of the rise of nationalists whose ideology is incompatible with effective management of international trade and global institutions. In contrast, the transnational interest bloc perspective argues that the contemporary crisis of liberal institutions is a direct product of a long history of capitalist class relationships and the dominance of corporate power, which liberal policies have encouraged and even celebrated. Similarly, realists who focus on state security interests obscure the way in which those interests are framed by powerful corporations whose profits are often the overriding consideration in determining the direction of a country's foreign policy. The extent to which the capitalist system has been put into crisis by a long-term tension between corporate profit-making and internal security and stability is outside the purview of most realist frameworks (Dunn 2009). Realists assume that a state's security interest can be formulated as an independent expression of state policy. Instead, the security interests of states are very much a product of sectoral competition among transnational interest blocs, with those firms that depend the most on military contracts having a vested interest in defining security threats in a manner to maximize profits and power (Cox 2014).

The role of the military-industrial complex in the United States is an illustration of how particular fractions of capital are bound together by a mutual interest in either the profits derived from military spending (military contractors and those who invest in military or military-related industries) or the benefits accrued by foreign investors from the geostrategic orientation of the military in protecting foreign investments. Today, U.S. military spending is the highest in post-WWII history, despite the absence of any geostrategic threat equivalent to the former Soviet Union during the Cold War. The reasons include a vast bipartisan level of support from the Republican and Democratic Parties for militarization that benefits military contractors that manufacture weapons whose production is dispersed throughout the United States. This ensures that the level of congressional support for such spending will be high across a range of districts that see the production of weapons as the foremost driver of jobs and employment, especially in districts where weapons production dominates the local or regional economy. The other factor keeping military spending at record-high post-WWII levels is the interrelationship between such spending and the protection of foreign direct investment, especially in areas of the global economy that disproportionately produce energy resources that much of the global capitalist system is still dependent on. Despite the turn in the U.S. toward a much more aggressive exploitation of domestic natural gas and oil extraction, the U.S. still bases much of its foreign military strategy, including the location of military bases and preparations for future use of military forces, on ensuring the security and delivery of oil and gas resources from areas such as the Persian Gulf and West Africa to global capitalist markets (Stokes and Rafael 2010). There is also a linkage between high levels of military spending and the use of that spending to protect market access for U.S. foreign investors and traders. Though the Trump administration has used nationalist rhetoric and protectionist measures within an aggressive "America first" posture, the basic outlines of U.S. military strategy, including the U.S. commitment to the NATO alliance, have not changed significantly in his first two years in office. In fact, Trump has presided over a significant hike in military spending with overwhelming support from congressional Republicans and Democrats (Hartung 2018).

The relationship between military spending and the maintenance of corporate-friendly trade and investment deals is noteworthy. As the U.S. state increased the level of militarization after the events of 9/11, the U.S. steadily expanded its military presence to as many as 135 countries, which represented a surge in the deployment of official military bases and special operations troops that are positioned within countries to undertake military training and counterinsurgency operations. This militarized expansion is both a geostrategic response to broadly defined "global terrorist networks" that was initially focused on Al Qaeda but has broadened to include a range of other organizations such as ISIS, and an effort to promote the "stability" of foreign markets, which includes ongoing access to natural resources and support for an expansion of foreign capital investment. In this way, militarization has been utilized as a complementary tool in the effort to promote global neoliberalism. What the rise of the Trump nationalists has meant is not a break with this relationship but a more aggressive deployment of military troops and special operations forces under the unilateral direction of U.S. military commanders—who have been given more power and discretion to identify the "targets of operation" under the Trump administration. The nationalism of Trump, then, should be viewed in the context of advancing a continuity in U.S. military spending whereby the U.S. lavishes military resources and aid on traditional U.S. allies while expanding the use of military "solutions" as the diplomatic components of the U.S. foreign policy bureaucracy is reduced—again continuing a long-standing trend but in a more aggressive way (Robinson 2018).

The imperial histories of the U.S., the E.U., and Japan provide a close linkage with the contemporary patterns of investment agreements that have radically expanded in recent decades. These three centers of global transnational accumulation have utilized long-standing geostrategic and military ties with developing countries, which includes lengthy histories of imperial domination of these developing countries, to advance more recent investment agreements that have built on these imperial relationships. The U.S. with CAFTA-DR, the E.U. with CARIFORUM, and Japan with its expansion of foreign direct investment into East Asia illustrate these patterns of historical continuity. Though not always a direct fit with specific imperial histories, given the gap between these histories and the details of the more recent investment agreements, in many cases imperial and military histories have provided the historical framework and pattern of political, strategic, and military relationships that have enabled a continuation of the "imperialism of free trade." In this way, the rules protecting investors in modern-day investment agreements have relied on the earlier relationships of military/imperial subjugation to provide a framework for advancing the privileges and power of transnational corporations (Pal 2017; Bhambra and Holmwood 2017).

TRANSNATIONAL INTEREST BLOC AS CRITICAL THEORY

The modern university in the United States, the E.U., and Japan is a product of a larger socioeconomic power structure that privileges corporate power within global capitalism (Cox 2013). As such, it is no surprise that the dominant ideologies that are taught in universities are what Robert W. Cox has called "problem-solving theories," which accept the current power structures in domestic and global capitalism as unproblematic (Cox 1981). Indeed, problem-solving theories orient themselves to assisting the current managers and leaders of the capitalist system—politicians and business elites—by advising them on how to make the current system function better. That means an emphasis of dominant theories on preserving status quo economic and political power arrangements by recommending changes that would purportedly increase the "stability" of the current power structure or allow for a better "optimization" of the use and deployment of resources within global capitalism to prolong the existing socioeconomic system. The fact that realism and liberalism have long dominated this "problem-solving" approach in international relations and political science is thoroughly predictable, given the status quo assumptions and acceptance of the existing social, political, and economic order embodied by a range of approaches within realism and liberalism and their compatibility with the mission of the corporatized university.

The transnational interest bloc approach offers an alternative firmly grounded in the critical theory tradition of international relations. This tradition does not take the existing socioeconomic and political structures as a "given" but instead examines the historical-structural dynamics of class power in creating and sustaining these structures. Unlike the realist tradition that privileges the concept of "national interest" in framing the foreign policy choices of nation-states, the transnational interest bloc approach, consistent with other Marxist and critical theory traditions, unveils the way that capitalist class interests use their material and ideological power and influence to shape the way that "national interests" are defined. Transnational interest blocs have competing definitions of what constitutes the "national interest" based on their degree of global competitiveness, their sectoral interests, and the size and scale of their global operations, as I have shown in previous chapters. Throughout this book, I have identified the transnational interest blocs promoting global neoliberalism as being led by information technology firms and financial firms. These firms have used their power within political systems and within global markets to promote policies that have established much of the neoliberal architecture of the new globalization.

These sectors of contemporary capitalism occupy a prominent organizational position within the most powerful transnational interest blocs on a domestic and global scale. They have been central to the emergence of transnational capitalist production that has led states to become more politically and economically dependent on transnational interest blocs for their survival. The use of the term "national interest" obscures the way that powerful actors within the transnational capitalist class define the "national interest." By grounding security within the framework of dominant class interests, specifically transnational interest blocs, security is revealed as a project of the vested interests of a socioeconomic class whose profits increasingly transcend the boundaries of the nation-state. In this way, the realist tradition is exposed as hopelessly outdated and a bit naïve in conceptualizing security within territorial boundaries. Increasingly, transnational capitalists have usurped nation-states in the interests of global profit, and definitions of national security have increasingly become ideological manifestations of corporate power on a global scale (Burchill 2005, 63–103).

To an extent this was always true, but at least in the previous period of "managed capitalism," the profits accruing to dominant class actors were more directly related to their ability to produce and to sell their goods within their home markets. Today, transnational capitalists in the most mobile sectors of global capitalism have used their hegemonic position within political systems and within global markets to segment their profit-making interests from the territorial boundaries of a nation-state. This has provided challenges of political legitimacy to capitalist institutions, which are less accountable to the citizens they purport to represent. In this way the transnational interest bloc approach offers distinct advantages over liberalism in explaining the way that contemporary trade and investment agreements operate in the new globalization.

The liberal tradition conceptualizes the market as distinct from political institutions. The prescriptive framework for the liberal tradition is governments that work to optimize market outcomes by establishing appropriate rules and regulations protecting and governing private property rights, while intervening with regulations and social welfare measures designed to mitigate the worst effects of the market. Liberals of course differ considerably on the extent of government intervention that is believed to be prudent. Orthodox liberals advocate minimal intervention, other than basic security guarantees and protection for individual property rights. Keynesian or interventionist liberals advocate more government spending and monetary stimulus during times of recession or depression to overcome the structural bottlenecks of capitalism. However, the basis of both orthodox and Keynesian economic theory is that political institutions and the market can be analyzed separately and function independently in a capitalist system (Vazquez-Arroyo 2008; Piereson 2012).

The transnational interest bloc theory diverges from liberal approaches by rejecting the artificial separation of politics from markets. Interest blocs are expressions of capitalist power within the market and within the state that have driven the capitalist system from the time that capitalism originated in the sixteenth and seventeenth centuries. Capitalist class fractions have long established the rules governing the system, and the notion that political institutions can be analyzed separately from socioeconomic power relationships was never accurate. However, in the period of the new globalization, the emergence of transnational production networks as a product of market and state power is dealing a further blow to the legitimacy of liberal theory. Orthodox liberalism has been exposed as an ideology that advances the interests of the most powerful transnational classes, which have used neoliberal theory to justify an ongoing political and economic assault on the welfare state. The Keynesian tradition that advocates government spending to check recession, alongside more regulation to check the negative effects of financial speculation, faces severe limitations on its effectiveness given the corporate domination of the capitalist state and the expansion of transnational production, which makes regulation of corporate behavior and redistribution of wealth harder to achieve (Wolff and Resnick 2012, 105–132). Transnational capital that is less dependent on profits in one country can much more easily sidestep regulatory, fiscal, and monetary signals by shifting its assets strategically in foreign locations, by relying on speculative financial investments to shield profits, and by betting either for or against government policies through currency speculation in international markets.

Liberal theory is also ill-equipped to explain contemporary trade and investment agreements through traditional models such as comparative advantage, which was based on a set of assumptions about traded goods being produced within territorial markets before being sold to foreign markets. Liberals argue that countries have historically done better when specializing in producing goods and services that maximize the most cost-efficient and productive use of domestic resources based on the factor endowments of the country, while importing goods and services that would be cheaper to acquire from abroad than to produce at home. This liberal approach to trade was always deeply flawed due to its failure to analyze the structural power of corporate actors to use their oligopolistic and quasi-monopoly power to dominate markets, a failure that is starkly magnified in the new globalization. Using global value chains, transnational corporations have relied on an extensive segmentation of production whereby component parts are produced in a wide range of locations. In this global market system, transnational firms structure transactions so that most profits from the value chain are captured by the lead firm. This is made possible by economies of scale and significant "rent capture" that reduces the amount of revenues and profits that flow back to developing economies. In other words, as we have seen through numerous examples documented in this book, countries that produce component parts that are exported and assembled in a wide range of locations in the global economy find that the "backward and forward linkages" traditionally associated with domestic production are captured outside the producing country, especially in locations where dominant transnational firms exercise ownership rights and privileges over intellectual property, branding, and marketing/distribution. This has led to a contemporary crisis of liberal trade theory, which has been discussed and documented elsewhere (Nolt 2018; Milberg and Winkler 2013).

In order to counter the power of transnational capital, interventionist liberals might look to the capitalist state or to capitalist institutions to challenge corporate power through higher taxation, stricter regulation, and more protection of workers' ability to bargain for higher wages and benefits. These may well help workers in the short term and certainly should be reforms that social movements on the left advocate. However, the size and power of transnational corporate production networks and capital investments dwarf the power of even the most advanced governments to implement social democratic policies that are capable of checking corporate power over the long term. Without a strong countermovement of working-class people organized across nation-states, especially the most powerful nation-states, where transnational corporations transfer most of their global profits, interventionist liberalism is likely to be successful only for limited durations. The social welfare aspects of interventionist liberal policies are in retreat even in the most advanced regulatory capitalist states of Western Europe (Palley 2018). The European Union, as documented in this book, has become a primary vehicle for advancing the interests of dominant sections of capital, or transnational interest blocs. With that in mind, the next section locates the transnational interest bloc approach within a larger framework of other critical approaches. I conclude by showing how an interest bloc approach suggests a praxis for left social movements that are trying to change the current system.

TRANSNATIONAL INTEREST BLOC AND PRAXIS

The transnational interest bloc traces the historical trajectories of capitalist political and economic power within the context of the political and economic histories of nation-states, then follows the expansion of transnational interest bloc power on a global scale. This approach includes an analysis of the capital-state-society-class-institutional relationships that are differentiated by national and regional histories. This starting point is also sensitive to sectoral differences among firms and to shifting patterns of transnational interest bloc conflict that occur within the nation-state and within the global system. Instead of starting with a structural framework of global capitalism and working down from those assumptions, the transnational interest bloc approach examines the varied histories of capital-state-society-class-institutional arrangements that structure and mediate corporate power.

The return to the centrality of production and class conflict certainly shares much in common with scholars who write about the "transnational capitalist class" (Sklair 2000; Robinson 2004; Harris 2008). Like these Marxist scholars, I argue that the structure of global capitalism is dominated by the political and economic power of transnational capital. However, I stop short of identifying the most dominant transnational capitalists as a "transnational capitalist class." In my view, "transnational interest bloc" best captures the fracturing and competing capitalist coalitions as they maneuver for favorable competitive positions, often disproportionately assisted by their location within geographical/territorial and state/regional boundaries. The transnational interest bloc approach does not deny that fractions of transnational capital organize their interests globally through the mechanisms of the market and in some cases through supra-state institutions. However, transnational interest bloc formation is a better way to frame how capitalists operate on a daily basis, where they are forced to confront political, institutional, sectoral, and class opposition to their hegemony—often expressed within territorially demarcated boundaries or within the socioeconomic histories of geographic regions. These boundaries and institutional frameworks have not been overcome by the overarching power of a transnational capitalist class, but they are being contested in ways that can best be appreciated by a mid-range theory that allows for deeper engagement with the specific historical trajectory of capitalist coalitions.

The transnational interest bloc approach is consistent with Marxist theories that focus on class exploitation at the point of production, particularly the extraction of surplus value, as integral to understanding the political economy of corporate power (Resnick and Wolff 1989). Power elite approaches within sociology, including the work of C. Wright Mills and William Domhoff, who examine the way that political networks of corporate power affect or determine state policy, share some common features with the transnational interest bloc approach (Mills 1956; Domhoff 2017). However, the transnational interest bloc approach, unlike power elite approaches, grounds corporate power within the structural dynamics of capitalism as a system of accumulation, consistent with other Marxist approaches. This book explains corporate behavior as a political response to periodic capitalist crises, especially the falling rate of profit during the period of 1965–1982. In doing so, I examine the extent to which corporations restructured their corporate organizational structure and their market position (within nation-states and on a global scale) and expanded their domestic and global lobbying networks in direct response to global capitalist crises. This approach borrows from corporate organization theory in economics and public policy, as well as a literature of capitalist crises that has been led by Marxist economists, sociologists, and critical theorists in international relations (Cowling and Tomlinson 2005; Tabb 2010).

The transnational interest bloc approach also links to a recent body of literature in non-Marxian economics that examines the political economy of global value chains. This includes scholarly works that analyze the economic implications of the dramatic expansion of global value chains for theories of international trade (Milberg and Winkler 2013). It also includes a distributional literature that examines the effects of value chain expansion on workers' wages and the growing inequality gap between classes on a national and a global scale (Timmer et al. 2013; Smith 2016). This literature returns economic theory to an analytic tradition that takes corporate power within the market seriously. The linkage of corporate power to increasing concentrations of market power and political power is inspired in part by the writings of neo-Marxist Michael Kalecki, for example, and others who used Marxist theory to examine the implications of corporate foreign direct investment, including Stephen Hymer (Hymer and Cohen 1979). These scholars examined corporate power as a set of strategies to exert greater control over the market and to more effectively meet the demands of an increasingly competitive global capitalism.

Therefore the corporate concentration of wealth was seen as a strategic market response to limit competition and to secure more control over resources and access to markets.

A Marxian analytical framework that operates at a mid-range level of analysis allows for the most thorough explanation of the political and economic factors that have contributed to the specific characteristics of global value chains. A focus on transnational corporations at the top of the global value chains, their linkages to a myriad of investment partners positioned at various levels within these supply chains, and the growing importance of a global subset of workers in production and logistics is crucial for a Marxism that seeks to understand the conditions of exploitation. Transnational corporations at the top of global value chains profit overwhelmingly from their concentration of ownership of patents, branding, and their favorable market position relative to powerful retailers and distribution networks. In turn, these firms are able to rely on contract manufacturers to produce products in a range of foreign locations, contracting in many cases at "arm's length" with independent producers whose cost margins are extremely tight. Ultimately, the political economy of global value chains rests on increasing the exploitation of workers locked into precarious conditions of part-time employment, the threat of long-term unemployment, and vigorous competition within a reserve army of laborers who are trapped by lack of mobility and relatively closed immigration systems.

The transnational interest bloc approach takes the politics of production seriously, using the latest and best economic data from scholars who have been on the cutting edge of analyzing value extraction in global supply chains. This process of analytical clarification is necessary for providing potential answers for working-class political organizations regarding the following: how transnational firms are able to make super-profits from a system of labor exploitation that dramatically increases labor productivity while keeping wages low or stagnant. For John Smith, who has used a version of dependency theory to examine global value chains, the consequences of this system of exploitation are most starkly revealed by the following observation: "Commodities produced mostly or entirely in low-wage countries and consumed mostly or entirely in imperialist countries expand the GDP of the nations where they are consumed by far more than the GDP of the nations they are produced" (Smith 2016, 37–38). This creates the optical illusion of value added in the developed states, which in reality is the ability of transnational corporations at the top of the global value chain to use their market power to capture more revenue as "profit" as a result of their privileged position.

From the transnational interest bloc approach, we start to get an appreciation of what a Marxian political economy of production would look like.

Transnational firms have particular characteristics embodied within their corporate structure, which includes who owns the firm, what the firm produces, how production is organized, and who works for the firm as contractors, managers, and employees. Transnational corporate power is contested by rivalries with other domestic and global actors, including rival firms and mobilized sectors of the population that have competing interests, such as workers, environmental movements, and consumer movements. According to a recent IMF study, it is the power of workers' movements, measured through trade unions (an imperfect measure to be sure), that explains, more than any other single variable, the extent to which inequality decreases or increases over time within a nation-state (Jaumotte and Buitron 2015). Of course, the relative strength of working-class movements disconnected from each other across the boundaries of nation-states cannot alter the crisis-prone nature of a capitalist system that rests on the global extraction of surplus value as its underlying feature.

What is needed more urgently than ever is working-class unity across the borders of capitalist nation-states. The material conditions of the new globalization have provided fractions of the global working class with increased power to challenge the system, if these workers are able to utilize their strategic locations in global production to advance their common interests. Contrary to the myth of the reduced importance of the "working class" in contemporary capitalism, the objective position of workers within the global capitalist system is at an all-time high numerically. Capitalism has never had a period where so much of humanity depends on selling their labor power for survival. And workers are increasingly concentrated in large numbers within logistical nodes of global value chains, meaning that the actions of thousands of strategically placed workers in logistics and distribution centers have power that is disproportionate to their numbers (Moody 2017).

Despite their increased importance to the system, the support infrastructure that exists to reproduce workers from one generation to the next is in the process of breaking down. The benefits that workers historically fought for in countries that have a social democratic history—health insurance, unemployment compensation, retirement benefits, and welfare assistance—are all being reduced in most advanced capitalist countries, and in countries where these benefits are still relatively extensive, prognostications for later decline have become the norm (Streeck 2017). Meanwhile, transnational corporations are replacing the labor of domestic workers with foreign workers who are trapped in a precariously competitive set of circumstances without any significant social safety net. A more recent trend, which I captured in chapter five, is the restructuring of the global workforce into fewer supply networks. This is being accomplished in part by the greater utilization of advanced technology, which has resulted in the substitution of workers for machines and the consolidation of supply networks into a more streamlined global production system. This process has made the remaining workers even more important to the process of production by locating a larger subset of workers within logistical nodes that are responsible for completing the production process and shipping the finished product to its market destinations. The just-in-time finished production and delivery of a product produced within global value chains has created a subset of workers who have strategic power within the global system.

The key for any emancipatory project is to forge unity between these groups of workers across the borders of countries. A critique of the political economy of global value chains, where profits are overwhelmingly concentrated at the top of the production hierarchy due to capitalist power within the market and within political systems, is an important place to start (Nolan and Zhang 2010; Milberg and Winkler 2013). What is apparent is that most workers cannot easily see these relationships by themselves, in isolation from other workers who are increasingly concentrated in distant locations. Therefore it is up to those within working-class political movements who can see these linkages, along with their allies in academia and in existing socialist organizing projects, to make this information available to them and to incorporate this knowledge within a framework of emancipatory and anti-capitalist political organizations. This is the best antidote to the rise of the far right in Europe and the United States. Instead, we often get a leftist response, dominated by identity politics discourse bereft of class analysis, which simply writes off working-class supporters of Brexit or of Trump as hopelessly irredeemable, outside the confines of a cosmopolitan sensibility that champions diversity and immigrant rights (Lapavitsas 2016). The problem, however, is that the liberal cosmopolitan ideology that defends diversity and immigrant rights rarely has anything to say about the contemporary conditions of workers under really existing capitalism (Sculos 2017). The ability of neoliberal capitalism to capture and utilize appeals to diversity and inclusion on its own terms has exposed the failures of identity politics as disconnected from class.

The task, then, of Marxist theory is to bring back a mid-range Marxism that takes class seriously as the starting point for engagement in meaningful political, economic, and social transformation. As critical scholars, we need to expose the fact that capitalism continues to rely on the same central techniques of labor exploitation, extraction of surplus value, and concentration of profits through capitalist power over markets and over states. We engage in this scholarly research as part of an emancipatory political project that aims to provide assistance for those who are central to changing the system, not because of any inherent "identities" that they may possess as individuals but because they are located collectively at the center of the most important exploitative relationships that determine who profits from the system.

The transnational interest bloc approach aims to bring mid-range class analysis to the center of discussions about how to strategically fight for radical reforms within capitalism and to help build working-class movements that are part of anticapitalist organizing efforts. For the past several decades, leftist scholars have minimized or dismissed the relevance of the working class for changing the system. Instead of class, there has been a disproportionate focus of critical theorists on "cultural signifiers" or the "multitude" in an attempt to develop an emancipatory politics. This "retreat from class" has meant that left scholars in universities have been writing less about production and working-class exploitation and more about ideological or cultural hegemony (Wood 1999). The transnational capitalist class approach is part of an effort to reverse that trend by focusing explicitly on class relationships within domestic and global production. By examining the political economy of surplus value extraction through global value chains, we are in a better position to analyze, interpret, and understand the exploitative relationships embedded in the new globalization. At the same time, our approach will then be more consistent in aligning with the material realities of those who are exploited and oppressed in global capitalism.

Bibliography

Afonso, Alexandre, and Line Rennwald. 2017. "The Far Right's Leftist Mask." *Jacobin* (March 17).

Aguiar de Medeiros, Carlos, and Nicholas Trebat. 2016. "Finance, Trade, and Income Distribution in Global Value Chains: Implications for Developing Economies and Latin America." CEPAL Paper, Santiago, Chile.

Aguiar de Medeiros, Carlos, and Nicholas Trebat. 2017. "Inequality and Income Distribution in Global Value Chains." *Journal of Economic Issues* 51, no. 2: 401–408.

Apeldoorn, Bastiaan Van. 2010. "Transnational Class Agency and European Governance: The Case of the European Round Table of Industrialists." *New Political Economy* 5, no. 2 (August): 157–181.

Autor, David H., and David Dorn. 2013. "The Growth of Low-Skill Service Jobs and the Polarization of the U.S. Labor Market." *American Economic Review* 103, no. 5: 1553–1597.

Baldwin, Richard. 2011. "21st Century Regionalism: Filling the Gap between 21st Century Trade and 20th Century Trade Rules." World Trade Organization Publications, Geneva.

Banga, Rashmi. 2013. "Measuring Value in Global Value Chains." Background Paper, no. RVC-8, UNCTAD Publication, New York.

Barkham, Patrick. 1999. "The Banana Wars Explained." *The Guardian*. https://www.theguardian.com/world/1999/mar/05/eu.wto3.

Bello, Walden. 2017. "Asia and Finance Capital: From the Japanese Bubble to China's Financial Time Bomb." Finance Working Papers, no. 3, Transnational Institute, Amsterdam.

Beshudi, Adam. 2018. "Trump Strikes Back at Chinese Tech Practices with New Tariffs." *Politico* (March 22).

Bhambra, Gurminder K., and John Holmwood. 2017. "Colonialism, Postcolonialism and the Liberal Welfare State." *New Political Economy* 23, no. 5: 574–587.

Bhargava, Rahul, and Donald R. Fraser. 1998. "On the Wealth and Risk Effects of Commercial Bank Expansion into Securities Underwriting." *Journal of Banking and Finance* 22, no. 4: 447–465.

Bohle, Dorothee. 2006. "Neoliberal Hegemony, Transnational Capital and the Terms of the EU's Eastward Expansion." *Capital and Class* 30, no. 1: 57–86.

Bohle, Dorothee. 2009. "Race to the Bottom? Transnational Companies and Reinforced Competition in the Enlarged European Union." In *Contradictions and Limits of Neoliberal European Governance*, edited by Bastiaan van Apeldoorn, Jan Drahokoupil, and Laura Horn, 163–186. New York: Palgrave Macmillan.

Bosch, Gerhard. 2015. "Shrinking Collective Bargaining Coverage, Increasing Income Inequalty: A Comparison of Five EU Countries." *International Labour Review* 154, no. 1: 57–66.

Brenner, Neil, Jamie Peck, and Nik Theodore. 2010. "Variegated Neoliberalism: Geographies, Modalities, Pathways." *Global Networks* 10, no. 2: 182–222.

Brenner, Robert. 1998. "The Economics of Global Turbulence." *New Left Review* special issue, no. 229 (May–June): 1–264.

Burchill, Scott. 2005. *The National Interest in International Relations Theory*. New York: Palgrave Macmillan.

Business Coalition for U.S.-Central American Trade. 2006. "U.S. Textile Sector Calls for Enactment of DR-CAFTA." Press release.

Caliari, Aldo. 2005. "CAFTA's Debt Trap." *Foreign Policy in Focus* (July 3), special report.

Canterbury, Dennis C. 2010. *European Bloc Imperialism*. Leiden, The Netherlands: Brill.

Caradaica, Mihail. 2013. "European Union in the Age of Neo-Liberalism." *Europolity* 7, no. 1: 21–33.

Chase, Kerry. 2005. *Trading Blocs: States, Firms and Regions in the World Economy*. Ann Arbor: University of Michigan Press.

Chomsky, Aviva. 2014. *Undocumented: How Immigration Became Illegal*. Boston: Beacon Press.

Cokelet, Benjamin. 2013. "The Mexican Council of Businessmen: Business, Politics, Elites and Decision-Making in Mexico." Project Poder Publication, Mexico City, Mexico.

Constantinescu, Cristina, Aaditya Matoo, and Michele Ruta. 2015. "The Global Trade Slowdown: Cyclical or Structural?" IMF Working Paper, Washington, D.C.

Cope, Zac. 2012. *Divided Work, Divided Class: Global Political Economy and the Stratification of Labor Under Capitalism*. Montreal: Kersplebedeb.

Cowling, Keith, and Philip R. Tomlinson. 2005. "Globalization and Corporate Power." *Contributions to Political Economy* 24, no. 1 (August): 33–54.

Cowling, Keith, and Philip R. Tomlinson. 2011. "The Japanese Model in Retrospective: Industrial Strategies, Corporate Japan and the 'Hollowing Out' of Japanese Industry." *Policy Studies* 32, no. 6: 569–583.

Cox, Ronald W. 2013. "The Corporatization of Higher Education." *Class, Race and Corporate Power* 1, no. 1, article 8.

Cox, Ronald W. 2014. "The Military-Industrial Complex and U.S. Military Spending after 9/11." *Class, Race and Corporate Power* 2, no. 2, article 5.

Cox, Robert W. 1987. *Production, Power and World Order: Social Forces in the Making of History.* New York: Columbia University Press.

Cox, Robert W. 1981. "Social Forces, States and World Orders: Beyond International Relations Theory." *Millennium: Journal of International Studies* 10, no. 2: 126–155.

Cox, Ronald W. 2008. "Transnational Capital, the U.S. State and Latin American Trade Agreements." *Third World Quarterly* 29, no. 8: 1527–1544.

Cox, Ronald W., ed. 2012. *Corporate Power and Globalization in U.S. Foreign Policy*. New York: Routledge.

Cox, Ronald W., and Daniel Skidmore-Hess. 1999. *U.S. Politics and the Global Economy: Corporate Power, Conservative Shift*. Boulder: Lynne Rienner Publishers.

Cronin, David. 2013. *Corporate Europe: How Big Business Sets Policies on Food, Climate and War*. London: Pluto Press.

Dao, Mai Chi, Mitali Das, Zsoka Koczan, and Weicheng Lian. 2017. "Why Is Labor Receiving a Smaller Share of Global Income? Theory and Empirical Evidence." IMF Working Paper 17/169.

Davis, Gerald F. 2009. *Managed by the Markets: How Finance Re-Shaped America.* London: Oxford University Press.

Davis, Mike. 2017. "The Great God Trump and the White Working Class." *Catalyst* 1, no. 1 (Spring).

Degain, Christophe, Bo Meng, and Zhi Wang. 2017. "Recent Trends in Global Trade and Global Value Chains." In *Measuring and Analyzing the Impact of GVCs on Economic Development*, edited by World Bank Group. Washington, D.C.: World Bank Publications.

Domhoff, William. 2017. *Studying the Power Elite: Fifty Years of Who Rules America*. New York: Routledge.

Drahokoupil, Jan. 2009. "The Rise of the Competition State in the Visegrad Four: Internationalization of the State as a Local Project." In *Contradictions and Limits of Neoliberal European Governance*, edited by Bastiaan van Apeldoorn, Jan Drahokoupil and Laura Horn, 187–208. New York: Palgrave Macmillan.

Drahos, Peter. 2003. "Expanding Intellectual Property's Empire: the Role of FTAs." Regulatory Institutions Network, Research School of Social Sciences, Australian National University.

Dreiling, Michael. 2000. "The Class Embeddedness of Corporate Political Action: Leadership in Defense of the NAFTA." *Social Problems* 47, no. 1 (February): 21–48.

Dunn, Bill. 2009. *Global Political Economy: A Marxist Critique*. Chicago: University of Chicago Press.

Economic Times. 2018. "Chip Wars: Tech Rivalry Underlies US-China Trade Conflict" (May 3).

The Economist. 2016. "The Rise of the Superstar Companies" (September 17).

European Central Bank. 2006. *July Monthly Bulletin*. Frankfurt: ECB Publications.

Ferguson, Thomas, Paul Jorgensen, and Jie Chen. 2018. "Industrial Structure and Party Competition in an Age of Hunger Games: Donald Trump and the 2016 Presidential Election." Institute for New Economic Thinking, Working Paper No. 66, New York.

Ferguson, Thomas, and Joel Rogers. 1987. *Right Turn: The Decline of the Democrats and the Future of American Politics*. New York: Hill and Wang.

Fichter, Michael. 2015. "Organizing In and Along Value Chains: What Does It Mean for Trade Unions?" *International Policy Analysis*, Friedrich Ebert Stiftung Institute, Berlin.

Foroohar, Rana. 2018. "Tech Companies Are the New Investment Banks." *Financial Times* (February 11): 57.

Gathii, James Thuo. 2011. "The Neo-Liberal Turn in Regional Trade Agreements." *Washington Law Review* 86: 421–474.

Gereffi, Gary. 2014. "A Global Value Chain Perspective on Industrial Policy and Development in Emerging Markets." *Duke Journal of Comparative and International Law* 33, no. 3 (Spring): 433–458.

Gereffi, Gary. 2014. "Global Value Chains in a Post-Washington Consensus World." *Review of International Political Economy* 21, no. 1: 9–37.

Gestrin, Michael. 2017. "Cross-Border Mergers and Acquisitions on the Rise." OECD Publications, Paris.

Gibbon, Peter, Sam Jones, and Lotte Thomsen. 2008. "An Assessment of the Impact of Export Processing Zones and an Identification of Appropriate Measures to Support Their Development." Danish Institute for International Studies, Copenhagen.

Gill, Stephen. 1990. *American Hegemony and the Trilateral Commission*. Cambridge: Cambridge University Press.

Giroux, Henry A. *Education and the Crisis of Public Policy: Challenging the Assault on Teachers, Students and Public Education*. Berkeley: Counterpoint Press.

Gittleson, Kim. 2018. "US Tax Cuts: Are They the Biggest in American History?" *BBC News* (April 17).

Gordon, Andrew. 2015. "Making Sense of the Lost Decades: Workplaces and Schools, Men and Women, Young and Old, Rich and Poor." In *Examining Japan's Lost Decades*, edited by Funabashi Yoichi and Barak Kushner. London: Routledge. Available online from Digital Access to Scholarship at Harvard (dash.harvard.edu).

Gourevitch, Peter. 2006. *Politics in Hard Times: Comparative Responses to Economic Crises*. Ithaca: Cornell University Press.

Grinberg, Nicolas. 2016. "Global Commodity Chains and the Production of Surplus-Value on a Global Scale: Bringing Back the International Division of Labor Theory." *Journal of World-Systems Research* 22, no. 1: 247–278.

Haller, Max. 2011. *European Integration as an Elite Process*. New York: Routledge.

Harris, Jerry. 2008. *The Dialectics of Globalization: Economic and Political Conflict in a Transnational World*. Newcastle: Cambridge Scholars Press.

Harris, Jerry. 2016. *Global Capitalism and the Crisis of Democracy*. Atlanta, Ga.: Clarity Press.

Hart-Landsberg, Martin. 2013. *Capitalist Globalization: Consequences, Resistanc and Alternatives*. New York: Monthly Review Press.

Hartung, William. 2018. "How the Pentagon Devours the Budget." TomDispatch .com (February 27).

Harvey, David. 2007. *A Brief History of Neoliberalism*. London: Oxford University Press.

Helleiner, Eric. 1996. *States and the Reemergence of Global Finance: From Bretton Woods to the 1990s*. Ithaca: Cornell University Press.

Heron, Tony. 2011. "Asymmetrical Bargaining and Development Tradeoffs in the CARIFORUM–European Union Partnership Agreement," *Review of International Political Economy* 18, no. 3: 328–357.

Hornbeck, J. F. 2006. "The Dominican Republic–Central American–United States Free Trade Agreement." Congressional Research Service, Washington, D.C. (April 4).

Horner, Rory, and Khalid Nadvi. 2018. "Global Value Chains and the Rise of the Global South: Unpacking Twenty-First Century Polycentric Trade." *Global Networks: A Journal of Transnational Affairs* 18, no. 2: 207–237.

Hymer, Stephen, and Robert B. Cohen. 1979. *The Multinational Corporation: A Radical Approach*. London: Cambridge University Press.

International Labour Office. 2015. "World Employment and Social Outlook: The Changing Nature of Jobs." International Labour Office, Geneva.

Itoh, Makoto. 2000. *The Japanese Economy Reconsidered*. New York: Palgrave Macmillan.

Jaumotte, Florence, and Carolina Osorio Buitron. 2015. "Inequality and Labor Market Institutions." International Monetary Fund Research Paper.

Jurenas, Remy. 2004. "Agriculture in the U.S.–Dominican Republic–Central American Free Trade Agreement." Congressional Research Service, Washington, D.C.

Karabarbounis, Loukas, and Brent Neiman. 2014. "The Global Decline of the Labor Share." *Quarterly Journal of Economics* 129, no. 1: 61–103.

Kim, In Song, Helen V. Milner, Thomas Bernauer, Iain Osgood, Gabrielle Spilker, and Dustin Tingley. 2018. "Firms and Global Value Chains: Identifying Firms' Multidimensional Trade Preferences." Forthcoming in *International Studies Quarterly*.

Kotz, David. 2015. *The Rise and Fall of Neoliberal Capitalism*. Cambridge: Harvard University Press.

Krasa, Stefan, and Mattias Polborn. 2013. "Party Realignment on Cultural Issues Is Responsible for Increased Political Polarization in Presidential Elections." London School of Economics Blog (March 3).

Krippner, Greta. 2005. "The Financialization of the American Economy." *Socioeconomic Review* 3: 173–208.

Krznaric, Roman. 2006. "The Limits on Pro-poor Agricultural Trade in Guatemala: Land, Labour and Political Power." *Journal of Human Development* 7, no. 1: 111–135.

Kufakurinani, Ushehwedu, Ingrid Harvold Kvangraven, Frutuoso Santana, and Maria Dyveke Styve. 2017. *Dialogues on Development, Volume 1: On Dependency*. New York: Institute for New Economic Thinking.

Kurth, James. 1979. "The Political Consequences of the Product Life Cycle." *International Organization* 33, no. 1 (Winter): 1–34.

La Monica, Paul. 2018. "These American Companies Could Lose in a Trade War with China." CNN Markets Now (March 22).

Lapavitsas, Costas. 2013. *Profiting Without Producing: How Finance Exploits Us All*. New York: Verso Books.

Lapavitsas, Costas. 2016. "Why They Left." *Jacobin* (July 7).

Lechevalier, Sebastien, ed. 2014. *The Great Transformation of Japanese Capitalism*. London: Routledge.

Lee, Joonkoo, and Gary Gereffi. 2015. "Global Value Chains, Rising Power Firms and Economic and Social Upgrading." Critical Perspectives on International Business 11, no. 3/4: 319–339.

Macartney, Huw. 2010. *Variegated Neoliberalism: EU Varieties of Capitalism and International Political Economy*. London: Routledge.

Mair, Peter. 2013. *Ruling the Void: The Hollowing of Western Democracy*. New York: Verso Books.

Marliere, Philippe. 2010. "The Decline of Europe's Social Democratic Parties." *Open Democracy* (March 16). Opendemocracy.net.

Maxfield, Sylvia, and James H. Nolt. 1990. "Protectionism and the Internationalization of Capital: U.S. Sponsorship of Import Substitution Industrialization in the Philippines, Turkey and Argentina." *International Studies Quarterly* 34, no. 1 (March): 49–81.

Meeropol, Michael. 1998. *Surrender: How the Clinton Administration Completed the Reagan Revolution*. Ann Arbor: University of Michigan Press.

Melville, Juliet. 2002. "The Impact of Structural Adjustment on the Poor." Caribbean Development Bank. Paper prepared for the Eastern Caribbean Central Bank 7th Annual Development Conference, 1–12.

Milanovic, Branko. 2016. *Global Inequality: A New Approach for the Age of Globalization*. Boston: Harvard University Press.

Milberg, William. 2007. "Shifting Sources and Uses of Profits: Sustaining U.S. Financialization with Global Value Chains." *Economy and Society* 37, no. 3: 420–451.

Milberg, William, and Deborah Winkler. 2010. "Financialisation and the Dynamics of Offshoring in the USA." *Cambridge Journal of Economics* 34, no. 2: 275–293.

Milberg, William, and Deborah Winkler. 2009. "Globalization, Offshoring and Economic Insecurity in Industrialized Countries." DESA Working Paper No. 87 (November), United Nations, New York.

Milberg, William, and Deborah Winkler. 2013. *Outsourcing Economics: Global Value Chains in Capitalist Development*. New York: Cambridge University Press.

Mills, C. Wright. *The Power Elite*. London: Oxford University Press, 1956.

Moody, Kim. 1995. "NAFTA and the Corporate Redesign of North America." *Latin American Perspectives* 22, no. 1 (Winter): 95–116.

Moody, Kim. 2017. *On New Terrain: How Capital Is Reshaping the Battleground of Class War*. Chicago: Haymarket Books.

Mooney, Pat. 2017. "Report: Big Data Is Accelerating Corporate Control of the Food Supply." *In These Times* (October 17).

Morgan, Glenn. 2014. "Financialization and the Multinational." *European Review of Labour and Research* 20, no. 2: 183–197.

Mosley, Lana. 2017. "Workers' Rights in Global Value Chains: Possibilities for Protection and for Peril." *New Political Economy* 22, no. 2: 153–168.

Mudge, Stephanie Lee. 2011. "What's Left of Leftism? Neoliberal Politics in Western Party Systems, 1945–2004." *Social Science History* 35, no. 3: 337–380.

Murray, Georgina, and John Scott, eds. 2012. *Financial Elites and Transnational Business: Who Rules the World?* London: Edward Elgar Publishers.

Ness, Immanuel. 2015. *Southern Insurgency: The Coming of the Global Working Class*. New York: Pluto Press.

Nielson, Jeffrey, Bill Pritchard, and Henry Wai-chung Yeung. 2014. "Global Value Chains and Global Production Networks in the Changing International Political Economy." *Review of International Political Economy* 21, no. 1: 1–8.

Nolan, Peter, and Jin Zhang. 2010. "Global Competition after the Financial Crisis." *New Left Review* 64 (July–August): 97–108.

Nolan, Peter, Jin Zhang, and Chunhang Liu. 2007. *The Global Business Revolution and the Cascade Effect: Systems Integration in the Global Aerospace, Beverage and Retail Industries*. New York: Palgrave Macmillan.

Nolt, James H. 2018. "The Global Crisis in Trade . . . Theory." ChinaUSFocus.com (May 16).

OECD. 2012. "Mapping Global Value Chains." Working Paper 9, OECD Conference Center, Paris.

Oxfam Briefing Paper. 2016. "An Economy for the 1%." Oxfam.org (January).

Pal, Timea. 2017. "Colonial Legacies and Foreign Direct Investment." Centre for International Studies, Lisbon.

Palley, Thomas. 2018. *Re-Theorizing the Welfare State and the Political Economy of Neoliberalism's War against It*. Dusseldorf, Germany: Macroeconomic Policy Institute.

Paus, Eva. 1988. *Struggle against Dependence: Nontraditional Export Growth in Central America and the Caribbean*. Boulder, Colo.: Westview Press.

Piereson, James. 2012. "John Maynard Keynes and the Modern Revolution in Political Economy." *Society* 49, no. 3: 263–273.

Powell, Jeff. 2013. "Subordinate Financialization: A Study of Mexico and Its Non-Financial Corporations." PhD Thesis, SOAS, University of London.

Prashad, Vijay. 2008. *The Darker Nations: A People's History of the Third World*. New York: The New Press.

Pratap, Surendra. 2014. *Emerging Trends in Factory Asia: International Capital Mobility, Global Value Chains and the Labour Movement*. Hong Kong: Asia Monitor Resource Center.

Prechel, Harland. 2000. *Big Business and the State: Historical Transitions and Corporate Transformation, 1880s–1990s*. Albany: State University of New York Press.

President's Council of Advisors on Science and Technology. 2017. "Ensuring U.S. Leadership and Innovation in Semiconductors." Washington, D.C., Executive Office of the President.

Price, John. 1994. "Lean Production at Suzuki and Toyota: A Historical Perspective." *Studies in Political Economy* 5: 66–99.

Quentin, David, and Liam Campling. 2018. "Global Inequality Chains: Integrating Mechanisms of Value Distribution into Analyses of Global Production," *Global Networks* 18, no. 1: 33–56.

Resnick, Stephen, and Richard Wolff. 1989. *Knowledge and Class: A Marxian Critique of Political Economy*. Chicago: University of Chicago Press.

Roberts, Michael. 2017. "Germany Stutters." Thenextrecession.wordpress.com, blog post (September 25).

Roberts, Michael. 2012. "Japan Election: Lowest Turnout since Records Began." Thenextrecession.wordpress.com, blog post (December 16).

Roberts, Michael. 2016. *The Long Depression*. Chicago: Haymarket Books.

Robinson, William. 2018. "Accumulation Crisis and Global Police State." *Critical Sociology* (March) 21: 1–14.

Robinson, William. 2014. *Global Capitalism and the Crisis of Humanity*. London: Cambridge University Press.

Robinson, William. 2004. *A Theory of Global Capitalism: Production, Class and State in a Transnational World*. Baltimore: Johns Hopkins Press.

Robinson, William. 2003. *Transnational Conflicts: Central America, Social Change and Globalization*. New York: Verso.

Rodrik, Dani. 2018. "What Do Trade Agreements Really Do?" *Journal of Economic Perspectives* 32, no. 2 (Spring): 73–90.

Ross, Robert J. S., and Kent C. Trachte. 1990. *Global Capitalism: The New Leviathan*. Albany: State University of New York Press.

Sanchez-Ancochea, Diego. 2008. "State and Society: The Political Economy of DR-CAFTA in Costa Rica, the Dominican Republic and El Salvador." In *The Political Economy of Hemispheric Integration*, edited by Diego Sanchez-Ancochea and Kenneth C. Shadlen. New York: Palgrave Macmillan.

Scott, Robert. 2011. "Chinese State-Owned Enterprises and U.S.-China Bilateral Investment." Testimony to Congressional Hearing, Panel II (March), U.S. Investments in China.

Segovia, Alexander. 2005. "Integracion Real y Grupos de Poder Economico en America Central." Friedrich Ebert Foundation, San Jose.

Selwyn, Benjamin. 2016. "Global Value Chains or Global Poverty Chains? A New Research Agenda." Working Paper No. 10. University of Sussex Centre for Global Political Economy, Brighton.

Serfati, Claude. 2008. "Financial Dimensions of Transnational Corporations, Global Value Chain and Technological Innovation." *Journal of Innovation Economics and Management* 2: 35–61.

Sklair, Leslie. 2000. *The Transnational Capitalist Class*. Hoboken, N.J.: Wiley-Blackwell.

Smith, John. 2011. "Imperialism and the Law of Value." *Global Discourse* 2, no. 1: 1–36.

Smith, John. 2016. *Imperialism in the 21st Century: Globalization, Super-Exploitation and Capitalism's Final Crisis*. New York: Monthly Review Press.

Soederberg, Susanne. 2009. *Corporate Power and Ownership in Contemporary Capitalism: The Politics of Resistance and Domination*. New York: Routledge.

Solis, Mireya. 2003. "Adjustment through Globalization: The Role of State FDI Finance." In *Japan's Managed Globalization in the 21st Century*, edited by Ulrike Schaede and William Grimes, 101–123. Armonk, N.Y.: M.E. Sharpe.

Solis, Mireya. 2013. "Business Advocacy in Asian PTAs: A Model of Selective Corporate Lobbying with Evidence from Japan." *Business and Politics* 15, no. 1 (April): 87–116.

Solis, Mireya. 2007. "The Japan-Mexico FTA: A Cross-Regional Step in the Path towards Asian Regionalism." *Pacific Affairs* 80, no. 2 (Summer): 279–301.

Solis, Mireya, and Katada, Saori N. 2007. "Understanding East Asian Cross-Regionalism: An Analytical Framework," *Pacific Affairs* 80, no. 2: 229–257.

Spieldoch, Alexandra. 2010. "NAFTA: Fueling Market Concentration in Agriculture." Institute for Agriculture and Trade Policy, Minneapolis, IATP Publication.

Srnicek, Nick. 2017. *Platform Capitalism*. Cambridge: Polity Press.

Starosta, Guido. 2010. "The Outsourcing of Manufacturing and the Rise of Giant Global Contractors: A Marxian Approach to Some Recent Transformations of Global Value Chains." *New Political Economy* 15, no. 4: 543–563.

Stokes, Doug, and Sam Rafael. 2010. *Global Energy Security and American Hegemony*. Baltimore: Johns Hopkins University Press.

Streeck, Wolfgang. 2014. *Buying Time: The Delayed Crisis of Democratic Capitalism*. London: Verso.

Streeck, Wolfgang. 2017. *How Will Capitalism End? Essays on a Failing System*. New York: Verso Books.

Tabb, William. 2010. "Marxism, Crisis Theory and the Crisis of the Early 21st Century." *Science and Society* 74, no. 3: 305–323.

Third World Network. 2009. "EU EPAs: Economic and Social Development Implications: The Case of the CARIFORUM-EC Economic Partnership Agreement." TWN Publications, Geneva.

Timmer, Marcel P., Abdul Azeez Erumban, Bart Los, Robert Stehrer, and Gaaitzen J. de Vries. 2013. "Slicing Up Global Value Chains." Paper for European Comission, Research Directorate General. Portions of this were later published in the *Journal of Economic Perspectives* 28, no. 2 (Spring 2014): 99–118.

Timmer, Marcel P., Bart Los, Robert Stehrer, and Gaaitzen J. de Vries. 2016. "An Anatomy of the Global Trade Slowdown Based on the WIOD 2016 Release." University of Groningen, GGDC Research Memoranda, no. 162.

Towers, Marcia, and Silvia Borzutzky. 2004. "The Socioeconomic Impact of Dollarization in El Salvador." *Latin American Politics and Society* 46, no. 3 (Autumn): 29–54.

UNCTAD. 2013. "World Investment Report." New York, United Nations Publication.

van Apeldoorn, Bastiaan. 2002. *Transnational Capitalism and the Struggle over European Integration*. London: Routledge.

van den Broek, Marjolein. 2014. "Intellectual Property for Development?" Master's Thesis, International Relations, Radboud University.

Van Der Pijl, Kees, and Yuliya Yurchenko. 2014. "Neoliberal Entrenchment of North Atlantic Capital: From Corporate Self-Regulation to State Capture." *New Political Economy* 20, no. 4: 495–517.

Vazquez-Arroyo, Antonio Y. 2008. "Liberal Democracy and Neoliberalism: A Critical Juxtaposition." *New Political Science* 30, no. 2: 127–159.

Vigna, Anne. 2018. "Brazil Goes Back to an Oligarch Past." *Le Monde Diplomatique* (May).

Vinik, Danny. 2018. "Trump's War on Regulations Is Real. But Is It Working?" *Politico* (January 20).

Weissman, Robert. 2004. "Dying for Drugs." *Multinational Monitor* 25, no. 4 (April).

White, Alan. 2017. "The Fate of Global Corporations in an Anti-Globalist World." *GreenBiz* (June 13).

Wigger, Angela, and Hubert Buch-Hansen. 2014. "Explaining (Missing) Regulatory Paradigm Shifts: EU Competition Regulation in Times of Economic Crisis." *New Political Economy* 19, no. 1: 113–137.

Wolff, Richard D., and Stephen Resnick. 2012. *Contending Economic Theories Neoclassical, Keynesian and Marxian*. Cambridge: MIT Press.

Wood, Adrian. 2017. "Variation in Structural Change around the World, 1985–2015: Patterns, Causes and Implications." United Nations University World Institute for Development Economics Research (WIDER), Helsinki.

Wood, Ellen Meiksins. 1999. *The Retreat from Class: A New True Socialism*. New York: Verso.

Yang, Y. Helio. 1998. "Post-NAFTA Production and Sourcing Development in the Maquiladora Program." *Industrial Management and Data Systems* 98, no. 6: 269–277.

Yi, Kei-Mu. 2003. "Can Vertical Specialization Explain the Growth of World Trade?" *Journal of Political Economy* 111, no. 1: 52–102.

Yoshimatsu, Hidetaka. 2005. "Japan's Keidanren and Free Trade Agreements: Societal Interests and Trade Policy." *Asian Survey* 45, no. 2 (March/April): 258–278.

Yoshimatsu, Hidetaka. 1998. "Japan's Keidanren and Political Influence on Market Liberalization." *Asian Survey* 38, no. 3 (March): 328–345.

Zhong, Raymond, and Paul Mozur. 2018. "For the U.S. and China, a Technology War That's Freezing Over." *New York Times* (March 23): A1.

Index

About the Author

Ronald W. Cox is Professor of Politics and International Relations at Florida International University in Miami, Florida. Professor Cox has written extensively in the areas of U.S. foreign economic policy, international political economy, American foreign policy, and the political economy of baseball. His previous books include *Corporate Power and Globalization in U.S. Foreign Policy* (ed.) (Routledge Press, 2012); *Free Agency and Competitive Balance in Baseball* (McFarland Press, 2006); *U.S. Politics and the Global Economy*, coauthored with Dan Skidmore-Hess (Lynne Rienner Press, 1999); *Business and the State in International Relations* (ed.) (Westview Press, 1997); and *Power and Profits: U.S. Policy in Central America* (University of Kentucky Press, 1994). In 2013, Professor Cox became the editor-in-chief of an open-access journal that he founded, titled *Class, Race and Corporate Power*.

www.ingramcontent.com/pod-product-compliance
Ingram Content Group UK Ltd.
Pitfield, Milton Keynes, MK11 3LW, UK
UKHW020209290926
15470UKWH00001B/92